W9-ATR-715

THE LIBRARY
ST. MARY'S COLLEGE OF MARYLAND
ST. MARY'S CITY, MARYLAND 20686

SOCIALISM AFTER COMMUNISM

Socialism after Communism

The New Market Socialism

Christopher Pierson

The Pennsylvania State University Press
University Park Pennsylvania

Copyright © Christopher Pierson 1995

First published 1995 in the United States and Canada by The Pennsylvania State University Press, 820 North University Drive, University Park, PA 16802.

All rights reserved.

ISBN 0–271–01478–4 (cloth)
ISBN 0–271–01479–2 (paper)

Library of Congress Cataloging-in-Publication Data

Pierson, Christopher,
    Socialism after communism : the new market socialism / Christopher Pierson.
       p.   cm.
    Includes bibliographical references ([p.   ) and index.
    ISBN 0-271-01478-4 (alk. paper)
    ISBN 0-271-01479-2 (pbk. : alk. paper)
    1. Socialism.   2. Post-communism.   3. Mixed economy.   I. Title.
HX73.P54   1995
335—dc20   94–47518
                                                            CIP

Typeset in 10 on 12 pt Palatino
by Best-set Typesetter Ltd., Hong Kong
Printed in Great Britain

It is the policy of The Pennsylvania State University Press to use acid-free paper for the first printing of all clothbound books. Publications on uncoated stock satisfy the minimum requirements of American National Standard for Information Sciences—Permanence of Paper for Printed Library Materials, ANSI Z39.48–1984.

Dedicated to the memory of my father
John Pierson
1921–1994

The travellers found themselves weary and lost in a strange land. They came upon a wise-looking local and asked to be put back upon the right road for their destination. 'Ah', said the local man after some thought, 'if that's where you are headed I wouldn't be starting from here.'

Anon.

When you have eliminated the impossible, whatever remains, *however improbable*, must be the truth.

Arthur Conan Doyle, *The Sign of Four*

Contents

Acknowledgements

I wish to express my gratitude to the University of Stirling, the University of California at Santa Barbara, the Carnegie Trust for the Universities of Scotland and the British Academy, all of which supported the research on which this book is based. I am also grateful for the advice of colleagues at seminars held at the universities of Oxford, Strathclyde, Edinburgh and Aberdeen, which has helped me to avoid still grosser errors than those which remain. I am greatly indebted to David Held, Virginia Bovell, the late Alec Nove and two anonymous referees at Polity Press for their attentive and helpful reading of the manuscript.

The book is dedicated to the memory of my father, John Pierson, who died while it was in the final stages of preparation.

The author and publisher would like to thank the following for permission to reproduce material in the book:

Basil Blackwell for table 2.1, from M. Bruno and J. D. Sachs, *Economics of Worldwide Stagflation* (1985); Cambridge University Press for figure 8.1, from A. Przeworski, *Capitalism and Social Democracy* (1985); and for figure 8.2, from A. Przeworski, *Democracy and the Market* (1991); Polity Press for Held's model, from D. Held, *Models of Democracy* (1987).

Preface

Norman Hunter, the hard-nosed England footballer, was surely not the first to offer the time-served political advice to 'get your retaliation in first'. Nonetheless, it still seems a wise counsel and I want here to offer one or two pre-emptive explanations of what is and what is not included in this study.

First, there is my use of the 'S' word. For some, it will seem at best archaic and at worst sheer wilfulness to write about the prospects for socialism. Either socialism belongs amongst that set of ideas which are fit only for deconstruction or else it is shorthand for a history of political hubris, bloodily misconceived and now entirely exhausted. Even 'on the left' (to use a favourite euphemism), it is something which is best kept at arm's length. I have some sympathy with the latter view at least. Socialism is an expression which has been so drained of meaning, and so abused by friend and foe alike, that we may be better to seek out alternative ways of describing those projects and practices which would once have been carried forward in its name. But if there may come a time to abandon the usage 'socialism', it should not be upon the terms given by the contemporary historians of its 'strange death'. As I seek to show in the early chapters of this book, the demise of socialism has been widely misrepresented and misunderstood. Any abandonment should not follow from the presumption that all we can look back upon is a history of accumulated failure. For two centuries, the ablest critics of capitalism and its consequences constructed their account under the rubric of socialism. In appraising this tradition we need to know what we should remember as well as what we must forget and any attempt simply 'to wipe the slate clean' is likely to draw our attention away from what remain the authentic insights of these earlier generations. Dangers also attend upon the attempt to rewrite the aspirations of socialism in some more acceptable idiom. It is simply not true, I think, that all that has been of value in socialism can somehow be rewritten under the rubric of, for example, democracy or freedom (themselves pretty much abused and misunderstood terms). Finally and most importantly, as I argue in the latter half of the book, social ownership (a key term of socialist discourse) is becoming not less but *more* central to the contemporary political aspirations of those 'on the left'.

I also feel the need to give some brief explanation of the very extensive discussion below of economic concepts and paradigms which certainly lie at (or indeed beyond) the outer limits of my professional competence. In part, this is a matter of necessity. Questions of economic organization are so central to this debate, above all to those invoking a *market* form of socialism, that they cannot be avoided. At the same time, it is important to try to bring to bear upon economic discussion ideas and experience drawn from political science and sociology. In recent years, economics has exercised an increasing influence upon political science, most prominently (though not exclusively) through the growth in rational choice explanations. This should not be one-way traffic and there is certainly space to apply political concepts in the heartlands of economic analysis. To paraphrase, markets are much too important to be left to the economists!

Finally, let me stress that this is a critical study of the 'death of socialism' debate and of the market socialist response to it. Whilst I try to indicate some revealing omissions from the market socialist position, I am more concerned with what is wrong with what is there than with those things that have been left out. I try to address the market socialists on their own terms. I do not generally seek to remedy their omissions, nor do I try to develop my own alternative 'blueprint'. It is in many ways extraordinary that a form of socialist advocacy which is directed towards contemporary problems and contemporary possibilities should have next to nothing to say about the politics of gender, ethnicity or environmental degradation. Consideration of these problems would raise issues which represent a severe and generic challenge to *all* forms of market advocacy. Unfortunately, their detailed evaluation lies beyond the scope of my discussion here.

Introduction

At the turn of the 1990s, it seemed for many commentators that 'the death of socialism' was a cliché whose time had come. Scarcely one hundred years after Lord Harcourt's declaration that 'we are all socialists now' had ushered in the collectivist age, political commentators were queueing up to bear witness that 'the Socialist Age was coming to an end' (Jenkins, 1987, p. 335). Characteristically, David Marquand argued that 'the epic struggle between capitalism and socialism is over; and capitalism has won', while Ralf Dahrendorf insisted quite simply that 'socialism is dead' (Marquand, 1991; Dahrendorf, 1990, p. 38). Of course, the 'death of socialism' has a long history, having been widely predicted in the 1930s and again in the early 1960s and it has long been a commonplace of conservative political rhetoric (in which it alternates with timely warnings about a dormant but still threatening red menace). What seemed to be different in the early 1990s was the ubiquity of the social changes identified with socialism's demise, the sorts of evidence taken to support it and the breadth of support for these positions even within the (erstwhile) political left. At the end of the 1980s, Francis Fukuyama achieved instant fame with his grandiloquent identification of 'the end of history' with 'the universalization of Western liberal democracy as the final form of human government' (Fukuyama, 1989, p. 4). But the problematic of systemic change was of longer standing and not confined to the political right. Thus, in another widely cited essay, written at the other end of the 1980s, André Gorz had suggested that 'in advanced industrial societies, socialism is already historically obsolete', while at the turn of the 1990s Bryan Turner, writing of 'the end of organised socialism', argued that 'we are now definitely into post-socialism' (Gorz, 1982, p. 12 n. 8; Turner, 1990, p. 134). The gradual exhaustion of the socialist idea which these authors record is seen to have reached its spectacular climax in the transformation of Eastern Europe in 1989. Ironically, when the long-awaited revolution finally came, it was 'a democratic and essentially anti-socialist revolution'. It was said that 'the ideas whose time has come are old, familiar, well-tested ones. (It is the new ideas whose time has passed)' (Selbourne, 1990, p. 274; Garton Ash, 1990, p. 154). Thus did socialism appear to perish with a resonant bang in the East and with a muted whimper in the West.

Socialism: A Terminal Decline?

There are few things which constrain our political judgement more than the dead hand of accepted wisdom and it seems as if, with a quite startling ease, 'the death of socialism' has already acquired the status of political common sense.[1] In the first part of this book I investigate this claim, with particular reference to experience in the developed West. It is not my intention to deny the profound changes upon which this new orthodoxy feeds. However, I do want to temper the aura of epochal generalization which has come to surround 'the death of socialism' by looking at some of the empirical evidence that is taken to support it. I also try to be a little more specific about what it is that has died. Does the 'death of socialism' mean the end of Soviet-style states in Eastern Europe or the decline of social democratic parties in the West or both? In what sense can the advanced capitalist societies of the developed West be said to be 'retreating from socialism'? Is it just the institutional apparatus of socialism that is under challenge or are the very ideas most frequently associated with socialism (above all, perhaps, equality and community) epochally unfashionable?

To anticipate a little, I shall argue that the more polemical celebrations of the 'death of socialism' are not really justified by the available evidence. Nonetheless, this rather exaggerated account is built upon a whole series of changes which taken together do pose a severe challenge to both the traditional beliefs and the established programmes of Western socialists and social democrats. Some of these traditional beliefs and much of the institutional apparatus through which they might be realized face fundamental reform. In the coming chapters, we shall see that it is perhaps above all else the traditional *political economy* of socialism that has been discredited by recent changes and certainly it is the seeming ubiquity of markets (in a 'global' economy) that is most frequently seen to be at the root of these difficulties. One of the boldest attempts to meet this particular challenge 'head on' has come from the advocates of a new form of *market socialism*. Market socialism has a lengthy history, primarily in the theoretical work of a number of distinguished Eastern European economists. In recent years, it has been revived by a number of Western socialist economists and political theorists who argue that, given a quite different institutional form, it represents a feasible way out of the strategic impasse which socialist forces are now seen to face. In a period dominated by theoretical and practical retreats, it is one of the most thoughtful and adventurous attempts to reconfigure socialist politics in response to a changed social environment. Parts II and III of this study are devoted to a detailed consideration of this initiative. In part II, I outline the principal elements of the contemporary market socialist position. In part III, I subject these to a detailed and critical scrutiny. In conclusion, I return to a consideration of some of the general problems facing contemporary socialist politics in the light of this investigation.

PART I

The Death of Socialism?

1

Socialism's Disappearing Social Base

The 'death of socialism' has spawned a large and diverse literature. The assessment of it here is organized around three broad and overlapping issues. First, there is the claim that the *social* bases of socialism are being undermined, most prominently through the 'withering away' of the political and industrial wings of the labour movement. The most serious symptoms of this process are seen in the declining density of trade union membership and the electoral misfortunes of parties of the left throughout the 1980s. A second and associated development is a decline in the *political economy* of socialism. The failure of 'planned' economies in the Soviet Union and Eastern Europe has a 'demonstration effect' for the advocates of planning in the West, whilst the transformation of the global economy is seen to render redundant those forms of the welfare state and of Keynesian economic macro-management upon which western social democrats have traditionally relied. Thirdly, it is suggested that in various ways the *ideological* coherence of socialism has been undermined. Whether as a 'crisis of Marxism' or as a 'crisis of labourism', through the countervailing appeal of consumerism or of the agenda of the new social movements, or under the corrosive impact of postmodernity, the traditional ideological appeal of the socialist idea is seen to be in retreat. In a final section, I shall consider the response of those who saw in the dramatic transformation of Eastern Europe in 1989 the consummation of socialism's collapse and draw some general conclusions about the status of the socialist project now. I begin by considering the 'withering away' of socialism's traditional social base in the industrial working class.

'Farewell to the Working Class'?

The advocates of socialism, even those who have imagined that it could be realized only through a period of protracted and fierce class struggle, have often insisted that the coming of socialism would be in (nearly) everyone's interest. However, almost as uniformly, at least since the rise of industrial capitalism, both reformist and revolutionary advocates of socialism have insisted that its progress would depend upon the political and industrial mobilization of the (normally urban) working class. Again, both reformers and revolutionaries anticipated that industrial development either had or would generate a majority constituency for the social and political programme of socialism. It was this belief that underwrote the confidence of Marxists in the inevitability of the coming of socialism and the expectation of social democrats that the majoritarian principles of parliamentary democracy would eventually generate a stable majority for their kind of socialism. This core societal component of the socialist case has come under increasingly critical scrutiny in recent years.

Like most elements in the argument for the decline of socialism, the claim about its eroding social base is not entirely new. It can be retraced at least to Eduard Bernstein's strictures upon the orthodoxy of the German Social Democratic Party at the turn of the twentieth century. But the consequences of Bernstein's arguments about the persistence of intermediary and agricultural strata were always rather ambivalent and, in practice, the general experience of social democratic parties in Western Europe was one of sustained growth throughout the first half of the century and beyond (Bernstein, 1909, pp. 48–9, 103; Przeworski, 1985, pp. 16–19; Flora, 1987; Mackie and Rose, 1991). It is only since the 1970s that commentators have widely seen 'the forward march of labour halted' (Hobsbawm, 1981; Piven, 1991; Lemke and Marks, 1992; though see the reservations expressed in Przeworski and Sprague, 1986).

At the heart of this concern lies the belief that, within a context of rapid social and economic change, the 'traditional' working class upon which the advance of socialism was seen to be premised is in numerical decline. As in most disputes about the salience of social class, much depends here upon the ways in which the working class is defined. It is undoubtedly the case that over the past hundred years the proportion of wage-earners within the working population has grown, so that those who make a living by selling their labour power for a wage or salary now constitute an overwhelming majority in all advanced industrial societies. In the European Union, for example, the figure is now well in excess of 80 per cent, whilst in the US it stands at more than 90 per cent (Eurostat, 1990, p. 59). If one accepts that this employee status defines at least the potential for a collective (class) interest in socialism, then the 'marginalization of the working class' is not a problem. There may be real political difficulties in mobilizing this potential class majority for socialism, but this is quite different from saying that this majority no longer exists. This, very broadly, is the position adopted by proponents of an 'orthodox' Marxism (see e.g. Wood, 1986; Mandel, 1978; Panitch, 1986 and 1990).

More common in recent years has been the argument that while this process of 'technical proletarianization' has indeed been continuing throughout the twentieth century, such a category does not define even the potential basis for a class interested in the promotion of socialism. Indeed, while this broader process of proletarianization has been proceeding, that more narrowly circumscribed working class which could form the basis for a socialist politics and which has, in practice, offered its support to social democratic parties throughout the advanced industrial societies is seen to be in long-term decline. While there is considerable disagreement about where precisely the parameters of this truly working class should be drawn, for most commentators there lies at its heart the category of manual (and frequently male) labour, in full-time employment, within traditional (and often strongly unionized) industries, located within long-established urban-industrial contexts (see e.g. Poulantzas, 1975; Hobsbawm, 1981; Przeworski and Sprague, 1986; Hall and Jacques, 1989).

Generally speaking, the core working class thus defined is a declining (though still substantial) minority in most advanced industrial societies. In Britain, where the process has been most spectacular, manual workers declined from around three-quarters of the working population in the first decade of the twentieth century to be something less than a half by 1981 (Price and Bain, 1988, pp. 162–4). In the US, their numbers fell from around 40 per cent in 1950 to less than a third by 1980 (cited in Lash and Urry, 1987, p. 120). Even in definitively social democratic Sweden, manual workers had fallen back from being a little more than half the working population in the immediate post-war years to constitute 47 per cent of the workforce by 1970 (Esping-Andersen, 1985, p. 52). In the same period, building upon a prior and continuing marginalization of agricultural employment, there has been a shift away from employment in extractive and manufacturing industries (in which many traditional blue-collar jobs were located), towards (often white-collar) jobs in the service sector. This process has accelerated over the past twenty years, so that by 1990 in the EC there were nearly twice as many people employed in the service sector (60 per cent) as in industry (32.5 per cent). Service sector employment was even higher in the US at around 70 per cent (Commission of the EC, 1991). Meanwhile, in Britain, manufacturing employment fell by more than a quarter in the course of the 1980s and this fall was most precipitate amongst those workers who have been widely regarded as the vanguard of the labour movement. Thus, in coal mining, for example, employment fell from 423,000 in 1971 to just 17,000 in 1993 (*Employment Gazette*, Feb. 1971; July 1994). In the US, the percentage of the population employed in manufacturing industry was halved between 1950 and 1970.

These sectoral changes have been accompanied by important changes in working practices and in the composition of the workforce itself. First, there has been a long-standing trend throughout the OECD countries towards increased female labour force participation. By 1988, women made up nearly 40 per cent of the working population in the European Community and in some countries (for example, Sweden), participation rates were still closer to parity. In the European Community, nearly three-quarters of all women in employment worked in the service sector. Although most women in paid employment work full time, more than a quarter of all women workers, and more than a third of married women, work part-time (Eurostat, 1989a; Rein, 1985). This helps to explain a long-term rise in part-time working, a trend which has become more pronounced over the past twenty years (OECD, 1985). There is, of course, no *prima facie* reason to believe that women workers are less responsive to a class appeal than are men, though it may be that typical domestic divisions of labour make their effective participation in political and trade union organization more difficult. However, trade union membership, described by Hobsbawm as 'the most elementary index of . . . class consciousness', has typically been lower amongst women, part-time workers and those in non-manual occupations. All of these categories have been expanding (Hobsbawm, 1981, p. 15; Blanchflower and Freeman, 1992, pp. 56–60).

A number of other aspects of industrial and economic change have seemingly weakened the bases for effective class mobilization. While economic restructuring has seen the creation of vast multinational and transnational corporations, firms within the expanding service sector are generally smaller and less frequently unionized than has traditionally been the case in manufacturing industry. This process has been heightened since the 1970s by a decline in average plant size in a range of industrialized countries and the relocation of employment from traditional urban-industrial sites towards semi-rural locations (Lash and Urry, 1987, pp. 84–160). In many of the largest economies, trade union membership has fallen substantially over the last ten years. In Britain, for example, membership fell from 13.4 million in 1979 to 9.0

million in 1994, while in the US the density of union membership was very nearly halved between 1970 and 1987 (*Social Trends*, 21 (1991), p. 183; Blanchflower and Freeman, 1992, p. 59; Visser, 1992, p. 19; *Employment Gazette*, June, 1994).

Finally, it has been suggested that recent changes in the structure of advanced capitalism have undermined what Hobsbawm called 'a common style of proletarian life' (Hobsbawm, 1981, p. 7). Although sectionalism has always been a problem for the labour movement, Hobsbawm, in his influential essay on the British working class, argues that these problems have become more acute in the period since the Second World War. With the growing influx of women and immigrant workers, the working class has become more internally diverse. Heightened social and physical mobility has eroded established communities of interest. The changing structure of industry and the growth of the public sector has made intra-worker disputes more common. For many workers, the targets of industrial action are no longer the owners of capital, but rather the government, 'the public' or simply other workers (Hobsbawm, 1981). According to Hyman (1992, 150–8), the difficulties of the 1980s may be summarized in terms of an accelerating process of working-class *disaggregation*:

1   a shift from collectivism towards individualism, reflected in declining levels of trade-union membership, and/or reduced responsiveness to collectively determined policies and disciplines;
2   a polarization within the working class (which may largely coincide with a division between union members and non-unionists) which many writers characterize in terms of core–periphery or insider–outsider relations;
3   a growing particularism of collective identities and projects in terms of employers, occupation, and/or economic sector or industry;
4   fragmentation within the 'organized working class' expressed in intra- and inter-union conflict, and a weakening of the authority of national leaderships and central confederations.

There are other ways of characterizing this diversity of interests within the broadly-defined working class. Some have stressed the ways in which growing affluence has transformed working class patterns of *consumption* under contemporary capitalism. Thus, the diversification of housing tenure, increases in car ownership, the expansion of leisure time and opportunities, the greater distance between place of work and place of residence, have all undermined collective patterns of consumption, which had tended to solidify the commonality of interest and experience of the traditional working class (Lash and Urry, 1987). Some have drawn attention to the existence of a dual labour market, in

which the interests and opportunities of full-time securely employed
workers within the primary sector are systematically different from
those of the more marginalized and intermittent workers within the
secondary labour market. Others have seen in this new division of
labour the emergence of a 'two-thirds, one-third' society in which a
substantial minority at the bottom of society (sometimes described as
'the underclass'), trapped in poverty, semi-permanent unemployment
and dependency upon state support, is increasingly divorced from that
of the 'respectable' majority, including the regularly employed working class (Wilson, 1987; Field, 1989; Therborn, 1989a).

Cumulatively, these changes have been taken by some to undermine
the capacity of the working class to act as the social basis for a
transformative political practice. In Gorz's iconoclastic formulation,
'the crisis of socialism is above all a reflection of the crisis of the
proletariat' (Gorz, 1982, p. 66). For him, the 'traditional working class is
now no more than a privileged minority [and] capitalist development
has produced a working class which, on the whole, is unable to take
command of the means of production and whose immediate interests
are not consonant with a socialist rationality' (Gorz, 1982, pp. 69, 15).
More measured, and more empirically grounded, is the judgement of
Lash and Urry that recent changes in the structure of 'disorganized
capitalism' have triggered 'the decline of working class capacities'.
Thus, 'not only has the size of the working class and especially its
"core" declined in disorganized capitalism, but spatial scattering has
meant the disruption of communicational and organizational net-
works, resulting in an important diminution of class resources'. As a
consequence, 'the power of a mass industrial working class to shape
society in its own image [is] profoundly weakened' (Lash and Urry,
1987, pp. 11, 311). Most bluntly, in Marquand's account, 'the classical
working class . . . has almost disappeared' and with it has gone the
classical socialist project for societal change. Indeed,

> To the extent that socialism is still the vehicle of the working class, that is
> now a handicap rather than an asset . . . in most developed societies, the
> majority [of the working class] has been absorbed, for all practical pur-
> poses, into a vast, almost boundaryless, middle class. The rest . . . have
> become an under-class, effectively excluded from full citizenship.
> (Marquand, 1993, p. 55)

The 'Gravediggers of Capitalism':[1] Dead and Buried?

To what extent do these societal changes justify the belief that the social
basis for the promotion of socialism has been eliminated? It is a truism

that we live (perhaps semi-permanently) in times of rapid social and economic change and, under these circumstances, it is perhaps more than usually difficult to adjudicate which changes are significant and in what their significance consists. It would certainly be foolish to say that nothing has *really* changed, but we have the benefit of some earlier projections of wholesale social transformation ('the post-industrial society', 'the end of ideology' and so on), to caution against too extravagant an exercise of the sociological imagination.

An initial problem in making an assessment lies not with the destination of social change, but with its point of departure. It is clearly presumptuous to speak of the period we are leaving as 'the Socialist Age'. Indeed, it is difficult to think of any OECD country having been 'socialist', without further and substantial qualification. It is also worth noting that those societies and periods in which class structure was deemed to be so much more promising for socialism were not characterized by uniform socialist advance.

Turning to more substantive questions, there has been a tendency (perhaps natural to Anglo-American authors), to concentrate too heavily upon the rather unusual experience of Britain and the United States. The 'exceptionalism' of the United States has been a common theme in the social science literature for a century and, however one understands the rise of the American New Right and American labour history, it is hard to see in the most recent period a reversal of previously highly favourable circumstances for the development of socialism (Sombart, 1976; Pierson, 1990; Mann, 1993). Britain may not immediately give the appearance of being so exceptional. Indeed, Britain has frequently been presented as the exemplar of class development under industrial capitalism and of the characteristically class-based politics to which this had been thought to give rise. Yet, as in other aspects of its development, Britain's status as 'the first industrial nation' has given it a distinctive history of class development and it is misleading to take it as the 'typical' case. For example, the numbers employed in agriculture were much lower much sooner than in continental Europe and its early twentieth-century preponderance of manual workers was also quite unusual. In 1911, 75 per cent of the British workforce was made up of manual workers. Fewer than 10 per cent were employed within the agricultural sector. In the most comparable European countries at this time, manual workers made up between 35 per cent (Germany) and 41 per cent (Denmark) of the workforce. As late as 1939, a quarter of all German workers were occupied in the agricultural sector (Esping-Andersen, 1985, p. 52; Lash and Urry, 1987, pp. 141, 144). In other European countries, for example in France and Italy, the steep decline of the agricultural sector was substantially a *post*-war development. In

France and the United States, the number of manual workers never exceeded 40 per cent (Bell and Criddle, 1988, p. 34; Lash and Urry, 1987, p. 119; Mitchell, 1975, p. 158). Thus, it was truly exceptional for manual workers to come to constitute a majority of the working population anywhere. Correspondingly, the decline of the manual working class has been much less precipitate than a cursory reading of the British and American evidence would suggest. In Britain, the proportion of manual workers has almost halved. But even here, in 1990, more than half of all male workers remained in manual occupations. The figure for the overall workforce was well over 40 per cent (*Social Trends*, 21 (1991), p. 74).

Nor have all the changes in twentieth-century class structure clearly militated against the socialist cause. Alongside the declining numbers of manual workers and despite some increase in the numbers of the self-employed during the 1980s, there has been a parallel long-term decline in the numbers of the petty bourgeoisie, the class which has been most implacably hostile to socialist forces (Eurostat, 1989b; Mann, 1993; on Scandinavia, see Esping-Andersen, 1985, p. 53). It is also a mistake to assume that the growth of the service sector necessarily means a growth in 'middle-class', white-collar positions or that it un-avoidably develops more conservative/market-supportive political at-titudes. Much of the rapid growth of the service sector in the US, for example, has been of menial, unskilled and part-time jobs, many of them in what has been styled 'the McDonald's proletariat' (Wood, 1989, p. 17; Esping-Andersen, 1992, p. 146).[2] At the same time, there have been very significant differences between countries in the extent to which their expanded service sector is in marketed or non-marketed (and generally state) services. In the US, for example, three times as many workers are employed in the marketed as opposed to the non-marketed services sector (54:17 per cent). In Europe, by contrast, only 50 per cent more workers are in marketed than in non-marketed ser-vices, (37:24 per cent) (Eurostat, 1990). Whether service workers are located in the public sector (largely in the welfare state), or the private sector may have a pronounced effect upon the capacity for (and the direction of), their political mobilization.

A broadly similar argument may be mounted in terms of the decline of trade unionism. How and whether trade unions can still act effec-tively are questions we return to below. If, however, we confine our-selves to considering trade union *membership*, the picture is again less drastic than the Anglo-American evidence would suggest. Certainly, the US and the UK are not alone in seeing union membership decline in the period since 1970, though the extent of this decline is exceptional. However, in the 1980s, only the Netherlands and Italy experienced a

Table 1.1 Union membership of non-agricultural workers as % of non-agricultural wage and salary employees, 1970–1986/7

Country	1970	1979	1986/7	Change 1970–87
Denmark	66	86	95	+29
Finland	56	84	85	+29
Sweden	79	89	96	+17
Belgium	66	77	76	+10
Ireland	44	49	51	+7
W Germany	37	42	43	+6
Australia	52	58	56	+5
Canada	32	36	36	+4
Switzerland	31	34	33	+2
Norway	59	60	61	+2
Italy	39	51	45	+6
UK	51	58	50	−1
New Zealand	43	46	41	−2
Austria	64	59	61	−3
Netherlands	39	43	35	−4
France	22	20	17	−5
Japan	35	32	28	−7
United States	31	25	17	−14
Unweighted average (exclusive of US)	48	54	53	+6

Source: Blanchflower and Freeman (1992, p. 59).

decline in union membership comparable to that in Britain and the US. In most of the other developed economies (with the exceptions of France and Japan), levels rose steadily in the 1970s and stagnated in the 1980s. In Sweden and Denmark, they exceeded the 'saturation' levels achieved in the 1970s, to stand at 96 per cent and 95 per cent respectively (see table 1.1). It is also clear that a significant part of the fall in densities can be attributed to the direct and indirect consequences of persistent mass unemployment (see Visser, 1992, p. 19).[3]

The following overall conclusions would seem to be justified. There has been a long-term and substantial decline in the proportion of manual workers within the economies of all the advanced industrial nations. This development has been unusually long-standing and steep in the UK. Nowhere outside of Britain (with the possible exception of parts of Scandinavia during the 1950s), did manual workers ever come to constitute a stable majority of the working population. Despite their declining numbers, manual workers continue to make up a substantial minority in nearly all industrialized countries. The numbers of employers and the self-employed have also fallen throughout most of the twentieth century. The major area of employment growth has been amongst white-collar employees particularly in the service sector. Wage-earners have now come to constitute an overwhelming majority of the working population in virtually all developed societies. Overall, we may judge (1) that the historical circumstances in which a *majority* of manual workers could have been mobilized behind the transition to socialism have almost never existed, (2) that manual workers form a declining but still substantial minority of the population in nearly all advanced industrial societies and (3) that trade union membership has fallen substantially from the historically high levels of the 1970s, but that this decline has been internationally quite variable and has left widely differing union densities throughout the OECD economies.

Now, if socialism's prospects depended solely upon the existence of a majoritarian manual working class, these developments would surely be fatal to its prospects (though the idea that something had changed very radically in recent years would be much reduced, since this majoritarian manual working class has hardly ever existed). But this is an argument which opponents of the 'death of socialism' fiercely resist. There is, they insist, no *prima facie* reason why the working class should be made up of manual workers or males or whites, or that it should be employed within certain traditional industries. Those who pare down the working class to a declining minority are said to be the victims of *technological* determinism. What is essential to the proletarian experience is not a particular technology, but the *social relations of production* founded in an exploitative wage-labour contract (see e.g. Wright, 1985). The belief that white-collar workers are, in some sense, 'middle-class' is entirely ungrounded. Braverman was perhaps the most influential exponent of the view that the growth of white-collar work in the twentieth century was contemporaneous with its deskilling and with the introduction of factory-like discipline in the office (Braverman, 1974). As we have already observed, the major change in the twentieth-century occupational structure has been from blue-collar to white-collar work, while the category of wage-earners or employees has continued to grow (though, of course, a growing proportion of these wage-earners do not sell their labour power to a capitalist employer).

The difficulty with this position is that, while wage-earning status may form *one* axis around which collective action could be taken, wage-earners do not look like, or act like, a class with collective social and political interests. More or less subtle qualifications about productive and unproductive labour, about non-productive positions in the division of labour which are 'functional for capital' or even the time-honoured distinction between 'class-in-itself' and 'class-for-itself' do comparatively little to address this problem.[4] Nor is the principal issue at stake here the old conundrum of the senior manager and the unskilled shopfloor worker 'sharing' the same class position. That managers are not owners in the nineteenth-century fashion may be important, but (senior) managers are comparatively few in number and there is evidence that, through control over the process of production or through participation in ownership, they are not exclusively sellers of their labour power. Much more important for class analysis, and its political consequences, are those divisions which exist among wage-earners 'proper'. In part, and broadly in line with Max Weber's analysis of class, these are differences in the control of marketable assets, but they are also differences in the terms and conditions of employment, in patterns of consumption and in attitudes to the interventionist state. Among the most important of these potential lines of division (and one to which we shall return below), is that between workers in the public and private sectors. This division has often been rather misleadingly presented. A large public sector does not, in itself, indicate the gradual abandonment of capitalism. Nor is it clear that those things that divide public and private sector wage-earners (for example, their attitude to public spending), are necessarily more important than those things which may unite them (perhaps, for example, a hostility to incomes policy). Yet, whatever its precise political salience, the expansion of (welfare) sate employment, often, but far from exclusively, under social democratic auspices, is one of the more remarkable and significant features of advanced capitalism.

In practice, explanations of the diversity of wage-earners' interests do not necessarily support the perspective of a declining salience of class. For example, counting against the 'two-thirds, one-third' argument, which would place much of the working class in society's 'comfortable majority', is the evidence of recent recessions that manual workers (especially in the private sector) remain particularly vulnerable to unemployment. Indeed, as Hobsbawm himself argues, any suggestion that history reveals a straightforward transition from class homogeneity to class heterogeneity is highly misleading (Hobsbawm, 1981; see also Marshall et al., 1989; and Hyman, 1992). Yet the countervailing expectation that all wage-earners share an overriding interest in socialization which will eventually make itself manifest is peculiarly unconvincing.

The Electoral Decline of Socialism

It would be difficult here to pass judgement definitively upon the profusion of explanations of the complex class structure of contemporary capitalism. Happily, there is a more modest alternative. For, while

witnesses to the 'death of socialism' have not abstained from some
fairly sweeping judgements about the changing class composition of
contemporary capitalism, the focus of their attention has been upon the
relationship between (a disaggregating) class and the (declining)
electoral fortunes of socialist and social democratic parties. Difficult
questions about the 'true' nature of class composition can largely be
avoided by concentrating upon the changing relationship between
some fairly conventional definitions of class and electoral support for
parties of the left.

At the heart of the critical argument lies the claim that the class
structure of contemporary capitalist societies does not (any longer)
provide a potential basis for the electoral success of parties of the
socialist and social democratic left. Either (1) social class (particularly
within the working class) is no longer a powerful indicator of voting
intention (the thesis of class dealignment), or (2) the shrinking of the
working class deprives the socialists of a potentially majority-securing
social base (the thesis of the 'disappearing' working class). (See e.g.
Crewe, 1985, 1991 and 1993; Heath et al., 1985 and 1991.)[5]

It is often in Britain that class voting was seen to have reached its
'purest' expression, and again it is in Britain that the electoral reverses
of the left have most often been associated with 'the rapid erosion of the
"pure" working class' (Butler and Stokes, 1974, p. 88; Crewe, 1984, p.
199). At its simplest, the class dealignment thesis suggests that social
class is no longer a secure indicator of voting intention. In the 1950s, it
is argued, occupation – and particularly the status of manual or non-
manual employment – was a very clear indicator of likely voting intention. In the UK, manual workers voted more than 2:1 in favour of the
Labour Party, while non-manual workers voted 4:1 for the Conservatives. Since the 1960s, occupational class is seen to have ceased to be a
useful indicator of voting practice. The argument at its crudest is that
the manual working class can no longer be relied upon to vote Labour
and class de-alignment is often seen to 'explain' the strength of the
Conservative Party in the UK. This tendency is seen to be exacerbated
by an *internal* division amongst workers between an old, 'traditional'
working class, which remains loyal to the Labour Party and a 'new'
working class, increasingly inclined to offer its support to other parties.
After the 1987 UK election, Crewe suggested that

> The [Labour] party has come to represent a declining segment of the
> working class – the traditional working class of the council estates, the
> public sector, industrial Scotland and the North and the old industrial
> unions – while failing to attract the affluent and expanding working class
> of the new estates and new service economy of the South. [Conservative]
> government policies are producing a steady expansion of the new work-

ing class, and a diminution of the old . . . The new working class is not only the dominant segment but increasingly dominant. Demography and time are not on Labour's side. (Crewe, 1987; see also Crewe, 1991 and 1993)

In a similar reassessment, Dunleavy and Husbands (1985), see class dealignment yielding new forms of electoral cleavage associated with the expanding role of the interventionist state. These new forms of *sectoral cleavage* turn upon the contrast between a private/commercial sector and a public/de-commodified sector, in areas such as employment, consumption (of, for example, housing and transport) and derivation of income. These sectoral cleavages are seen to cut across the traditional lines of working/middle class and to offer a better guide to voting intentions. Where private sector production and consumption is expanding for working-class electors they may be expected to transfer their support away from the party identified with public provision, that is, the Labour Party.

A broadly parallel process has been identified in the United States (though here, of course, the baseline of existing class structure and public provision, as well as the parameters of the traditional electoral alignment, are very different). As in the UK, attention has been focused upon the repeated victories of right-wing candidates in (Presidential) elections. Evidence from the 1980s suggested that the working class, which had been a core component in the Democrats' general electoral ascendancy since the 1930s, was now much more divided in its loyalties. Whilst ethnic minorities voted for Democrats in consistently high numbers (more than 80 per cent of black voters supported the Democrats), there were significant defections amongst the white working class, with a majority supporting Reagan in 1980 and 1984. Working-class support for the Democrats, which had been secured in the realignment of the 1930s, 'dropped precipitously in the presidential contests of the 1950s, recovered briefly in the 1960s, and then plunged again' (see Piven, 1991, pp. 235–41). Some commentators argue that the US now has a new alignment in which the Republicans have replaced the Democrats as the party with a 'natural' electoral majority. In fact, this perspective of *re*alignment could only be sustained by ignoring the continuing strength of the Democrats in Congressional and sub-federal elections, and is anyway rather weakened by the election of Clinton in 1992. Evidence of a *de*alignment (ticket-splitting, greater voter volatility, declining partisan identity and so on) is rather stronger. (For further discussion, see Ladd, 1981; Schneider, 1981; Beck, 1984; Lowi, 1985; Burnham, 1989; McKay, 1993).

Although the perspective of dealignment probably defines the dominant view of recent developments, it has certainly not gone unchallenged and, in the UK (where the loss of social democratic voters has been unusually severe), it has come under sustained attack by Anthony Heath and his colleagues (Heath et al., 1985 and 1991). Buttressed with substantial statistical support, the essence of their response is that (1) while *absolute* class voting (the numbers of middle-class Conservative or working-class Labour voters) has declined substantially since the 1960s the decline of *relative* class voting (measuring the extent to which parties draw their support from given classes, allowing for general changes in across-the-board political support and changes in the size of the classes) has been 'very modest' (Heath et al., 1991, p. 78); (2) while 'the working class . . . is certainly fragmented, most notably by region, ethnicity, housing and, to a lesser extent, by union membership', this is not a new phenomenon, and 'while Crewe and others have been right to note the spread of owner-occupation and the decline of union membership within the working class, these changes can go only a little way towards explaining the crumbling of the Labour vote' (Heath et al., 1991, pp. 113–14); (3) while there is some evidence of a public ector/ private sector division in 'middle-class' Labour voting, this is substantially to be explained by the largely overlapping division between 'welfare and creative professions' in both public and private sectors and 'others'; 'Sector has no statistically significant effect once we control for the welfare and creative occupations' (Heath et al., 1991, p. 94). 'Political differences between working-class public and private sector employees are rather modest', suggesting to Heath and his colleagues a 'rejection of the theory of distinct interests based on production sectors' (1991, p. 104).

It is impossible here to do full justice to the arguments over dealignment. However, what is probably more significant (and the more remarkable given the profound divergence over the central claims of dealignment), is the breadth of agreement over underlying changes in the class structure. Thus both the studies co-ordinated by Heath (Heath et al., 1985 and 1991), and Gordon Marshall (Marshall et al., 1989), are highly critical of Crewe's version of the dealignment thesis. Yet both are agreed that the working class has shrunk. Heath finds that 'in 1964 the working class . . . amounted to 51 per cent of the electorate but by 1987 this has fallen to 36 per cent' (Heath et al., 1991, p. 67). Marshall, using a similar class schema, but rather different criteria and bases, finds a decline in the manual working class from 48 per cent to 35 per cent of the working population (Marshall et al., 1989, p. 101). It is a part of Heath's ambition to show that the loss in Labour Party support between 1964 and 1987 (of about 13 per cent) is to be attributed as much to immediately *political* factors, perhaps most notably to the rise of third-party candidacies, as to social changes (including changes in the class structure). Yet he estimates that changes in the class structure between 1951 and 1981 should have increased the Conservative share of the vote by about 3.8 points, the Liberal/Alliance by about 0.7, and entailed a loss of about 4.5 points in the Labour vote (Heath et al., 1991, p. 203). What we have is an image of 'avoidable' political losses for Labour, including backing the 'wrong' policies, piggybacking on some 'scarcely avoidable' changes in social structure (see also Harrop and Shaw, 1989). Similarly, Marshall argues that there is limited evidence of changes in the sociological behaviour of the working class (little evidence of new levels of sectionalism, privatism, or of a dissipating class consciousness), but that the size of this class has fallen substantially (Marshall et al., 1989, pp. 98–142, 196–224). Thus it appears that, even among the opponents of class dealignment, there is substantial support for the thesis of the declining working class. In the US, explanations of the decline of the Democrat vote are more varied, including an important emphasis upon changes in the ethnic and regional composition of the vote, but here too the changes are set against the background of a long-term decline in blue-collar employment (see e.g. Piven, 1991; Esping-Andersen, 1985).

Of course, it could be that the political consequences of change in the class structure are largely confined to the Anglo-American context. Indeed, comparative scrutiny of the recent electoral fortunes of parties of the left suggests both that there is substantial international variation and that the performance of the American Democrats and the British Labour Party has been unusually poor. At the same time, while support for the Democratic Party may have fallen, it is not clear that this should be seen as a decline in the 'pro-socialist' vote. Walter Korpi, for example (1983, p. 38), describes the left vote in the US as having fallen from 1 per cent in the period 1946–60 to 0 per cent in the period 1961–80! Similarly, Britain's unusually proletarian class structure may have left greater space for a fall than exists elsewhere. However, there is some evidence of dealignment in Germany and France (though in the latter this is 'very limited'), while, most instructively, Esping-Andersen, Sainsbury and Lafferty all find evidence of Social Democratic Party 'decomposition' penetrating into the heartlands of Scandinavian social democracy (Lash and Urry, 1987, pp. 214–19; Esping-Andersen, 1985, pp. 114–41; Sainsbury, 1993; Lafferty, 1990). As interestingly, Esping-Andersen's discussion of the *differential* pace of incipient party decomposition in Denmark, Norway and Sweden focuses upon the governmental performance of their respective Social Democratic administrations and the differential capacity of the parties to forge effective alliances of interest between the manual working class and other wage-earners. There have also been some spectacular

defeats for the left outside the Anglo-Saxon world, perhaps most dramatically in France, where support for the Socialist Party in the 1993
National Assembly elections was virtually halved to stand at 19.2 per
cent (*Electoral Studies*).

Despite all this evidence, the long-term electoral decline of the left is
easily exaggerated (see Merkel, 1992). Thus, the combined electoral
strength of the left in Western Europe, which had stood at 40.1 per cent
through the 1970s, advanced to 42.5 per cent in the years 1980–3 (Lane
and Ersson, 1987, p. 112; Pierson, 1991a, pp. 171–2). In the 1980s, while
the right took or retained power in the UK, the US and West Germany,
the left retained or was restored to office in Sweden, Norway, France,
Spain, Portugal, New Zealand and Australia (Mackie and Rose, 1991).
In Australia, the Labour Party won five consecutive election victories
(Mackie and Rose, 1991; *Electoral Studies*). In France, the Presidential
candidate of the left was elected in 1981 and re-elected in 1988. But
perhaps the most dramatic electoral success of the 1980s belonged to
the Spanish Socialist Workers Party (PSOE). Having achieved an aston-
ishing 48.7 per cent of the vote in the 1982 elections, the PSOE went on
to win the elections of 1986 and 1989, albeit with a rapidly depleting
share of the vote (Share, 1989, p. 29; *Electoral Studies*). In trying to
evaluate the electoral performance of the left, we should be mindful of
those difficulties which they have shared with parties of the centre and
right. Virtually *all* mainstream parties have faced a 'crisis of representation' which has seen their support eroded by third parties or voters'
abstentions. Thus in 1993 the collapse of the French Socialists was
actually outstripped by the rout of the Canadian Conservatives, whose
vote tumbled from 43 per cent in 1988 to just 16 per cent (and from 154
MPs to just 2!), and it was in a similar context of electoral difficulty for
mainstream parties that the Irish Labour Party (as a third force) was
able to double its representation at the 1992 general election and force
its way into the new governing coalition (*Electoral Studies*). We should
also bear in mind that socialist parties are not always looking to win an
elusive 51 per cent of the popular vote. In plurality voting systems, 40
per cent will often be enough to deliver a majority of parliamentary
seats, whilst in systems with proportional representation the com-
plexities of alliance-building and coalition formation will often mean
that (socialist) parties have strategic ambitions other than simply maximizing their vote (for a detailed evaluation, see Kitschelt, 1994).

All of this suggests that even under contemporary circumstances a
social democratic party *can* win and retain governmental office. However, it is also clear that this is becoming increasingly difficult and
indeed it is only possible if a successful appeal is made beyond the
'natural' constituency of social democrats in the traditional working

class. Thus, for example, the PSOE's remarkable victory in 1982 could not have been achieved simply on the basis of traditional working-class votes, and in fact the party secured the votes of a little less than half of skilled and unskilled workers even in this historic triumph. In practice, the PSOE draws its electoral support from all classes. In 1982, it gained the votes of rather more than a third of white-collar workers, and more than one-quarter of all 'entrepreneurs' (cited in Share, 1989, pp. 111–12). Nor is this really such an innovation. Most European social democratic parties have at some stage sought to redefine themselves as *Volksparteien* (people's parties), none more successfully than the Swedish SAP, whose aspiration to constitute Sweden as the 'People's Home' can be retraced to the writings of Per Albin Hansson in the 1920s, perhaps even to the thought of Hjalmar Branting at the end of the nineteenth century (Tilton, 1990).

Whilst social democratic parties share with others the problems of declining support and withering partisan loyalty, they are clearly not 'unelectable'. Much more disturbing for socialism's supporters is the evidence seemingly to be derived from the Spanish, French and Australasian experience, that contemporary social democratic parties can *only* achieve electoral success by abandoning even the most modest attachment to traditional socialist or even social democratic goals. The *locus classicus* of this jettisoning of socialist principle is often found in Mitterand's early abandonment of Keynesianism and the inauguration of an austerity programme in 1982. But it can also be seen in the Spanish experience. Writing in 1985, Antonio Garcia Santesmases reflected that 'in only ten years, the Spanish Socialists have gone from republicanism, neutralism, anticapitalism, *autogestion*, to defender of Spain's entry into NATO, and a strong supporter of the efficiency of the market economy' (cited in Share, 1989, p. 150). Throughout much of the 1980s in Spain, sustained economic growth was coupled with unemployment rates above 20 per cent (Share, 1989, pp. 76–7). This experience has been reproduced elsewhere. Writing of the election of New Zealand's fourth Labour Government in 1984, David Denemark cites 'a political-economic "about face" as sweeping as any seen in the western industrial world. Labour, historically committed to the virtues of collective provision, state interventionism, and Keynesianism, has become a "New Right" advocate of individual provision, "the free market", and monetarism' (Denemark, 1990, p. 62).

One long-popular account of the 'U-turns' of social democrats in office is the 'betrayal' of the socialist movement by its pusillanimous leaders. This is not generally a satisfactory explanation. While leaders are surely as vulnerable as anyone else to a loss of political nerve, it is curious that the socialist movement should have been so unlucky in

uniformly choosing for high office those who have subsequently be-
trayed their core constituency. The waywardness of socialist leaders
notwithstanding, we do better to seek the origins of these reversals in
the circumstances in which socialist and social democratic leaders find
themselves operating. On the one hand, it may be that to secure an
election-winning plurality, social democratic leaders have to appeal
beyond the minoritarian working class, and thus to dilute their socialist
political agenda. While this necessity may be becoming more pronounced, it is certainly not new (see Przeworski, 1985; Przeworski and
Sprague, 1986; and below pp. 195–205). What may be newer and still
more daunting is the prospect that the economic world order within
which socialist and social democratic governments have now to operate is one in which even the modestly progressive strategies of
Keynesianism and the welfare state are no longer sustainable. It may be
that even if socialists prove to be electable, they can no longer pursue
even a mildly socialist political agenda. It is this prospect that we
investigate in chapter 2.

2

The Declining Political
Economy of Socialism

Despite common usage, it is not certain that socialism is best understood as an economic or politico-economic theory.[1] Certainly, for many of its advocates, the socialist organization of economic life (however this is understood) is not an end in itself but rather the necessary means to achieving some ulterior moral or political goal and, as we shall see later in our discussion, this last claim is central to contemporary socialists' reappraisal of the market. Yet, while the *ambition* of socialists has often been the promotion of a system that is morally and ethically superior to capitalism, for most socialists (though certainly not for all), the principal *mechanism* for achieving this superior form of social organization has been a reconstituted economy.

This is especially clear in, though by no means confined to, the political economy of Marxism. The 'anarchy of production' under capitalism is seen to generate 'crises, internecine competition, and wars' (Bukharin and Preobrazhensky, 1969, p. 89). It promotes the irrational exploitation of resources and the irrational distribution of goods and services. It combines 'crises of overproduction' with the underutilization of labour and capital and the persistence of vast unmet need. At the same time, the capitalist organization of the economy is seen to be profoundly anti-democratic. Whilst decisions about economic life are of fundamental importance to every member of society and to 'the community' more generally, effective decision-making powers are concentrated in the hands of those with significant holdings of private capital and the formally free and equal institutions of political democracy are in fact subservient to the economic power of private capital-holders.

The dominant socialist response to these irrational and undemocratic elements within capitalism has been to offer the alternative of a democratically planned socialist economy. Models for exercising this control of the economy have been very different in the (Soviet) East and the (social democratic) West. While the economies of Eastern Europe (even excluding the former Yugoslavia) were quite varied, the essence of the Soviet model was a centrally planned economy, which in its more extreme forms could embrace the forced direction of labour and the rationing of consumer goods (see Ellman, 1989).[2] In the West, some industrial undertakings were taken into public ownership, and this 'socialization' of the economy was often given great political prominence. But, more generally, it was some variant of the Keynesian model, in which government manipulation of a few macro-economic levers would yield effective management of the wider economy, which described the preferred form of (indirect) control of economic life. Of course, we should be cautious about the extent to which economies, in either East or West, were ever effectively 'planned'. A great deal of government conduct has been not so much 'planning' as 'muddling through', and there is some evidence that, even within the Soviet Union, 'planning' may often have been an *ex post* justification for developments which had already taken place (Schmidt, 1983; Ellman, 1989, p. 17; Rutland, 1985). In the British social democratic experience, a general sympathy for 'planning' was sometimes coupled with an extremely hazy conception of what such planning might entail in practice (Marquand, 1988, pp. 42–3). Despite this, political control of the economy has retained a central place in the *justification* of the case for socialism.

It is the credibility of this economic alternative which is now under serious challenge. We now face a situation in which the two most prominent and quite divergent forms which 'real socialism' took in the twentieth century – the Soviet model and Western social democracy – seem both to have run out of steam at the same time. Both the Soviet model (and the derivative 'reform' models of Eastern Europe) and Keynesianism now stand condemned for having failed (literally) 'to deliver the goods' and having concentrated economic power in the hands of state bureaucrats rather than dispersing it amongst the general population. This simultaneous decline in the political economy of socialism in both East and West is seen to have many causes, not all of which can be attributed to the weaknesses of socialist theory and practice (for example, the consequences of the changing composition and distribution of the industrial workforce or of the globalization of capitalist markets). Nonetheless there is a widespread sense that both of the major twentieth-century variants of the socialist tradition have failed to deliver on their promise to rationalize and democratize economic life.

I shall consider these arguments about the decline of the political economy of socialism under two heads. First, I shall discuss (very briefly) the crisis of the Soviet model. This has been amply investigated elsewhere and I am principally interested here in the 'demonstration effect' that the difficulties of the Eastern economies have had for those seeking reform in the West. Secondly, I shall assess in a little more detail the crisis of social democratic Keynesianism in Western advanced industrial countries. In particular, I shall consider the argument that, whatever its residual strengths, a Keynesian social democratic strategy of the kind pursued in the post-war period has been rendered impractical by changes in the global economic order.

The Decline of the Planned Economy

In their several ways, Marxism, Marxism-Leninism and Stalinism all presumed that socialist economic organization would be more efficient, more equitable and more productive than its capitalist counterpart (see Marx, 1973a; Brus, 1972; Lenin, 1960; Stalin, 1955, pp. 40–1; Bukharin and Preobrazhensky, 1969, pp. 119–20). Further, according to Brus, all these Marxist approaches were 'rooted [in] the conviction that the socialist economy is centrally planned' (Brus, 1972, p. 27). Whatever institutional form Marx and Lenin had expected this planning to take, in practice, the Soviet model, pioneered in the Soviet Union and later forcibly exported to the communist societies of Eastern Europe, bore the imprint of the Stalinist conception of a highly centralized 'command' economy. The 'traditional' centralized Soviet model may be identified around the following features:

1   The concentration of practically all economic decisions at the central level (except for individual choice in the fields of consumption and employment).
2   The hierarchical nature of plans and the 'top – down' structure of plan implementation.
3   Imperative rather than indicative planning.
4   Economic calculation and planning stipulated in direct and physical (rather than monetary) terms.
5   Money having a largely passive role within the state sector.
6   Planning embodied within an authoritarian political system (Brus, 1972, pp. 65–71; Ellman, 1989, p. 18).[3]

In the period between Stalin's death in 1953 and the revolutions of 1989 (and, of course, rather sooner in Yugoslavia), this system was subjected to repeated attempts at reform. Typically, these involved the attempt to address the many rigidities of the traditional model by introducing a greater element of market decision-making and decentralization within what remained essentially 'planned' economies. Some of these reforms met with a limited measure of success, as, for example, in Hungary under the New Economic Mechanism of 1968 (Berend, 1989; Kornai, 1986; Xavier, 1989; Swain, 1992), and we shall return to their significance for the specification of market socialism in a later chapter. However, few would now argue that these reforms offered an optimal mix of plan and market or even that they effectively addressed those generic weaknesses which have been widely identified with existing forms of planned economy. The impact of the reform process was further weakened (to the point of being overwhelmed) by the revolutions of 1989. Not only were the economies of Eastern Europe subject to a much more sudden and wholesale marketization but also many of those who had been the most articulate defenders of the reform process themselves now called for a much more enthusiastic and unqualified embrace of the market principle (see e.g. the discussion of Hungary in Hankiss, 1990; Brus, 1989; Kornai, 1990b; Kornai, 1993; Swain, 1992).

With the 'failure of the Soviet economy' having already passed into the received wisdom of Western political commentary, we need to exercise some caution in judging the weaknesses of the planned economy. Those who have sought seriously to contrast the economic records of market and planned economies have warned against too unqualified an endorsement of the superiority of the market (see e.g. Bergson, 1987 and 1989; Ellman, 1989; Nove, 1983 and 1988). Yet, whatever reservations they may have entered against the workings of the market, they have commonly identified profound structural weaknesses that seem to undermine the competence of existing models of the planned economy. Few would dissent from Adam Bergson's very modest claims that 'socialist economic performance tends to be undistinguished by Western standards' and that 'socialism and centralist planning probably contributed significantly to results that are subnormal by Western standards' (Bergson, 1989, pp. 1, 51). I confine myself here to a brief indication of the most prominent generic weaknesses identified in these planned economies:

1 *Poor responsiveness to the final consumer*   Under a planned economy, production is geared to the plan not to the demands of consumers. The consequence is a sellers' market, with chronic shortages and queueing, a limited range of goods and services, poor quality,

forced substitution or postponement of purchases and forced saving.

2   *Irrational incentives structure*   In general, the aspiration is to satisfy planned targets, not to satisfy demand in the most cost-effective way possible. Managers have an incentive to seek slack plans which it is well within the capacity of their enterprises to satisfy and to hoard labour and producer goods. Quality is extremely difficult to control where outputs are measured in direct physical terms and not according to consumers' preferences. The bureaucratic redistribution of profit, soft budget constraints, the lack of effective competition and the lack of incentives to innovate undermine productive efficiency, institutionalize risk aversion and retard economic growth.

3   *The 'Curse of Scale'*   Economy-wide planning leads to problems of scale, complexity and information processing. It encourages poor intersectoral allocative efficiency, aggravates bottlenecks and shortages and intensifies the tendency towards the bureaucratization of economic decision-making.

4   *The second and third economies*   The irrationalities and inefficiencies built into the planned system themselves have a chronic tendency to generate both a second economy (of 'illicit' and unregulated private activity) and a third economy (of unsanctioned exchanges between state enterprises aimed at circumventing the malfunctioning of the official planning mechanism). (Nove, 1983; Kornai, 1980 and 1990a; Bergson, 1989; Ellman, 1989)

Ellman summarizes the experience of the traditional planned economy thus:

> The traditional model of socialist planning is of an economy almost entirely administered and controlled by the state which developed in accordance with the plan. Experience has shown that efficient implementation of this model is not feasible . . . The fact that 'socialist planning', in the original sense of a rational economy which replaced market relationships by direct calculation and direct product exchange, has nowhere been established, reflects not the malevolence of this or that social group, not the backwardness of the countries concerned, but the theoretical inadequacy of the traditional conception. (Ellman, 1989, p. 327)

Crisis in the Political Economy of Keynesian Social Democracy

In fact, social democrats in the West have long since abandoned any ambitions they might once have entertained of moving towards a centrally controlled planned economy and, as a consequence, the failures of the Soviet model have a limited salience for our discussion here. Of much greater importance are the problems that have increasingly beset the traditional political economy of Western social democracy over the past twenty-five years. In the rest of this chapter, I want to concentrate upon the evolution of these problems and to consider the *programmatic* political difficulties to which they have given rise.

Of course, there is a long-standing view that social democracy is simply the name for a particular brand of unprincipled expediency and that it lacks anything so grandiose as a political programme (however modestly conceived). Amongst its socialist critics, it is condemned not so much for its pragmatism as for its opportunism. Yet it is possible to unearth a larger rationale for social democratic practice and this has been a part of the self-understanding of at least some social democratic politicians and theoreticians – although these have been rather exceptional within the 'practical-minded' Anglo-Saxon tradition (Kesselman, 1982; Keman, 1993). In its various forms, this social democratic strategy is based upon the claim that under advanced capitalism, given certain favourable circumstances, social democratic governments may exercise effective control over the context of economic decision-taking and the distribution of the economic product in such a way as to promote an incremental advance towards a more socialist society.

It is important to grasp that the modern social democratic programme was shaped by a particular historical context (see Przeworski, 1985, pp. 7–46). Down to the 1930s, what principally divided the revolutionary and revisionist wings of the socialist movement (at least so far as their programmatic ambitions were concerned), was a disagreement not so much about *aims* as about *methods*. Admittedly, Lenin, Kautsky and Bernstein (to cite but one tradition) probably saw the coming socialist society rather differently, but each would have expected such a society to be premised upon the abolition of large-scale holdings of private capital. Since neo-classical economics insisted that capitalism required the free play of untrammelled market forces, it seemed that for its socialist (including social democratic) opponents, socialism must by contrast be premised upon some form of centralized and directive planning and investment. However, the social, political and economic costs of transition to such a socialized economy were great, perhaps insurmountable, for social democrats pledged to the introduction of socialism through the medium of liberal parliamentary democracy. This was more especially the case as social democrats in the 1920s found themselves coming into office in minority governments with the backing of minoritarian working-class forces (see Emmanuel, 1979;

Offe, 1985; Przeworski, 1985; Przeworski and Sprague, 1986). The 'solution' to this social democratic dilemma was found in the development of Keynesian economic policy in association with the promotion of an expanded welfare state – the complex conveniently and conventionally summarized as the *Keynesian Welfare State*.[4] It is in this way that Keynesianism and the welfare state came to assume their familiar centrality in social democratic thinking.

The Political Economy of Keynesian Social Democracy

For social democracy, the vital importance of Keynesianism resided in its status as 'a system of political control over economic life' (Skidelsky, 1979, p. 55). Its great strategic elegance lay in its promise of effective political *control* of economic life without the dreadful social, economic and political *costs* that social democrats feared 'expropriation of the expropriators' would bring. For the social democrats, Keynes's great contribution lay in his refutation of the neo-classical belief that the operation of a self-regulating market mechanism under capitalism could secure full employment. Say's Law – that under capitalism supply created its own sufficient demand – held true, Keynes claimed, only under the peculiar conditions of full employment. It did not, however, itself *guarantee* this equilibrium at full employment. Such a balance could only be secured *outside* the market, by the state's manipulation of those key economic variables which can be 'deliberately controlled or managed by central authority' (Keynes, 1973). It was, Keynes argued, the duty of governments to intervene within the market to generate an enhanced level of 'effective demand', promoting the propensity both to consume and to invest, so as to ensure sufficient economic activity to utilize all available labour and thus to secure equilibrium at full employment. To achieve this, a whole range of indirect measures – including taxation policy, public works, monetary policy and the manipulation of interest rates – were available to the interventionist government.[5]

Keynes's advocacy of a 'managed capitalism' seemed to offer a neat solution to the social democratic dilemma of how to furnish reforms for its extended constituency and maintain its long-term commitment to socialism without challenging the hegemony of private capital. Economic *control* could be exercised through the manipulation of major economic variables in the hands of the government. The owners of capital could be *induced* to act in ways which would promote the interests of social democracy's wide constituency. The traditional socialist aspiration for socialization of the economy could either be dismissed as irrelevant or else postponed to some rather uncertain (and more favourable) point well into the future. At the same time, social democratic governments could shape the propensity to consume, through taxation and monetary policy, as well as through adjusting the level of public spending. They could also rectify the disutilities of the continuing play of market forces through the income transfers and social services that came to be identified with the welfare state.

In fact, this programme has been quite differently understood by the right and the left within social democracy, in line with their differing understandings of the nature of advanced capitalism. In contrast to classical Marxism, those on the right or 'revisionist' wing of social democracy have tended to structure their critique of capitalism not around the private ownership of the means of production nor around exploitation at the point of production, but rather around the *inequalities* of wealth and consumption that it generates, and its *inefficiency* in employing the nation's human and material resources.[6] They afford definitive status to the winning of parliamentary democracy, to the efficacy of purely *political* power and to the manipulation of the *consumption* side of the economy. They insist that through judicious Keynesian economic management and the expansion of the welfare state it is possible to attenuate class antagonism, to mitigate inequality, and thus to move incrementally towards a more socialist society.

Those on the left of social democracy, especially advocates of the recently influential 'power resources model', have taken a quite different view of the relationship between advanced capitalism and social democracy (see e.g. Korpi, 1983 and 1989). At the heart of their position is a perceived division between the exercise of economic and political power. In the *economic* sphere, the decisive power resource is control over capital assets, the mechanism for its exercise is the (wage labour) contract and its principal beneficiary is the capitalist class. However, in the *political* sphere, power typically flows from the strength of numbers, mobilized through the democratic process, and tends to favour 'numerically large collectivities', especially the organized working class. Unlike the revisionists, supporters of the power resources model insist that the logic of Marx's analysis of the contradictions of capitalism and the centrality of class struggle still hold under these new circumstances, but that parliamentary democracy and the interventionist state provide new media for the prosecution of the class politics of socialism. Social democratic governments elected under universal franchise are seen to constitute an effective counter to the power exercised by capital within the privately owned economy and, where such governments become more or less permanently entrenched in office (and this may in itself be an essential precondition), an effective balance or at least stalemate may be established between the political powers of social democracy and the economic powers of capital. Under these circumstances, some sort of (temporary) compromise between capital and labour is likely to emerge, but in the expectation that in the long run the position of labour will be strengthened in ways which will make possible socialization of the investment function.

'The Rise and Fall of the Keynesian Welfare State'

For the greater part of the post-war period, both wings of the social democratic movement sought to advance their political strategies broadly through the medium of the Keynesian Welfare State. Undoubtedly, this period saw circumstances for social democracy that were more favourable than those that either preceded or succeeded them (the 1930s and the later 1970s and 1980s respectively), and it is from this period that we tend to derive our understanding of what social democracy is. Yet we should be cautious in positing too close an identity between the Keynesian Welfare State and social democracy *per se*. We certainly need to distinguish between 'Keynesianism plus the welfare state' as (1) the typical form of economic and social policy adopted by social democrats and (2) the typical form of economic and social policy under a particular and distinctive 'regime of capital accumulation' (see Aglietta, 1979; Harvey, 1989). In fact, in the period between the end of the Second World War and the early 1970s (the much-vaunted epoch of 'Fordism'), *all* political parties and economic actors pursued their interests within this particular institutional context, leading some commentators to characterize these years as 'the Golden Age of Social Democracy' (Jenkins, 1987). Yet, as recent work on both the welfare state and Keynesianism makes clear, the interventionist policies of this period could have very differing political intentions and outcomes, and could serve quite differing social and political forces (see e.g. Esping-Andersen, 1990).

It is certainly not a mistake to identify the practical experience of social democracy, and its (declining) fortunes, with the history of the Keynesian Welfare State. It is, however, an error to think that social democracy means simply the politics of economic intervention plus welfare or, correspondingly, that policies of intervention and welfare must always be the product of social democratic forces. Insofar as the history of the post-war period has been rather crudely depicted as 'the rise and fall of the Keynesian Welfare State' this misplaced correspondence has probably encouraged commentators to be too sanguine about the successes of social democrats in the 1950s and 1960s and to be too damning of their prospects in the period since the early 1970s. Undoubtedly, in *practice*, the day-to-day problems of managing consensus must always have loomed large in the consciousness of social democratic politicians. Given this, however, it is important to stress that the *theorists* of social democracy have always depicted it as something more than simply the amelioration of capitalism and that, in principle, the strategic amalgam of 'Keynesianism plus the welfare state' is but one *historically contingent* context within which to pursue the politics of social democracy. This qualification becomes particularly important at a time when a number of social democrats are seeking to recast their political programmes in ways that differ decisively from this traditional welfare state pattern (a reassessment which, we shall see, includes the advocacy of 'marketized' forms of socialism).

This important qualification having been sounded, it remains the case that any assessment of the programmatic difficulties (and successes) of social democracy must focus upon the post-war experience of the Keynesian Welfare State. Simply put, the argument of its detractors is that the political economy of post-war social democracy, based upon Keynesian macro-management and the expansion of the welfare state, while seemingly successful in the twenty-five years following the war, is now exhausted. In that earlier period, even parties of the right had been forced to work within the parameters defined by the social democrats. Now the position is reversed with social democratic governments in office finding themselves obliged to pursue the policies of the neoliberals (see pp. 22–3 above).

In its broad outlines, this story is by now a familiar one. In a succession of Western industrialized economies, the process of post-war reconstruction saw the entrenchment of a new and distinctive set of political and economic institutions. At its simplest, this new order could be identified around (1) Keynesian economic policies and a mixed economy to secure full employment and economic growth domestically within the agreed parameters of an essentially liberal capitalist international market; (2) a more or less 'institutional' welfare state to deal with the dysfunctions arising from this market economy and to guarantee certain minimum standards of public service; and (3) broad-based agreement between left and right, and between capital and labour, over these basic social institutions (a market economy and a welfare state), and the accommodation of their (legitimately) competing interests through elite-level negotiation (Bowles and Gintis, 1986; Taylor-Gooby, 1985; Kavanagh, 1990; Kavanagh and Morris, 1989). These liberal democratic or social democratic institutions were seen as the best guarantee of avoiding both the economic disasters and the concomitant political polarization of the inter-war years. For social democrats, they were seen as the most effective way of advancing the social and economic condition of their core constituency in the broad working class.

For a period of twenty-five years following the war, this system met with considerable success, securing for 'the advanced industrial countries of the Western world . . . an extended period of prosperity for which it is impossible to find a precedent' (Shonfield, 1965, p. 61). Throughout the 1950s and 1960s average annual growth rates within the OECD economies stood close to 5 per cent while inflation, though rising slowly, stayed below 4 per cent until the late 1960s. These were also years of unusually low unemployment. The period 1950–67, in which the average levels of unemployment in six major OECD countries stood at 2.8 per cent, contrasts markedly with the experience in 1933 at the height of the depression, when unemployment had reached 13 per cent, and with the period after 1980, when average unemployment rates in the EC were persistently above 10 per cent (OECD, 1991; Eurostat 1988). At the same time, there was a rapid growth in spending on the welfare state. Social expenditure, which had averaged 12.3 per cent of GDP in the OECD countries in 1960, had advanced to 21.9 per cent of a much-enhanced GDP by the mid-1970s. Over the 1960–75 period, average annual growth in deflated social expenditure for the OECD countries was in excess of 6 per cent per annum (OECD, 1988, pp. 10–11). It was in this period and under these circumstances that the emergence of a broadly social democratic consensus over the management of advanced capitalism was most confidently identified.

The 'Social Democratic Consensus' in Decline

Recent years have seen the authenticity of consensus in this period widely challenged. It has been suggested that the bipartisanship of the post-war years, while genuine, depended in substantial part upon the favourable climate of sustained economic growth that made positive-sum resolutions of distributional conflicts a viable policy. Where such positive-sum solutions were not available, political conflict could still be acute (Pimlott, 1988; Deakin, 1987; Taylor-Gooby, 1985; Esping-Andersen, 1985). There has also been a tendency to redraw (and shorten) the parameters of the period of sustained economic growth and comparative social peace with which consensus is identified, to cover little more than the fifteen years between 1950 and 1965 (see Gamble, 1988; Deakin, 1987; Kavanagh and Morris, 1989). Even amongst its keenest admirers, there is a fairly broad-based agreement that the politics of consensus always rested upon the capacity to generate a growing economic surplus. Economic growth was the basis of Keynesian policies to induce capital investment, the stimulus to support economic activity at levels securing full employment and the fount of resources for increased expenditure on health, education, welfare and social services. It was economic growth that made a reconciliation of the opposing interests of capital and labour viable and sustainable. Fittingly, the most successful phase of the Keynesian Welfare State was also a period of unprecedented and unparalleled growth in the international capitalist economy.

Wherever one chooses to place 'the beginning of the end' of this era, by the early 1970s the signs of economic difficulty were unmistakable and the fivefold increase in oil prices which OPEC was able to impose in 1973 precipitated (rather than caused) a severe slump throughout the Western industrialized world. A few figures will illustrate the contrast between the 1950s and 1960s and experience after 1973. Between 1965 and 1973, the economies of the OECD countries showed an annual average growth rate of about 5 per cent. In 1974, this annual growth rate fell to 2 per cent and in 1975, nine OECD economies 'shrank', bringing the annual average growth rate below zero. Although there was some recovery from this low point, there was to be a second oil-price 'shock' in 1979, and for the decade 1974 to 1984 annual average growth was little over 2 per cent (Alber, 1988a, p. 187). Nor were these economic difficulties confined to sluggish growth. By 1975, unemployment in the OECD area had risen to an unprecedented 15 million, a figure that had doubled within a decade (OECD, 1991). At the same time, inflation accelerated and there was a growing balance of trade deficit throughout most of the OECD. The 'misery index' (the rate of inflation plus the rate of unemployment) which, for the seven major OECD countries, had averaged just 5.5 per cent through the 1960s had risen to 17 per cent by 1974/5. At the same time, levels of investment and levels of profitability fell, while the value of disposable incomes stagnated. Governments throughout the developed West found themselves simultaneously failing to achieve the four major economic policy objectives – growth, low inflation, full employment and balance of trade – on which the post-war order had been based (Gough, 1979, p. 132; Goldthorpe, 1984, p. 2).

The economic crisis of the early 1970s represented a peculiarly severe challenge for social democrats. Their accommodation with a reformed capitalist economy was premised upon the expectation that this economy could generate low-inflationary growth and fund an expanding social dividend under circumstances of full employment. Not only did low growth undermine the commitment to full employment,

Table 2.1   Macroeconomic performance in the OECD,
1960–1981 (%)

Economic Indicator	1960–73	1973–81
Unemployment rate	3.2	5.5
Inflation	3.9	10.4
GNP growth	4.9	2.4
Productivity growth	3.9	1.4

Source: Bruno and Sachs (1985, p. 2).

it also had severe consequences for the welfare state, which was now faced with rapidly growing demands which had to be met from a depleting tax revenue. This manifested itself in a 'yawning gap between expenditure and revenues' and the growing indebtedness of the public household. The coincidence of high unemployment with high inflation (the coming of 'stagflation') seemingly ruled out the traditional Keynesian remedy of responding to a rise in unemployment with a government-led injection of economic demand (see Scharpf, 1991, pp. 35–7).

The initial response of social democrats (and others) to the crisis of the early 1970s was to see it as a temporary interruption in a soon-to-be-resumed pattern of economic growth. Upon this view, the essentially sound and well-ordered international economic order had been subjected to an 'external shock' or series of shocks (of which OPEC's quintupling of the price of oil was the most spectacular), which had temporarily thrown it out of equilibrium. What was crucial about all these 'shocks' was that they were essentially *exogenous* (from outside the system) and if not non-replicable (after all OPEC could, and did, impose a second oil price hike), then certainly *contingent*. This view was well represented in Paul McKracken's 1977 OECD Report, which concluded that the recession of the early 1970s arose from 'an unusual bunching of unfortunate disturbances unlikely to be repeated on the same scale' (OECD, 1977).

The Crisis of Keynesianism and the Keynesian Welfare State

As the severity of the economic problems of the 1970s became clearer, this essentially optimistic view – of a 'hiccup' in economic growth leading to a temporary pause in the advance of the Keynesian Welfare State – was increasingly overtaken by studies which stressed the contradictions within the post-war settlement as the real source of crisis.

The fivefold increase in crude oil prices was simply the dramatic pre-cipitating event which disclosed the deep-seated structural weaknesses of the post-war political economy which had been in the making for twenty-five years, and manifest to the discerning eye since at least the late 1960s. At the heart of this account is the claim that the end of the period of post-war economic growth was not externally caused but *inherent* in the social, political and economic order of the social demo-cratic consensus and especially in its ameliorating institutions for the management of economically based political conflict. This challenge was heard from both the neo-Marxist left and the neo-liberal right. Despite their profound differences, both were agreed that the problems of social democracy in the 1970s could not be understood as 'simply' economic. Rather, they were an expression of the cumulative effect of the economic and political contradictions which had always underlain the new social democratic order established after 1945 under the rubric of the Keynesian Welfare State.

For the neo-Marxists, the post-war settlement represented a set of institutional arrangements for managing the consequences of what classical Marxism had always identified as the central contradiction of capitalism – that between the social forces and the private relations of production. For them, at the heart of the Keynesian Welfare State lay the process of managing the crisis tendencies of advanced capitalism through the mechanisms of the interventionist state. Under the post-war settlement, the state took increasing responsibility for negotiating relations between capital and labour, for creating opportunities for investment and for meeting the dysfunctional costs of a regime of economic growth. For twenty-five years following the Second World War, this social democratic form of crisis management had proven to be remarkably effective. But in the long run, it was unsustainable, as the interventionist state became increasingly vulnerable to a cumulat-ive crisis logic of its own (the 'crisis of crisis management'). The costs of the 'compensatory' measures embodied in the welfare state had begun to erode the incentives for economic growth, which was itself the only sustainable basis of welfare state funding. This core contradiction of the Keynesian Welfare State expressed itself in a fiscal crisis of state indebt-edness, declining economic growth, declining effectiveness of state policies and a corresponding loss of legitimacy for the post-war social democratic order (Offe, 1984; for a fuller account, see Pierson, 1991a, pp. 49–61).

Even more influential and dramatic as an account of the exhaustion of the Keynesian Welfare State in this period were the writings of the New Right. In fact, the neo-liberal hostility to social democracy was not so much new, as newly influential. Friedrich Hayek, who remains the most sophisticated and articulate representative of this position, had maintained his hostility to the post-war settlement since its inception in the later years of the Second World War (Hayek, 1944). Yet it was the difficulties of social democracy in the 1970s that gave the arguments of the neo-liberals a renewed authority. At the heart of their position lay the belief that the spontaneously arising market economy, or what Hayek had called 'catallaxy', offered the best means of securing both optimum individual and social welfare and the surest guarantee of individual liberty. To the extent that social democracy and the Keyensian Welfare State countermanded this 'natural' order, they had always, even in the years of their greatest successes, offended against justice and economic rationality. However, by the 1970s, the cumulative consequences of usurping 'catallaxy' meant that the social democratic programme was no longer simply immoral or sub-optimal. It was now threatening the continuing integrity of liberal democracy itself. At the heart of the New Right's economic argument was the insistence that the Keynesian Welfare State was:

1 *uneconomic* It displaced the necessary disciplines and incentives of the marketplace, undermining the incentive (of capital) to invest and (of labour) to work.
2 *unproductive* It encouraged the rapid growth of the (unproductive) public bureaucracy and forced capital and human resources out of the (productive) private sector of the economy. Monopoly of state welfare provision had enabled workers within the public sector to command inflationary wage increases.
3 *inefficient* The state's monopoly of welfare provision and its creation and sponsorship of the special interests of trade unions led to the inefficient delivery of services and a system which, denuded of the discipline of the market, was geared to the interests of (organized) producers rather than (disaggregated) consumers.
4 *ineffective* Despite the huge resources dedicated to it, the welfare state had failed to eliminate poverty and deprivation. (Pierson, 1991a, pp. 40–8, 149–52)

By the mid-1970s, the crisis tendencies of social democracy were seen to be rampant throughout the Western industrialized world and the problem of social democratic governments overloaded with demands for spending and intervention seemed to threaten a descent into ungovernability. Neo-Marxists hoped that the crisis would be resolved through the inauguration of socialism. The New Right sought redemption through the dismantling of the social democratic order and the reassertion of a liberal, market-based regime.

The Death of Social Democracy?

From the distant perspective of the 1990s, these accounts of the crisis of governance in the 1970s look unduly apocalyptic. While the intervening years have seen some evidence of increased political instability (growing electoral volatility, declining deference to government, the abandonment of bipartisanship), there has been no real threat of a breakdown of liberal democratic government and limited interest in major constitutional reform. Certainly, no one has suggested that the crisis of the 1970s was resolved through a radical transformation into socialism! However, it has been widely argued, and not only on the triumphalist wing of the New Right, that the crisis was effectively resolved by jettisoning the apparatus of social democracy and embracing a revivified form of liberal capitalism. Upon such an account, the end of the welfare state consensus, the abandonment of corporatist economic institutions and the commitment to full employment, along with the reimposition of the disciplinary rigour of the market, 'saved' liberal democracy by abandoning social democracy. Clearly, this has profound consequences for the programmatic integrity of social democracy. We have already seen that the *electoral* recovery of social democratic parties would have a quite different resonance if it had to be premised upon the abandonment of the traditional social democratic *programme*. We need then to consider the extent to which changes since the mid-1970s have indeed rendered the traditional social democratic programme built around Keynesianism and the welfare state redundant.

The Demise of the Welfare State?

There was a measure of agreement in the critical literature of the 1970s that in the long run the redistribution of resources through the welfare state and the governmental support of full employment might prove incompatible with the maintenance of a viable capitalist economy. In the late 1970s, there was again agreement amongst practising politicians of the social democratic left and the neo-conservative right that one of the issues that divided them most clearly was the right's growing hostility to the existing structure of the welfare state. In no country was the breach this promised with the post-war regime more explicit than it was under the first Thatcher administration voted into office in the UK in 1979. In the 1979 election campaign, the Conservatives presented themselves as a party breaking with the exhausted legacy of social democratic consensus. This break included the abandonment of the governmental commitment to secure full employment. On the welfare state, there was to be a drive to cut costs by concentrating resources upon those in greatest need, to restrain the bureaucratic interventions of the 'nanny state' in the day-to-day life of citizens, a greater role for voluntary welfare institutions and the encouragement of individuals to make provision for their individual welfare through the private sector. Nowhere offers a more clear-cut testing ground for the abandonment of the social democratic consensus than the UK.[7]

Certainly, the 1979 General Election in the UK may be described as a 'watershed'. Labour had been in office for eleven of the previous fifteen years and this election brought to power a Conservative government that remained in office throughout the 1980s and won four consecutive elections. Yet in judging the breach with consensus that it represented, one must be circumspect. First, the breach with traditional social democratic governance *predates* the election of the Conservatives in 1979. As has been frequently observed, it was the Labour government of 1974–9 that presided over the earliest retrenchment in welfare spending and a (then) unprecedented rise in post-war unemployment. Secondly, the political practice of the post-1979 Thatcher government did not always match its political rhetoric. Certainly, unemployment was allowed to reach unheard of levels (officially in excess of 3 million), a string of major public corporations and utilities were returned to the private sector, and there was a major (and popular) drive to sell off public housing and limited cuts in expenditure on education. Yet in the period of the first Thatcher administration total social expenditure showed a significant growth of about 10 per cent, rising as a proportion of GDP from 21.6 per cent to 24.1 per cent, largely as a consequence of extremely high levels of unemployment and low economic growth (Eurostat, 1988, p. 135).

Whilst the second Thatcher administration had promised 'the most fundamental examination of [the] social security system since the Second World War', it was only really with the election of a third Thatcher government in 1987 that the process of wholesale reform within the welfare state can be said to have begun (DHSS, 1985; Kavanagh, 1990, p. 217). Glennerster, Power and Travers write of the period between 1988 and 1990 as initiating 'the most decisive break in British social policy since the period between 1944 and 1948', the years in which the modern British welfare state was created (1991, p. 389). As well as the implementation of the government's Social Security Act (of 1986), these years saw the passage of the Education Reform Act (1988), the Housing Act (1988), the National Health Service and Community Care Act (1990) and the prosecution of wholesale reform of the NHS following the publication of the White Paper *Working for Patients* in 1989. The current policy climate is still dominated by the contested process of putting these reforms into practice and certainly these new developments in the mainstream welfare state areas of education, health and, perhaps above all, pensions suggest that a major change *may* be on the horizon. But, at present, change is substantially focused upon institutional reform (dividing the *purchasers* of welfare services from their *providers*), in the delivery of what remain largely publicly funded services. On the basis of past experience, it must be doubted whether this will mean a wholesale withdrawal of the state or that it will enable a substantial reduction in levels of public expenditure. In 1991, more than a decade after Mrs Thatcher's first electoral triumph, social expenditure still stood at 24.7 per cent of GDP (Eurostat, 1993, p. 163). (For a more extended discussion, see Pierson, 1993b.)

The US reveals a remarkably similar pattern. The Reagan administration was rhetorically hostile to the 'dependency culture' of the welfare state and life was certainly made much more unpleasant for the poorest and most marginal in American society during the 1980s. But the mainstream (and most expensive) social security programmes proved extremely difficult to restrain and, however Clinton's pre-eminent concern with the reform of health care is resolved, it is likely to mean an increase in its public administration (Katz, 1986, p. 274). In continental Europe, there have also been reforms and retrenchment but, even under conservative regimes, the 'backlash' against welfare was never so pronounced as in the US or the UK. Here again, the possibility of a new era of reduced expenditure and policy reversals must be taken seriously. But the actual pattern of policy and spending throughout the OECD countries since 1975 has been much more one 'of consolidation rather than of welfare state dismantling' and social expenditure throughout the EC has stood remarkably firm in recent years at about 25 per cent of GDP (Alber, 1988b, p. 463; Eurostat, 1993, p. 163).

In sum, the experience of the Keynesian Welfare State since the 1970s has not been as the literature of that decade had anticipated. Certainly, there has been retrenchment and a significant worsening of conditions for those most reliant upon the state to secure their well-being. But this owes rather less to the 'contradictions of the welfare state' and rather more directly to low levels of growth and faltering economic performance. There has not (as yet) been a wholesale reversal of welfare policy, nor massive cuts in public provision, nor (as yet) a general transfer of welfare effort into the private sector. In contrast to the rather grand generalizations of both New Right and neo-Marxists, Manfred Schmidt is probably right to identify 'muddling through' as the generic form of government policy throughout this period (Schmidt, 1983, pp. 14ff).

Yet this is not an especially comforting outcome for the integrity of the social democratic programme. For the dramatic prognoses about the demise of the welfare state which were a common feature of both left and right in the 1970s were premised upon a misunderstanding of the nature of the welfare state. Under certain circumstances (probably those in which welfare measures insulate workers from the imperatives of the marketplace), the welfare state *may* constitute part of a social democratic strategy. However, those social policies which are summed up under the rubric of the welfare state have been a common feature of *all* regimes under advanced capitalism (and beyond). Conservative and liberal governments, as much as social democratic ones, have fashioned policies for the public administration of welfare. As Esping-Andersen has explained, what is most important (and most vulnerable to change) is not the existence of the welfare state itself (which may be close to a necessity under market-organized forms of society), nor even of the level of resources devoted to public welfare, but rather the *type of welfare state regime* (Esping-Andersen, 1990).

What we have seen over the past quarter-century is a move away from the circumstances that favoured or at least tolerated the promotion of social democratic forms of welfare state regime. Thus, sustained levels of social spending and continuing public endorsement of the popular elements of the welfare state may well prove to be consistent with an internal transformation from a solidary, universalistic, citizenship-based welfare state (of the kind to which social democracy aspired) towards a system based on the more generous provision of insurance-style entitlement and a further deterioration in the position of the poor and stigmatized (Alber, 1988a, pp. 187–9; see also Parry, 1986, pp. 155–240). Very broadly, in recent years welfare state provision has been made *more* dependent upon labour market status and *more* subservient to (a changing) economic policy. Changes in welfare policy (including the widespread abandonment of full employment as a real policy goal) have been designed to deliver greater economic *flexibility*, especially in the labour market. Everywhere there has been an increasing concern with controlling costs. We can observe these changes in the circumstances surrounding the social democratic type of welfare state, throughout the advanced industrial societies and *almost irrespective of regime type* .

A number of commentators comprehend these changes under the logic of a transition from the post-war Fordist regime towards a new and post-Fordist international order (see Pierson, 1994). In Bob Jessop's view, 'Whereas Fordism facilitated a policy of full employment and welfare rights to secure demand and thereby created the basis for a class compromise between capital and labour, the new post-Fordist

regime poses serious problems for full employment and the class alliances which this entails' (Jessop, 1991, p. 90). According to Albertsen,
these changes are part of a much wider 'restructuring of state interventionism' in which 'Keynesian policies aiming at full employment
through national regulation of general social demand' are increasingly
giving way to 'austerity policies aiming at international competitiveness in wage levels and directed primarily against the public-sector
service class and the lower strata of the working class' (Albertsen, 1988,
p. 349). To understand this process and its political consequences, we
need to turn to the second element in the Keynesian Welfare State
amalgam, and consider the recent experience of Keynesianism.

The Death of Keynesianism?

If anything, the institutions of Keynesianism have been even more
basic to the post-war social democratic programme than the securing of
the welfare state. It has long been recognized that the improvement of
the economic condition of social democracy's constituency in the working class had principally to be achieved not through the institutions of
the welfare state but through economic growth under circumstances of
full employment. Social democrats as different as Beveridge (1944) and
Esping-Andersen (1985) have insisted that without the underwriting of
full employment (to maximize tax revenues and minimize claims to
benefit) a comprehensive welfare state may be insupportable. Others,
including Scharpf (1991), have seen full employment as *the* overriding
political imperative of the social democratic cause. Correspondingly,
the 'decline of Keynesianism' may be even more damaging to the social
democratic cause than a 'crisis of the welfare state'.

Of course, there is some (well-founded) scepticism as to whether
social democratic practice was ever truly Keynesian. Several economists argue that the unprecedented period of economic growth
after 1945 owed comparatively little to Keynesian economic management, and rather more, for example, to the leading role of the US
and the dollar, a new international trading order and the commercial
application of new technologies derived from the war (see Keane
and Owens, 1986; Skidelsky, 1979). Matthews argued in the late
1960s that throughout the 'Golden Age' of economic growth, British
governments had in fact run (deflationary) budget *surpluses* and,
when the long-standing post-war boom began to falter, precipitating
the circumstances in which a Keynesian intervention might have had
a real impact, there was a reassertion of the traditional doctrine
of 'sound finance' (Matthews, 1968). According to Andrew Gamble,

'Keynesianism when it was tried was not needed and when it was needed was not tried' (1988, p. 43).

Nevertheless, it does seem appropriate to describe social democratic policy in this period as broadly Keynesian, at least in its intent. Keynes's policy was centrally concerned with securing full employment within a market economy through the government's guarantee of sufficient aggregate demand. The support of full employment was the cornerstone of social democratic policy and, throughout the post-war period, parties (of varying political complexions) pledged their support to the governmental support of full employment, a 'mixed economy' and the extension of public expenditure (Webber, 1986, p. 19; Marquand, 1988; Kavanagh, 1990). While the policies adopted were not always 'classically' Keynesian, including, for example, public investment in housing and the expansion of public sector employment, they did entail the belief that fiscal policy and public expenditure should be used to promote full employment. From the early 1960s onwards, it seemed that the classical 'indirect' Keynesian device of adjusting the parameters of the macro-economy were increasingly ineffective and this heralded a period of what in the UK Marquand has called 'hands on' Keynesianism, in which governments became increasingly involved in mediating the day-to-day market arrangements between (organized) capital and (organized) labour (Marquand, 1988). In some European countries, such corporatist institutions were of much longer standing and more institutionally and constitutionally entrenched (Scharpf, 1991). While the development of corporatist institutions through which the interests of state, capital and labour elites could be negotiated differed significantly from the original Keynesian blueprint for aggregate demand management, it was still motivated by the desire to use the state to promote economic growth and the fullest possible employment.

Some commentators would now locate the first signs of the breakdown of this Keynesian regime as early as the mid-1960s and see the heightened importance of corporatist institutions as a *symptom* of this decline. Certainly, the difficulties of the Keynesian Welfare State became more pronounced from the late 1960s onwards and by the mid-1970s even some social democrats themselves, quite spectacularly in the case of Prime Minister Jim Callaghan at the 1976 British Labour Party conference, seemed to have abandoned the belief that Keynesianism, in whatever form, offered a viable policy for economic macro-management.[8] The ill-fated 'Social Contract' negotiated by the incoming UK Labour government in 1975 may itself be seen less as the high-point of post-war collaboration of capital, labour and the state than as a last desperate attempt to hold together forms of corporatist bargaining which had already been undermined. These continued to unwind through the later 1970s culminating in the 'Winter of Discontent' of 1978/9 and an election which swept Labour out of power for more than a decade (Deakin, 1987, pp. 2–3). The incoming Conservative government pledged itself to break with the exhausted legacy of Keynesian social democracy. There was a commitment to sustained or enhanced economic growth, but this was to be achieved by an *abandonment* of Keynesian economics and the commitment to full employment in favour of monetarism and supply-side reforms. Of course, the incoming government faced a formidable task in breaking the institutions of the post-war consensus, most notably the power of organized labour, and certainly the semi-permanance of the Thatcher regime looks much more secure with a decade's hindsight than it did in 1981. Nonetheless, the authority of the Conservative government was undoubtedly strengthened by the sense that its social democratic opponents had no alternative to offer other than a version of the consensual politics which they had themselves been forced to abandon in the mid-1970s.

Elsewhere in Europe, the nemesis of Keynesianism was neither so swift nor so comprehensive. Scharpf's (1991) comparative survey of British, Austrian, German and Swedish experience shows Britain's social democrats to have been probably the *least* successful in responding to the economic difficulties of the 1970s and early 1980s. In Sweden and, above all, in Austria, social democratic forces were able to weather the economic shocks of the early 1970s, sustaining something close to full employment and, in the Austrian case, doing so without fuelling an unacceptable rise in levels of inflation. Scharpf explains much of this divergence in terms of institutional differences in the European labour movements, especially in terms of the much greater governmental capacity which social democrats enjoyed under Austria's 'corporatist Keynesianism' when compared with the 'purely statist Keynesianism' of the UK (1991, p. 166). But by the end of the period which Scharpf reviews (the early 1980s), these institutional advantages enjoyed by Swedish and Austrian Keynesianism had largely been eroded and Keynesianism everywhere seemed to be facing a common fate (Scharpf, 1991, pp. 238–55).

What precipitated this crisis of Keynesianism? At its simplest, it seems that by the mid-1970s the background conditions for the successful pursuit of classical Keynesian policies no longer held. Perhaps the clearest manifestation of this was the emergence of 'stagflation'. Keynesian demand management in the post-war years had rested on the supposition that there was a 'trade-off' between unemployment and inflation. If unemployment rose unacceptably, it could be controlled by a government-led injection of demand which might exact a small but acceptable price in raising inflation. If inflation rose to unacceptable levels, this could be met with a modest deflation and a small rise in unemployment. The 'stop–go' policy that this implied might have an undesirable effect in retarding overall economic growth, but it did deliver into the hands of government an albeit blunt instrument for managing the level of activity within the economy. 'Stagflation' – the coincidence of rising unemployment and rising inflation – seemingly eliminated this balancing act, and in the mid-1970s, as we have seen, both were rising to unprecedented post-war levels.

The causes of this stagflation are undoubtedly complex. But a number of commentators, prevalently though not exclusively from the New Right, have argued that it is primarily to be understood as a surface manifestation of underlying weaknesses inherent in the institutional structure of Keynesian social democracy. Two mutually reinforcing arguments have been especially influential. First, it is maintained that, in the long run, the empowering of (organized) labour that is implied by a governmental commitment to full employment makes such a policy unsustainable. Most familiarly this was an argument deployed by the New Right. Thus Samuel Brittan insisted that 'in the last analysis the authorities have to choose between accepting an indefinite increase in the rate of inflation and abandoning full employment to the extent necessary to break the collective wage-push power of the unions' (Brittan, 1975, p. 143). But it was a tendency which has also been identified on the left. Kalecki had argued during the Second World War that the institutionalization of full employment would greatly strengthen at least the obstructive power of organized labour and some on the left argued that the contradictions of 'full employment capitalism' to which this gave rise simply demonstrated the desirability of replacing it with full employment under socialism (Kalecki, 1971).

The difficulties entailed in pursuing full employment are seen to be amplified by a second weakness inscribed in the constitutional structure of liberal democracy. Liberal democratic governments (most particularly social democratic governments with their ties to organized labour and their commitment to full employment), face enormous pressures to increase public spending, without the countervailing discipline of a firm budget constraint. This tends to generate what Rose and Peters call a 'one-eyed Keynesianism' (in which deficit budgets in periods of economic downturn are not balanced by budget surpluses in years of prosperity and growth). By running a (semi-permanent) budget deficit, governments can enjoy the present electoral benefits of their *largesse* while deferring the costs upon future governments (and/ or generations). But this has a cumulatively damaging effect on the long-term stability of the economy – by, for example, encouraging inflation, squeezing out private sector investment and making domestic industries internationally uncompetitive. Without some sort of constitutional constraint upon the action (and spending) of governments, politicians, bureaucrats and voters *acting rationally* will tend to generate economic policies which are, in the long run, unsustainable.

For a number of commentators these tendencies suggest not so much that Keynes was 'wrong' as that Keynesian social democracy was radically incomplete. In part, these reflect oversights of Keynes himself. If Keynes recognized the strengthening of the bargaining position of labour that full employment would bring, Skidelsky argues, he seems to have believed that trade unionists, from reasons of either social deference or collective self-interest, would refrain from the full exercise of this power. Again, he seemed to believe that policy makers would be sufficiently insulated from the pressures of a mass democracy to ensure that they would always act in ways which were fiscally, if not politically, prudent (Skidelsky, 1979). Similar weaknesses are seen to undermine the premises of Keynesian social democratic practice. According to Marquand, 'although Keynesian social democracy had a theory of the economy . . . it had no theory of the political economy'. Lacking such a theory, 'Keynesian social-democratic politicians and officials could not come to terms, either with the political implications of their economic policies, or with the economic implications of their political assumptions' (Marquand, 1988, p. 58). Thus, for example, even when they came to recognize that full employment with low inflation could only be secured through the implementation of some sort of incomes policy, they lacked either the will or the ability to forge the institutional reforms which might have made such policies sustainable. Again, government seemed to take upon itself increasing responsibility for the consequences of day-to-day micro-economic decisions without enjoying the power effectively to enforce its decisions upon either labour or capital. For Marquand, the failings of Keynesian social democracy in the UK were above all political and constitutional, the failure to evolve a 'developmental state' adequate to the managerial demands of the late twentieth century (1988, pp. 146–51).

As with the 'transformation' of the welfare state, British experience cannot be taken as 'typical'. If anything, it is, as we have seen, a 'worst case' of reversal for the Keynesian imperative. In those countries which fared rather better in the 1970s, notably Sweden and Austria, there was some recognition of the difficulties of simultaneously achieving full employment and low inflation. It was precisely the self-discipline of these European labour movements (in both their governmental and union wings) that made possible their successes in the 1970s. In

Scharpf's view, this institutional self-discipline had even to embrace the social democrat's management of a redistribution of income *from* labour *to* capital, as the only way of securing full employment under the prevailing circumstances. But even in these most favourable circumstances, the problems of Keynesianism were only delayed rather than defused.

A Changing International Context

In fact, explanations of these ubiquitous difficulties have increasingly to be sought not in domestic circumstances but in the changing international context of Keynesianism. It is above all changes in the international political economy that have undermined the circumstances for the promotion of national Keynesian institutions. The powers of national governments, national labour movements and nationally based capital – between whom agreements about economic and social policy were typically constructed – have been undermined by the greater internationalization and deregulation of the modern world economy. Even the domestic difficulties of Keynesian social democracy must often be understood as the local expression of international processes. At the risk of some oversimplification, one could say that Keynesianism and its characteristic welfare state form are increasingly incompatible with the new international political economy.

Changes in this international economic context are complex and contested, but we can identify certain broad tendencies which have a particular salience for Keynesianism. While Keynesianism has been understood as above all a *domestic* political economy, it can only operate effectively within a particular *international* structure. In the successful post-war years, this international order was secured around the hegemonic role of the US economy and the reserve currency status of the dollar. It was the epoch of what Keohane calls 'embedded liberalism', in which domestically interventionist states operated within a context of essentially liberal world trade, guaranteed by the hegemonic presence of the US (Keohane, 1984). From the early 1970s, this order was undermined by the declining economic authority of the US, the loss of the reserve currency status of the dollar and the consequent loss of exchange rate stability. At the same time, other economic changes rendered industrial and financial institutions increasingly independent of given governments' authority. There was a growth in the number and power of transnational corporations. These transnational corporations, producing and marketing on a world scale and operating with budgets which often exceeded those of individual nation states, were able to operate without tutelage to any particular nation state. Increasingly, it was nation states which had to make themselves attractive to the corporations in order to secure inward investment. At the same time financial institutions became increasingly global and there was a growth in international credit markets which operated beyond the control of national central banks (Scharpf, 1991, p. 241). With the advent of new developments in information technology, capital became almost instantaneously transmittable around the globe. Indeed, the traditional social democratic fear of 'capital flight' seems increasingly archaic, when capital is in a constant flurry of movement around the world economy. Similarly 'speculation against the national currency' becomes not the feared consequence of enforcing a radical socialist programme but a day-to-day fact of economic life. Under all these circumstances, we may expect that domestic conflicts and domestic divisions of interest will increasingly be shaped by an *international* political economy over which individual nation states have declining control.

These changes in the international political economy have had at least two profound consequences. First, they have tended to strengthen the bargaining position of capital over against labour, which cannot match capital's new-found international mobility, and secondly, they have undermined the authority and capacity of the interventionist state. These developments clearly present acute difficulties for a policy which is premised upon 'taming private capital' *within national boundaries* and is likely to prove extremely damaging to traditional Keynesian Welfare State strategies. The greater openness of the international economy since the 1970s has made it increasingly difficult to pursue reflationary policies within one country. As 'national monetary policy lost its sovereignty over interest rates', greater weight fell upon the capacity of governments to manipulate the economy through fiscal policy and deficit budgeting (Scharpf, 1991, p. 245). But in a context of internationally conditioned high interest rates, this was likely to prove to be prohibitively expensive. Keynesianism had been a strategy for national governments to be pursued essentially within national economies. But by the mid-1970s, even the largest economies no longer enjoyed that relative autonomy from wider economic circumstances that would allow the pursuit of a genuinely national economic policy. What the British government discovered in the mid-1970s, the Mitterand government was to find after 1981 – 'that "Keynesianism in one country" is not possible' (Harrington, 1987, p. 140). For Scharpf (1991, p. 238), this evidence suggests that we have now reached 'the end of the Keynesian interlude'.

Social Democratic Political Economy Transcended?

How compelling is this general account of an epochal transcendence of the social democratic political economy of 'Keynesianism plus the welfare state'? Certainly, changes in the global political economy have curtailed opportunities for the further development of national social democratic strategies. The deregulation of international markets and of financial institutions, in particular, have tended to weaken the capacities of the interventionist state, to render all economies more 'open' and to make national capital and more especially national labour movements much more subject to the terms and conditions of international competition.[9] The prospects for sustaining long-term, corporatist arrangements within particular nation states (including the institutionalization of a 'social wage'), seem even less promising in a deregulated international economy. Of course, decline in the capacity of the nation state, and with it the *potential* for a social democratic strategy, can be exaggerated. Certainly, within most developed welfare states, the state itself remains the single largest and most decisive economic actor and much taxable activity (especially outside the corporate sector) is still resolutely national (since we all have to live, shop and work *somewhere*). At the same time, whilst growth of the welfare state has been effectively halted, there has (as yet) been no wholesale reversal from existing (historically high) levels of social expenditure and, insofar as welfare state interventions have an *efficiency* effect, we might expect these to *increase* under internationally more competitive circumstances (see Therborn, 1989b; Barr, 1987 and 1992). And whilst the powers of the nation state may have been reduced, the changing international political economy has also seen the rise of supranational institutions (EU, NAFTA, ASEAN and so on), which may enhance economic co-ordination and social policy interventions beyond the level of the nation state.

Nonetheless, the cumulative consequences of these changes for the traditional social democratic project are severe. Under the new economic order, there are still opportunities for governments to intervene in the economy and to underwrite the public provision of welfare. However, it seems as if these interventions must normally be confined to, or at least be consistent with, the interests of highly mobile international capital. Increasingly, it seems impossible for governments' social and economic interventions to be reconciled with the traditional social democratic aspiration for a 'citizens' welfare state premised upon full employment and welfare *rights*' (Offe, 1987). It is this, as much as anything, that defines the theoretical impasse of contemporary social democracy. A changed political economy, above all the renewed weight placed upon the supply-side, has left social democrats without a coherent political programme of their own. Through much of the 1980s, when in office, they found themselves rather sheepishly pursuing the policies of their opponents, prosecuting the interests of capital (with as benign a face as they could muster), under circumstances where it appeared that there was no alternative.

At some historical point, social democracy abandoned the traditional socialist aspiration to socialization of the economy and attached its political aspirations to the Keynesian Welfare State project. But under the changed international economic order, it seems that Keynesianism can no longer deliver those political goods which social democrats seek. More or less reluctantly (and more or less optimistically), a number of sympathizers have been driven to the conclusion that social democracy can only be revived (if at all) with a new political programme that is no longer premised upon the manipulation of demand and the *indirect* shaping of the investment function (for two contrasting discussions, see Esping-Andersen, 1985, and Scharpf, 1991). This is the agenda we take up in part II.

3

The Ideological and Epistemological Crises of Socialism at the 'End of History'

Ideology is an ambivalent and elusive term and the ideological crisis of socialism defines a correspondingly broad and ambiguous field of inquiry.[1] Yet it is an issue that is not easily avoided. Central to socialists' self-understanding and legitimizing their actions has been the claim that socialism represents a coherent and distinctive set of values and beliefs. Similarly, amongst its critics, it is the deep-seated exhaustion of this 'idea of socialism' which is seen to underpin many of its other difficulties (see Fukuyama, 1989). For many of these critics (and not a few erstwhile supporters), this long-standing process of ideological degeneration reached its spectacular denouement in the revolutionary events of 1989 in Eastern Europe. For many commentators, these transformations gave dramatic and definitive expression to the final and universal collapse of the Socialist Idea.

This suggested process of decline can be understood in terms of the interaction of two rather differing conceptions of ideology. First, the ideology of socialism may be understood as that connected set of values and beliefs which is taken to justify and to mobilize the movement to create socialist institutions and societies (values such as equality, community and equity). In this sense, ideology has often been seen as a positive element within the socialist heritage. Contrasting with this is a second and perhaps today a dominant conception of ideology in which it corresponds to 'meaning in the service of power' (J. Thompson, 1990, p. 7). In this second sense, ideology has a strongly pejorative connotation of *mis*representation and the attempt to mask the exercise of power and domination under the rubric of 'the forward march of socialism'. In its most decadent form, such ideology descends

into a stylized routine in which the positive terms of traditional socialist discourse are milked of their meaning, and in which the cynicism of
its propagators is matched only by the indifference of its intended
targets.

The ideological crisis of socialism embraces both of these elements.
On the one hand, it appears to many that the values and ideas for which
socialism has traditionally stood are irrelevant or unattainable or simply unpopular. As a consequence, socialism is seen to be increasingly
ideological in the second and pejorative sense of masking 'the will to
power' with an appeal to values in which no one (including its own
spokespersons), any longer believes. Of course, connections between
ideology and the 'real world' and especially the suggested lines of
causation between the two are peculiarly perplexing and fiercely contested. Nonetheless, it has been widely suggested that the kinds of
problems of socialism which we have already discussed (the numerical
decline of the working class and the decline of Keynesianism, for example), exacerbate the ideological problems of socialism while, con-
versely, weaknesses in the 'idea of socialism' contribute further to the
undermining of those social and political forces from which support for
socialist objectives is most likely to be derived.

Once again, we must not proceed from the assumption that the
worst-case scenario of socialism's fiercest detractors gives us an accu-
rate picture of the current fortunes of the socialist idea. Throughout its
history, and throughout its 'Golden Age' wherever and whenever you
choose to locate this, the ideas of socialism have been, by turns, cen-
sured and lampooned by its opponents. Nonetheless, in recent years
the ideology of socialism has been subjected to a sustained assault,
sometimes coming from rather unexpected quarters and culminating in
the identification of the revolutionary events of 1989 as history's final
settling of accounts with the Socialist Idea.

The Crisis of Marxism

Historically, it is Marxism that has furnished the most systematically developed defence of the socialist idea and, even though ideology
has generally had a secondary place within the Marxist schema, it is
also the site of an elaborate (and quite diverse) ideology critique
(J. Thompson, 1990). It is therefore of some importance that this authoritative Marxist tradition should be so widely perceived to be 'in
crisis' (Gouldner, 1980; Gorz, 1982; Cohen, 1983; Laclau and Mouffe,
1985; McLennan, 1989; Mouzelis, 1990; Wright, 1993). This idea of
'crisis' must itself be treated with some caution. It is not especially new.

Kolakowski's influential study dates 'the breakdown of Marxism' from the 1920s, but an 'internal' challenge might just as well be retraced to the 'Revisionist Debate' within German social democracy at the turn of the twentieth century (Kolakowski, 1978; Bernstein, 1909; Pierson, 1986). If we date the codification of Marxism from the propagation of the Erfurt Programme in 1891, this might give us eight years of untroubled orthodoxy followed by one hundred years of crisis! The point is not an entirely frivolous one. Even in the period of its greatest political and intellectual authority, the power of Marxist thinking lay quite as much in its dissenting as in its orthodox tradition. Indeed, its competence as social theory was probably enhanced rather than undermined by this heterodoxy. Nowhere is this diversity clearer than in disputes over the epistemological status of classical Marxist explanation and a critical approach to Marxism's epistemology amongst those broadly sympathetic to its critique of classical political economy can be sensibly retraced to the work of the critical theorists in the 1920s and 1930s (see Held, 1980; Habermas, 1972).

Despite this long-standing history of fruitful dissent, it is appropriate to suggest that Marxism has faced a very particular challenge since the early 1970s. This long predates the dramatic transformation of Eastern Europe and the Soviet Union. While these changes may have important consequences for the future of socialism (which are discussed below), these societies labouring under the maxims of Marxism-Leninism had long since been abandoned as models of socialism by almost all (academic) Marxists in the West.[2] More important for the declining authority of Marxism amongst the Western left has been the sustained attack upon the epistemological premises of the traditional Marxist position and the promotion of a 'post-Marxist' alternative.

At its simplest, the post-Marxists' claim is that 'classical' forms of Marxist reasoning have been undermined by their incorporation of a series of poorly vindicated epistemological assumptions. Their corresponding counter-suggestion is that what remains of value in the Marxist tradition can now only be salvaged by purging 'classical' Marxism of these debilitating elements. The substance of the post-Marxist critique can be summarized around four principal themes.[3] First, there is the claim that Marxism has placed a misguided faith in the possibilities afforded by a 'philosophy of history'. Historicism – as confidence in immanent if tendential laws of historical development – and the more specific expectation that continued societal development will tend to favour progressive social forces with an interest in socialism is seen to be extraordinarily deep-seated in Marxist theory. With hindsight, this optimism is seen to be misplaced and even, under some circumstances, pernicious. Secondly, it is suggested that Marxist analysis has a tendency to 'derive' political and ideological phenomena from other (and logically prior) aspects of a materialist analysis. This privileges the explanatory power of the categories of 'class' and 'labour' in ways which contemporary experience is seen not to justify. Thirdly, there is a belief that the explanatory framework of classical Marxism tends to treat economic, political and ideological categories as *essences* rather than as *capacities*. This both draws attention away from the contingent, historical and contestable elements *within* given state and democratic practices and promotes strategies for socialist transformation which are themselves seen to be 'essentialist' – for example, 'smashing the state' or replacing 'bourgeois democracy' with 'proletarian democracy'. Fourthly, it is suggested that classical Marxism's analytical strengths are heavily concentrated upon the explanation of society-wide or even world-wide social phenomena. But not all forms of social and political struggle are best understood in this global context. This is true not only of inter-state struggles, which are massively evident but rather poorly explained in conventional Marxist analyses, but also of (conceptually) localized disputes within societies, disputes which may not have a national or class-based significance but which are nonetheless strategic sites of the struggle to secure autonomy. The possibility this raises of socialist pluralism is said to be very poorly conceptualized by a Marxism which is overwhelmingly committed to holistic patterns of social explanation. In fact, 'post-Marxism' covers a broad range of revisionists, from those, such as E. O. Wright (1993), who seem to wish to preserve as much as is possible of the classical approach, to those (such as Laclau and Mouffe, see below pp. 59–60), who end up jettisoning just about everything that could be described as distinctively Marxist. 'Post-Marxists' also show a very variable sensitivity to the existence of diversity and flexibility within what is in practice a far from uniform 'classical' Marxist tradition. However, *all* the post-Marxists share the conviction that without significant reconstruction of its explanatory premises, Marxism will be unable to understand, let alone change, the contemporary world.

The Declining Centrality of Labour

This epistemological challenge to classical Marxism is buttressed by a number of further difficulties which it is seen to share with the socialist tradition more generally. In chapter 1 we discussed the (contested) evidence of a sociological and electoral 'decline of labour' in recent times. We have now to consider the corresponding claim that the category of labour, which has been the privileged subject of the ideology of the left for two hundred years, is losing its centrality. This claim can itself take a variety of forms. It may primarily be a response to the empirical evidence that the working class fails either to achieve majority status or to realize its 'historical mission' (Gorz, 1982; Przeworski and Sprague, 1986). It may, as in the work of the rational choice Marxists, rest upon the belief that the category of labour does not normally define a community of interest around which collective political action may be mobilized or the supposition that, under advanced capitalism, workers do not have a rational interest in initiating a transformation towards socialism (Przeworski, 1985; see pp. 195–205 below). It may be that the transition to a post-industrial society or, at least, to a radically new form of capitalism has displaced work as 'the key sociological category' (Offe, 1985, pp. 129–50; Habermas, 1990b). Under these circumstances, new constellations of interests, new political identities and new social movements may be displacing the 'old' social movement built around organized labour. As the symbols and discourse of 'collective labour' increasingly fail to correspond to the 'lived experience' of social and political subjects, these become available for mobilization around other ideologies, perhaps, most notably, around feminist and ecological ideas (Offe, 1985; Laclau and Mouffe, 1985; Dobson, 1990; Boyne and Rattansi, 1990).[4]

The Challenge of the Postmodern

In recent years, the idea of socialism has also faced an increasingly corrosive challenge from the advocates of the postmodern. It is not always clear in what this postmodernism consists. Ihab Hassan writes of its having shifted 'from awkward neologism to derelict cliché without ever attaining to the dignity of concept' and it has an uncentred quality befitting its celebration of diversity and 'otherness'. Even the clearest of discussions are rather diffuse (see e.g. Smart, 1993). Close to its heart lie a general scepticism about the positivistic logic of modernity, hostility to a 'grounded' project of social change and the advocacy of plurality, idiolect and indeterminacy (Hassan, 1985, p. 119; Boyne and Rattansi, 1990; Harvey, 1989, pp. 39–118). Yet however 'diverse' postmodernism itself may be, the main themes in its iconoclastic reaction against the socialist idea, with which we are centrally concerned, are relatively clear.

Socialism, and most explicitly Marxism, is seen to be deeply infused with the positivistic and constructivist logic of modernity to which postmodernism is most vigorously opposed. The idea of socialism has often been celebrated by its advocates as a product of the Enlightenment and of the application of Reason to human affairs which the thinkers of the Enlightenment recommended. The Enlightenment heralded a world, including a human world, which could be subjected to control and transformation by human agents according to the imperatives of revealed reason. It promised the replacement of myth and religion by science, and of tutelage to superstition and irrationality by self-direction through the exercise of reason; the displacement of the cyclical fatalism of human existence by the promise of evolution and progress; the expectation that reason and philosophy could be married to (indeed, could only be realized in) the requirements of practical, sensuous life. The more optimistic Enlightenment thinkers 'had the extravagant expectation that the arts and sciences would promote not only the control of natural forces, but would also further understanding of the world and of the self, would promote moral progress, the justice of institutions, and even the happiness of human beings' (Habermas, 1981, p. 9). The Enlightenment seemed to offer the spectre of a global project of 'universal human emancipation through mobilization of the powers of technology, science, and reason' (Harvey, 1989, p. 41).

It is this 'meta-narrative' of overall social change guided by the dictates of a universal Reason towards which the scepticism of the postmodernists is most witheringly directed. Indeed, for Lyotard, postmodernism can be simply summed up as 'incredulity towards metanarratives' (Lyotard, 1984, p. 4). Postmodernists refute the claimed association between reason and emancipation that modernity shares with the Enlightenment. Their counter-argument is that the relationship between the practical application of (Western, instrumental) reason and emancipation is precisely the opposite of that indicated by the Enlightenment. The meta-narratives of reason and of modernity do not foster self-realization; they do not disclose but rather mask the exercise of power – so that 'Reason itself destroys the humanity it first made possible' (Habermas, 1987, p. 110). 'Depth knowledge' of the underlying structures of human existence is unavailable. Acting as if this knowledge were available, and reforming and directing society in accordance with the consequent 'dictates of Reason', will always yield institutions and practices which are repressive and unjustified.

Socialism is seen to be deeply implicated in this flawed 'project of modernity'. Its ambition is the global transformation of the social world in correspondence to the revealed requirements of a rational social order. Even in its non-Marxist variants, if not quite graced with a philosophy of history, it nonetheless embodies a presumption that history favours the transition towards a more benign, reasonable and socialist order. It shares those very assumptions of Enlightenment thinking – the coherence of meta-narratives, the availability of 'depth knowledge', the plasticity of the social world – to which the postmodernists are most trenchantly opposed. For the postmodernists, the consequences are dire. However well-intentioned may be the political intervention of socialists, their ambition for social transformation in accord with the imperatives of a global reason will always tend towards totalitarian outcomes. The more rigourously and systematically do socialists apply the presumptions of modernity, the more oppressive and distorting will the consequences prove to be.

Clearly, this critique of the application of reason has a long history on the political right (retraceable at least to Burke's strictures on the French Revolution and well represented in the more recent past by Hayek), and for some of its critics on the left postmodernism does little more than offer 'a rationale for lying back and enjoying late capitalism' (Burke, 1910; Hayek, 1982; Callinicos, 1990, p. 114). Others on the left have seen postmodernism as a much more promising development. They welcome the breach with the totalizing and homogenizing 'imaginary' which they understand to have dominated the traditional left. They welcome the celebration of open-endedness, pluralism and the space for 'other voices' which postmodernism permits, seeing in this a respect for the plurality of contemporary emancipatory struggles over against the privileging of the discourse of class. Rather than the 'one great struggle for socialism' whose consummation is (indefinitely) postponed, they identify a range of localized emancipatory struggles, for racial and sexual identity or penal reform, where real advances may be won (see Boyne and Rattansi, 1990).

Probably the most sustained, and certainly the most ambitious, attempt to marry this 'left face' of postmodernism with the characteristic sensibilities of the post-Marxists is to be found in Laclau and Mouffe's *Hegemony and Socialist Strategy* (1985; see also Laclau, 1990; Mouffe, 1992). Laclau and Mouffe locate themselves firmly and explicitly within the domain of discourse analysis. While attacking the postmodernist opening to the right, they are also quite explicit in their rejection of the traditional discourses of the left. They insist that

> What is now in crisis is a whole conception of socialism which rests upon the ontological centrality of the working class, upon the role of Revolution, with a capital 'r' . . . and upon the illusory prospect of a perfectly unitary and homogeneous collective will that will render pointless the moment of politics. (Laclau and Mouffe, 1985, p. 2)

Reworking the (neo-Gramscian) conception of hegemony, within 'a post-Marxist terrain', they reject the characteristic epistemological claims of Marxism and most notably the privileged explanatory status of the productive process and the leading political role of the working class. For them, there is no 'necessary' relationship between socialism and the working class (nor between economic and political struggles) and socialism may be as effectively advanced by other and 'new' social movements. Whether or not the workers' or any other movement is 'progressive' 'depends upon its hegemonic articulation with other struggles and demands' (Laclau and Mouffe, 1985, p. 87). This disprivileging of the economy and of the working class, along with a trenchant hostility to all forms of 'essentialism' ('classism', 'statism', 'stagism', 'economism' and 'the foundational character of the revolutionary act'), leads Laclau and Mouffe radically to recast the political aspirations of the contemporary left. Upon this discursive terrain, 'the task of the Left . . . cannot be to renounce liberal-democratic ideology, but on the contrary, to deepen and expand it in the direction of a radical and plural democracy' (1985, pp. 176–7; italicized in the original). The politics of socialism is thus recast as a process of open-ended, multi-sited democratic struggle to achieve varying forms of emancipation. Socialism increasingly becomes democracy, in a process which is not only open-ended but also unending (1985, pp. 176–93).

Defending Marxism

In chapter 1, we assessed claims about the 'declining social base for socialism' and found that, while there was evidence of real and deep-seated change, this does not reflect quite the sort of wholesale transformation that its most drastic proponents have suggested. The claims of the post-Marxists and the postmodernists have been just as fiercely contested. It is possible to isolate four main elements in the critical response to post-Marxism. First, there is the claim that post-Marxists have created a rather careless caricature of vulgar Marxism against which to direct their critical fire. Norman Geras, for example, accuses a wide range of post-Marxists of 'obloquy', of the casual disparagement of Marxism in terms which even its most vulgar apologists would not recognize. It is only by denying the real sensibility, adaptiveness and variety of Marxist analysis as, for example, by construing 'determinism' in an absurdly mechanistic way, that the arguments of the post-Marxists can be sustained (Geras, 1990). Secondly, the grounds upon which the post-Marxists stand in their assault upon Marxist rationalism is seen to lay them open to the very same charge. To suppose that Marxism can be described as, *in its essence* and *of necessity*, deterministic suggests 'a suspiciously rationalist construal of the theoretical problem which marxism faces' (McLennan, 1989, pp. 153–4). The post-Marxists have also been criticized upon more substantive grounds. Some have insisted that the decentring of the politics of class, which follows from the post-Marxists' emphasis upon the plurality of emancipatory struggles, cannot be justified. They insist that a recognition of the diversity of emancipatory struggles is not inconsistent with a continuing emphasis upon the primacy of the politics of class (Geras, 1990; Wood, 1986). Abandoning the politics of class, at a time when the institutions of the organized labour movement face their sternest challenge, is to abandon the most effective weapon in resisting the neo-conservative assault precisely at the moment when it is most desperately needed. Others suggest that, however innovative may be the intellectual context, the *post*-Marxists do little more than reproduce the criticism of an earlier generation of *anti*-Marxist writers, most notably, of Karl Popper, (McLennan, 1989, p. 203; Popper, 1961 and 1962). In so doing, they tend to give succour to forms of classical pluralist thinking which even many of its most celebrated proponents have now abandoned.[5] Finally, there is the issue of the post-Marxists' claim to endorse a socialist political programme. It is argued by their critics that such an endorsement is inconsistent with their anti-foundationist perspective. Even those, such as Laclau and Mouffe, who have broken most radically with the Marxist tradition, insist that 'of course, every project for radical democracy implies a socialist dimension' (Laclau and Mouffe, 1985, p. 178). But it is unclear from their theoretical apparatus just why this may be presumed. In his more recent work, Laclau explicitly voices the question 'why prefer one future over another?' There can, he argues, 'be no reply if the question is asking for a kind of Cartesian certainty that pre-exists any belief. But if the agent who must choose is someone who *already* has certain beliefs and values, then criteria for choice . . . can be formulated.' He comments that 'such an acceptance of the facticity of certain strata of our beliefs is nothing but the acceptance of our contingency and historicity' (Laclau, 1990, p. 83). It is not clear that this rather Weberian-sounding formulation will satisfy those who want to know why it is the project of socialism that we should endorse.

Defending Modernity

The criticisms of the postmodernists have met a similarly robust response, perhaps most systematically in Habermas's defence of *The Philosophical Discourse of Modernity* (1987). Habermas's ambition is to show that criticisms of modernity (from Nietschze to Foucault) are mistaken. He concedes that, in practice, the project of modernity has been *distorted* but insists that the weaknesses and distortions which the postmodernists have identified are not intrinsic to the project of modernity itself. The drastic conclusions that they draw – that the project of modernity should be abandoned – are not justified by their critique. Indeed, Habermas argues that even the fiercest critics of modernity have not themselves been able to step outside the domain of the discourse of reason or 'the philosophy of consciousness' which they seek to condemn. Thus, for example, in assessing Derrida, he insists that he 'inherits the weaknesses of a critique of metaphysics that does not shake loose of the intentions of first philosophy'. Of Foucault, he writes that his approach 'cannot lead to a way out of the philosophy of the subject, because the concept of power that is supposed to provide a common denominator for the contrary semantic components has been taken from the repertoire of the philosophy of the subject itself' (Habermas, 1987, pp. 181, 274).

The one point in the critique of modernity that Habermas endorses is that 'the paradigm of the philosophy of consciousness is exhausted' (1987, p. 296). But he entirely rejects the conclusions to which this insight is said to give rise. For Habermas, the recognition of this difficulty is as old as the philosophical discourse of modernity itself and can be responded to in terms of a *reconstruction* of the philosophy of modernity, built upon a reversing of those 'wrong turns' taken at strategic points in its development. In essence, this means replacing the model of subject-centred reason 'with the model of unconstrained consensus formation in a communication community standing under cooperative constraints' (1987, p. 295). According to Habermas, the advocates of postmodernity have made the mistake of identifying the limitations of a particular form of (subject-centred) reason as a limitation of *all* forms of reason. Habermas's claim is to have reconstituted the traditional but problematic claims of the supporters of modernity by purging this tradition of its association with an (exhausted) subject-centred reason and redeeming it through the appeal to the claims of intersubjective or communicative reason.

'Post-everything Means Capitalism Forever'?[6]

We cannot hope here to resolve definitively the (sometimes wilfully) arcane debate swirling around post-Marxism and postmodernism. However, some insights can be drawn from the very terms and nature of the debate. Indeed, that the debate over the nature of socialism (as more generally over the modernist application of reason), should be engaged at quite so fundamental a level is itself indicative of a widespread loss of confidence in the traditional aspirations (and guarantees) of the socialist project. That the politics of class and of the realm of production more generally should be so widely questioned also indicates uncertainty over the future direction of the politics of work and labour. Making the relationship between socialism and democracy so problematic (once again) underlines the tension that has always existed between two of the 'great' projects of the modern period.

This debate over ideology illustrates yet again the severity of the challenge that confronts contemporary advocates of socialism. But it does not, I think, demonstrate that the latter is necessarily in terminal decline. First, we must insist that ideology be put in its proper place. It is very natural that the *ideology* of socialism should have held such a fascination for intellectuals and academics, but it has probably never been such a powerful and coherent force as those who bear witness to its collapse suppose. At least in the West, occasional invocations of the 'New Jerusalem' have always been heavily outweighed by the mundane and sometimes rather grubby business of securing the short- and medium-term interests of those who have supported socialist and social democratic parties. Thus socialist politics has been very much more (or less) than the realization of a socialist ideology. Again, the 'crisis of Marxism' is profoundly important, not least because of the intellectual authority which Marxism has enjoyed on the left most especially in its 'renaissance' from the mid-1960s onwards. However, as we have seen, recognition on the left of theoretical weaknesses in the Marxist position is of very long standing and if these weaknesses are above all *epistemological*, then they cannot be new and can hardly be taken to explain a historical *decline* in socialism's fortunes. Nor is it clear that the loss of a privileged historical status which Marxism supposed socialism to enjoy should necessarily prove fatal to the latter's prospects. While it will be alarming to some to find that history is not on the side of socialism (nor, of course, it follows, of anyone else), it may not seem so disturbing to others that socialism should have to be fought for, or defended perhaps even on *ethical* or *moral* grounds. Indeed, outside the community of intellectuals, it is often upon *moral* grounds that socialism's claim to be superior to capitalism has been most convincingly redeemed. To say that socialism's victory is not assured tells us nothing about the value of its aims, and it is not the same as proving it to be unattainable. It is not even clear that the ideas of socialism (at least as this has been practised in the West) *are* just so uniformly unpopular. Democratic publics have good reason to be cynical about any politician (of left *or* right) who insists that a little present suffering is all that is needed to carry them into the Promised Land. But there is plenty of evidence of continuing public sympathy with classical social democratic ambitions (for universal health care, decent standards of public housing, and so on), even in some of those countries which have only recently freed themselves from Communist tutelage (Taylor-Gooby, 1989; Smith, 1989; Swain, 1992). What we can see is less a wholesale withdrawal of popular support for the *ideals* of socialism (at least in their social democratic form), but rather a growing scepticism about the *capacity* of socialist and social democratic movements to deliver. Finally, the more thoroughgoing is the negative, system-refuting moment of postmodernism, the more difficult it is to see upon what defensible political ground its advocates may stand. If postmodernism really does lack a political pragmatics, there are surely grounds for indulging Daniel Singer's suspicion that in practice 'post-everything' would mean 'capitalism for ever'. The problem here is not with 'scepticism towards all meta-narratives' but with the more political question 'what is to be done?' If *something* is to be done, then socialists seem as well placed to propose policy as anyone else. This is, of course, rather less than carrying through the 'inevitable laws of history', but it is also rather more than the architects of a new 'end of ideology' would seem to permit.

The Revolutions of 1989 and the Collapse of Socialism

If some of these qualifications might once have been entertained, there is a very broadly held view that they were effectively swept away by the sheer scale of the social transformation effected by the revolutions of 1989. Almost as uniformly on a demoralized left as on the triumphalist right, there was a sense that for socialists 'the game was up'. For those on the left who had spent half a lifetime or more condemning the regime in Eastern Europe, it could hardly be the collapse of the Soviet Empire that occasioned regret (though one suspects that Gerry Cohen (1992), was not alone on the left in harbouring a rather shame-faced and lingering attachment to 'the first socialist state'). Rather, it was the chosen route out of Soviet socialism, not down 'a Third Way' but through the restoration of capitalism, and with it the conviction that 'socialism can no longer be considered as an alternative socioeconomic system that is viable and superior to capitalism' (Lukes, 1990, pp. 573–4). It seems appropriate to conclude our review of the 'death of socialism' by turning to this, its synoptic denouement. I shall not add to the wealth of commentary and speculation about the likely outcome of the continuing process of change in the East (even though there is some evidence that developments since 1989 have not been just as the harbingers of freedom had anticipated). Indeed, I am not interested so much in these developments in themselves as with the consequences that they have had for socialism in the West. In part, these are changes in the practical circumstances in which socialist and social democratic parties are required to act. Thus, for example, the emergence of a new area of comparatively underdeveloped and newly marketized economies on the eastern edge of the European Union, the process of partial disarmament, the possibility of mass migrations and perhaps above all the reunification of Germany radically alter the strategic context in which socialist forces (along with others) have now to operate. But I am less concerned with these strategic changes than with the 'demonstration effect' that the transformations in the east are thought to have had for Western socialist and social democratic forces.

One view, admittedly that of a small minority, is that whatever the transformations in Eastern Europe connote, they cannot be understood as a reversal for socialism. In Alex Callinicos's spirited account:

> What is dying in the disintegrating eastern bloc is not socialism, of however a degenerate and distorted form, but the negation of socialism [i.e. Stalinism]. (1991, p. 2)

Since the societies of Eastern Europe were not socialist but state capitalist, the spectre of the economic self-management of the associated producers (and with it the explanatory apparatus of an orthodox Marxism), emerges unscathed from half a century of bureaucratic autocracy. Such a view, while internally consistent, requires us to accept a version of the 'science of historical materialism' which few will now find it possible to support. It also requires us to endorse what I take to be the analytically unhelpful judgement that the societies of Eastern Europe and the Soviet Union were 'not socialist'. Here we find ourselves thrown into the midst of the dispute as to 'what is to count as socialism'. Surely, it is objected, societies which were so oppressive for the ordinary working population and in which the workers were so evidently not in control of the means of production should not properly be described as socialist. While there is substance to this objection, I think greater analytical clarity is achieved if we describe those societies in which the greater part of economic assets are not in formally private ownership as 'socialist' (however 'unsocialist' their institutions and practices may seem in other respects). In this limited sense, it seems to me that it is appropriate to describe the societies of Eastern Europe and the USSR as socialist and to this extent, and especially where linked to the call for a restoration of private ownership of property and of a capital market, to consider the revolutions of 1989 as anti-socialist. In this sense, 1989 saw the wholesale abandonment of socialism in a string of Eastern European countries. However, if we do choose to call these societies 'socialist', it is only proper to point out that hardly any Western socialists aspired to or even defended political and economic arrangements in these countries, and then only in the most highly qualified terms. There is no reason why the overturning of 'socialism' in this very limited sense and in itself should be especially distressing or embarrassing for Western socialists and social democrats.

But there are other elements in the experience of 1989 which are potentially much more damaging to the integrity of 'the socialist idea' in the West. There is, for example, a long (if largely theoretical) tradition in Eastern Europe of advocating the internal reform of communism, of bringing autocratic and oppressive regimes under Soviet tutelage towards a humane and democratic form of self-governing socialism. This agenda for 'reform communism' was often advocated under the title of Ota Sik's famous study *The Third Way* (1976). This process of gradual and internal reform towards a democratic socialism was also dealt a death blow by the revolutions of 1989. The reform agenda was simply overwhelmed by the pace and ferocity of anti-communist feeling and by a desire for Western-style institutions (multi-party parliamentary democracies, the market and affluence). After the events of 1989, many of those who had been the leading advocates of the reform process revealed themselves as advocates of a much more traditional form of capitalist market economy, (see e.g. Brus, 1990; and Kornai, 1990b). The transformations of 1989 also provided further proof, were it needed, of the global interconnectedness of the world economy, (as indeed of the media of information and communication). It provided socialists in the West with (perhaps unwelcome) evidence of the impossibility of insulating national or even regional economies from the dictates of a global (market) economy. In this sense, the transformations in the East were final proof of the impossibility of 'socialism in one empire'.

In the short-term at least, the revolutions of 1989 also gave considerable succour to the political opponents of socialism in the West. By the end of the 1980s, and after a decade in government, the economic performance of the most enthusiastic neo-conservative regimes (in the US and the UK) was, at best, unimpressive. In Western Germany, the popularity of Christian Democrat Chancellor Helmut Kohl had slumped to an all-time low. Under pressure at home, the transformations in Eastern Europe could be represented by governments of the right as a victory for liberal democracy and the tenacity of the West in facing down the totalitarian threat. Leaders of the Eastern revolutions were fêted by right-wing parties in the West. Their newly-unleashed enthusiasm for the market, the sclerotic incompetence of the old communist order and the qualitatively-different economic problems of the former communist regimes lent support to conservative claims that 'the whole world' was moving towards neo-liberal solutions. While its impact is unquantifiable, the neo-conservative right sought every opportunity to repeat this claim about 'the worldwide march *from* socialism'.[7]

'The Strange Death of Socialism': Three Views

Of course, there exists a still more apocalyptic view of the consequences of the revolutions of 1989 for the prospects of socialism. Upon this account, the transformation of Eastern Europe in 1989 marks not just the passing of communism or Marxism-Leninism, but indeed allows us to recognize the historical passing of the socialist project in *all* its forms. In fact, this thesis received its most grandiose expression in Francis Fukuyama's charting of the 'end of history', *before* the revolutionary events of 1989. Shrouding itself (rather unconvincingly) in the mantle of Hegel's philosophy of history, Fukuyama's argument was that the 1980s had witnessed the definitive 'triumph of the West' and 'the total exhaustion of viable systematic alternatives to Western liberalism'. This was not just an epochal victory but consummated 'the end of history as such: that is, the end point of mankind's ideological evolution and the universalization of Western liberal democracy as the final form of human government'. In actuality in the West, and as an aspiration elsewhere, we live in the best of all possible worlds, a world of 'liberal democracy in the political sphere combined with easy access to VCRs and stereos in the economic' (Fukuyama, 1989, pp. 3, 4, 8). Undoubtedly, Fukuyama was much more widely cited than read and there is a suggestion that the more fully elaborated treatment of his theme in *The End of History and the Last Man* (Fukuyama, 1992), is much less certain about the final victory of liberal democracy (see McCarney, 1993). Nonetheless, it was the much-simplified version of Fukuyama's thesis that gained such prominence in 1989–90 as a suitably grandiloquent but simple explanation of what were widely recognized to be complex but world-historical events.

More measured, though little less apocalyptic in terms of their prognoses for socialism, are Ralf Dahrendorf's *Reflections on the Revolution in Europe* (1990). Given that Dahrendorf describes his essay as 'a homily to Popper' and that it celebrates the achievements of 'the Open Society', it is perhaps unsurprising that he sees Fukuyama's self-styled Hegelian historicism as 'a caricature of a serious argument' (p. 35). Yet he is little less damning in describing the consequences of the revolutions of 1989 for the prospects of socialism, in both East and West. Indeed, he insists that 'the point has to be made that socialism is dead, and that none of its variants can be revived for a world awakening from the double nightmare of Stalinism and Brezhnevism' (p. 38). He endorses the view of the coming of communism, through revolution in the USSR and through military imposition in Eastern Europe, as 'a developing-country phenomenon' which seemed to promise 'a quick and painless way out of authoritarian rule and preindustrial poverty'. In this, it failed. The peoples under communism got 'dictators and misery' and a 'combination of ineffectiveness and suppression [which] eventually set in motion the process of self-destruction which we have watched in recent years' (pp. 44, 46).

> In other words, socialism is not only a developing country phenomenon, but it is one which cannot be upheld beyond the initial stages of development. Sooner or later it has to give way to more open and effective modes of economic advancement and probably political involvement as well. Really existing socialism cannot last . . . In this sense [and inverting the historical logic of Marxism], capitalism succeeds socialism. (p. 46)

If communism has been a victim of its failures, social democracy in the West is seen by Dahrendorf to have fallen victim to its own successes. To the extent that social democracy managed to temper the worst excesses of an unconstrained liberal capitalism, it has made itself redundant. As it has ameliorated the condition of the working population, so has the working class diminished and increasingly attached its aspirations to individual mobility rather than collective advancement. As the welfare state has secured unprecedented levels of health and welfare provision for the general population, so have the apparatuses of state and bureaucracy been felt to press more heavily upon a population which now craves greater choice, independence and self-direction. Dahrendorf recognizes that social democracy in the West has been *incorporated* into existing political and economic institutions, rather than being straightforwardly rejected. Nonetheless, as an independent political force and cause, its energies are largely spent.

In the end, Dahrendorf rejects the belief that the future in either East or West can be restructured around the pursuit of some 'third way', with a system that incorporates 'the best of capitalism' and 'the best of socialism'. In part, this reflects Dahrendorf's hostility to the logic of 'systems'. What we need is not a capitalist 'system' (hence his hostility to Hayek), nor a socialist 'system', but rather the more effective pursuit of 'the open society'. But there is also a more hard-edged and substantive point, to the effect that in reality there is little to be learnt and still less to be borrowed form the unhappy experience of 'actually-existing socialism' (pp. 53–7). Overall, Dahrendorf's judgement is straight-forward: 'communism has collapsed; social democracy is exhausted' (p. 71).

Finally, we might consider the political judgements delivered by the celebrated ethnographer of the 1989 revolutions, Timothy Garton Ash, whose brilliant cameos of revolutionary events had such a profound (and probably inordinate) effect upon the perceptions of the reading public in the West. For Garton Ash, the revolutions of 1989 reaffirm 'the value of what we already have, of old truths and tested models, of the three essentials of liberal democracy and the European Community as the one and only, real existing common European home' (Garton Ash, 1990, p. 156). 'The ideas whose time has come', he concludes, 'are old, familiar, well-tested ones. (It is the new ideas whose time has passed)' (1990: 154). If, within the new order arising in Eastern Europe, there is one 'message' upon which all parties are agreed, it is this:

> There is no 'socialist democracy' there is only democracy. And by democracy they mean multi-party, parliamentary democracy as practised in contemporary Western, Northern and Southern Europe. They are all saying: there is no 'socialist legality', there is only legality. And by that they mean the rule of law, guaranteed by the constitutionally anchored independence of the judiciary. They are all saying, and for the left this is perhaps the most important statement: there is no 'socialist economics', there is only economics. And economics means not a socialist market economy but a social market economy . . . the general direction is absolutely plain: towards an economy whose basic engine of growth is the market, with extensive private ownership of the means of production, distribution and exchange. (1990, 151)

Socialism: Past, Present and Future

There are important differences in the substance (and plausibility) of these three commentaries upon the revolutions in Eastern Europe. However, they are more or less united in their judgement that the dramatic events of 1989 signalled the final dissolution of socialism in both East and West. While Dahrendorf recognizes that social democracy may have been *subsumed* rather than rejected in contemporary Western societies, they are all quite clear that *actually existing* liberal democracy has been seen to be historically superior to socialism in any existing or realistically imaginable form. Despite some twitching in its more remote limbs, socialism as both theory and practice is effectively dead.

Is this conclusion justified? Certainly, there are grounds for maintaining that some of the central elements of the traditional socialist outlook are no longer sustainable and it may be that the term 'social-ism' has itself been so comprehensively abused that it now has a radically diminished analytic or political value (see e.g. Kaldor, 1991, pp. 41–2). Nonetheless, it does not follow from this that Western liberal democracy represents the crowning achievement of humankind's moral and political development nor that all those historical forces identified with socialism are themselves exhausted. Insofar as these commentaries embrace just such a judgement, the consequences of 1989, not least for Western social democracy, have been grossly overstated.

Thus, if we wish to speak of a 'crisis of socialism – East and West', we must be clear that what passes for 'socialism', and what constitutes its 'crisis', are quite different in these two spheres. While socialists and social democrats have been less ready than those on the political right to condemn the Soviet Union and all its works, almost no one on the Western social democratic left defended the USSR and its satellites in Eastern Europe as even the most deformed expression of a socialism suited to the more advanced industrial societies. Indeed, the historical split between social democracy and communism may be retraced with some precision to disagreement over the status of the October Revol-ution and the nature of the post-revolutionary society, and there is a long tradition, even within the Marxist canon, of hostility to Marxism-Leninism and the Bolshevik Revolution (for the classical exchanges, see Kautsky, 1920 and 1964; Lenin, 1960; see also the commentary in Pierson, 1986). Alongside the strategy of 'reform communism', there has always been the claim on the left that Eastern Europe and the nations of the Soviet Union would have to pass through a period of 'restored' capitalism before a more attractive form of socialism could be historically viable. Under these circumstances, to speak of both Soviet and Western models as forms of 'state-administered socialism' may establish a quite misleading identity between the two. The Soviet model has collapsed. But, while the institutional and electoral chal-lenge to socialism in its characteristic Western forms is, as we have seen, severe, to suggest that its traditional institutions are on the verge of disappearing or that its parties are 'unelectable' is very poorly vindi-cated by the available evidence (see, Pierson, 1991a; Esping-Andersen, 1985; Flora, 1987). Indeed, within Eastern Europe itself, and scarcely five years on from the events of 1989, ex-communist parties have topped the polls in a number of national elections (in Lithuania, Poland and Hungary; see *Electoral Studies*).

While not entirely consistent, commentaries on 1989 have also tended to contrast the decline of socialism not so much with the con-tinuing rude health of capitalism, as with the strength of liberal democracy. There is an asymmetry here. For while the economies of the Western societies may still properly be described as capitalist, they do not look like the Hayekian model of liberal capitalism so widely touted for the East. As Galbraith has argued, 'the Smithian free market . . . is something we in the West do not have, would not tolerate, could not survive . . . for Eastern Europeans pure and rigorous capitalism would be no more welcome than it would be for us' (Galbraith, 1990, p. 7). If the contrast which 1989 highlights is not that between socialism in the East and capitalism in the West, but rather that between socialism in the East and liberal democracy in the West, the latter must be recognized to have been shaped, reformed and compromised by a century of social democratic pressure. Whatever the recent ascendancy in some quarters of neo-liberal parties and/or policies, social democratic forces remain deeply entrenched in the social fabric. In practice, social democratic and socialist parties within the constitutional arena in the West have almost always been involved in a politics of compromise with existing capitalist institutions (to whatever far distant prize its eyes might from time to time have been lifted). These have always been grounds for condemnation by those 'further to the left'. Yet, if advocates of the death of socialism accept that social democrats belong within the socialist camp, as I think they must, then the contrast between socialism (in all its variants) and liberal democracy must collapse. For *actually existing* liberal democracy is, in substantial part, a product of socialist (social democratic) forces.

A similar argument may apply to the message that Timothy Garton Ash reads into 1989. He may be right to suppose there is no 'socialist democracy', only democracy; no 'socialist legality', only legality; no 'socialist economics' only economics. But, of course, Garton Ash claims very much more than this. In essence, he argues that these is no socialist democracy, only *actually existing* liberal democracy as we have it in the West; no socialist legality, only *actually existing* liberal legality as we have it in the West and no socialist economics, only *actually existing* liberal economics as we have it in the West. But it does not follow from the implausibility of specifically 'socialist' invocations of these ideas and institutions that they can *only* be found in their existing liberal formulations. To take but one example, it is quite possible to accept that there is no such thing as 'socialist economics', while defending the idea that there could be and should be a socialist economy, indeed, as we shall soon see, this is a core contention of Alec Nove's influential *Economics of Feasible Socialism* (1991). Again, being critical of the aspiration to constitute a 'socialist democracy' does not commit one to the view that existing liberal democratic institutions represent the best available redemption of the promise of democracy *per se*.

This brings us finally to the issue of the availability of a 'third way'. It has not always been clear to what the 'third way' is an alternative. For some, it has represented an alternative to either capitalism or socialism; for others, it represents an alternative to either traditional social democracy or Soviet communism. I have already suggested that the 'third way' as a 'reform communism' route out of the *impasse* of Eastern European authoritarian regimes is defunct. I have also indicated that those who were the keenest exponents of the third way as a process of internal reform within communist societies seem, under the newly prevailing circumstances, to be much more willing to embrace a traditional form of the capitalist market. Yet I am here more concerned with the general question of whether the possibility of alternatives to *actually existing* liberal democracy has been exhausted by the demise of Eastern European socialism and the problems of Western social democrats.

It is hard to see why in principle this should be so. To accept that no alternatives to *actually existing* liberal democracy remain, we should have to agree that we could not imagine ways in which the democratic and economic credentials of Western societies could be improved upon or could not conceive of social forces which might seek to mobilize change in this direction. At the end of a century which has witnessed genocidal excesses committed in the name of competing 'totalizing' social projects, it is one of liberal capitalism's greatest assets that it seems to offer a low-risk, 'least worst' future. But this judgement must depend, in part, upon where you are looking from and what you are looking for. It is only perhaps the dramatic difficulties of socialism that have so effectively drawn our attention away from the continuing problems of capitalism. After all, the *last* 'end of ideology' was premised upon the unparalleled growth and prosperity which the West enjoyed in the twenty-five years following the Second World War. This age has gone. We now have societies with sluggish growth, permanent mass unemployment, impoverished public services and chronic, long-term environmental problems. At the end of the twentieth century, many of those things that have made global capitalism unattractive and irrational remain (indeed, they may be highlighted by the elimination of the vices of the Soviet alternative), and the ecological imperative presents new and ever more pressing grounds for an exercise of enhanced *collective* control over our (global) appropriation of natural resources. At the same time, it is unclear that those economies which have been in the front line of the neo-liberal revival and most hostile to the institutions of social democracy have been the most economically successful over the past decade (see Scharpf, 1991). Whilst the basis of traditional social democratic strategies based upon the Keynesian Welfare State may be disappearing, the growth of new supra-national institutions (including those of the EU) seems to offer new terrain upon which social democratic practices and institutions may already be set in train.

Socialism after Communism

We should now be in a position to make a more informed, if still somewhat provisional judgement, on the 'death of socialism'. It will be clear that I believe that, for whatever reasons (an over-concentration on the ideology of socialism or on the experience of the Soviet Union, the tendency to draw comparisons between a confused present and an idealized past), the demise of socialism has been overstated. As we saw in chapter 1, the social base of socialist forces has been eroded, but not quite in the way that its critics have imagined and certainly not so as permanently to exclude socialist and social democratic parties from governmental office. Again, whilst the ideological claims of socialists (particularly to be able to direct the process of social and political change) are very much weakened, it is not clear that many of the things for which socialists have in practice stood (such as full employment and publicly guaranteed welfare) are so very unpopular. It seems that it is a loss of confidence in the capacity of socialist forces to deliver these public goods in acceptable ways and at a tolerable social cost, rather than an aversion to the ends in themselves, that best summarizes the change of opinion amongst democratic publics.

This brings us to the erosion of the traditional political economies of socialism, in which area I think its severest difficulties lie. On the traditional model of central planning (and its derivatives), I follow Nigel Swain's rather melancholy judgement: the centrally planned economy 'does not seem inherently implausible and is quite consistent with popular variants of economic components of a "socialist project"; but it does not and cannot work' (Swain, 1992, p. 53). We should not necessarily foreclose on the possibility that at some future date an effective form of democratic fully planned economy might be ventured (though there is a neo-libertarian argument that, since this type of planning proceeds from an epistemological error rather than an institutional problem, this is an option which we should indeed reject out of hand) (see Lavoie, 1986). But, whilst an enhanced level of economic intervention may be defended, I think we are obliged to abandon the model of an economy whose central directing force is the plan.[8] Despite the difficulties outlined in chapter 2, it seems to me that the abandonment of (what has generally passed for) Keynesianism need not be so comprehensive. In practice, socialists and social democrats coming to office have little option in the short term but to make use of what remains of the Keynesian paradigm to pursue their constituents' interests. Social democrats, at least, have always been involved in the rather delicate and inglorious business of trying to manage capitalism insofar as they were able in the interests of their natural supporters. Even under the present inauspicious circumstances those on the left may well feel that it is better that the consequences of a globally untamed capitalism should be managed by social democratic rather than neo-conservative political forces. In a period of global capitalist ascendancy, as Scharpf has pointed out (1991, pp. 274–5), social democrats and their trade union partners may find themselves faced with little option but to allocate the burden of a redistribution of wealth in favour of capital. But we may be confident that, in neo-conservative hands, this redistribution would be still less equitable and still more damaging to the long-term interests and institutional integrity of social democracy.

In the rather longer term, it seems clear that the possibilities of a socialist political practice need to be far more fundamentally rethought. We should not underestimate the achievements of the social democrats, but it seems clear that even were the much more favourable balance of forces of the post-war period somehow to be reproduced, 'Keynesianism plus the welfare state' would not now constitute a viable and socialist strategy. And if there are grounds for continuing to advocate a socialist political practice, or at least an alternative to existing forms of capitalist regime, it can only be with a recognition that certain elements of traditional socialist belief are unambiguously finished, including the supposition that socialism is the privileged historical project of the messianic urban-industrial working class or that the 'anarchy' of the market can give way to the seamless organization of a planned economy. Indeed, any form of political advocacy which wishes to draw upon that which is still vital in the socialist tradition must of necessity be able to address at least the following recurring empirical and theoretical problems: (1) economic inefficiency, (2) the failures of centralized planning, (3) the lack of economic democracy, (4) the limits of state action, (5) the ineffectiveness of economic intervention and (6) the unitary vision of the good society. Above all, I think it must reactivate a debate which was foreclosed by the rise of modern social democracy, that is, the classical question of the nature and form of a regime of social ownership.

One of the boldest and theoretically most sustained attempts to meet this challenge has come from the recent advocacy for, and in, the West of a new form of *market socialism*. At the heart of the market socialist project lies (what is for socialists) a radically unconventional view of the market economy and its capacity to realize socialist goals. It proposes a correspondingly much-attenuated role for (and faith in) planning and the capacities of the interventionist state. It offers a highly distinctive account of the circumstances for promoting traditional socialist values such as equality, equity and community. Yet, at the same time, (and in the face of Keynesian practice), market socialists restore the very traditional imperative of the collective ownership of society's productive assets. A careful investigation of the theoretical and practical agenda of the market socialists should tell us a great deal about the possibilities of socialist revisionism under contemporary circumstances. It is to such an evaluation that I turn in the rest of this study.

PART II

The Case for Market Socialism

4

A Model of Market Socialism

If the evidence of part I suggests that socialism may not be entirely exhausted, it does nonetheless show that, at the very least, its aims and values have now to be promoted under quite different (and much more difficult) circumstances than was the case some twenty or thirty years ago. It also makes it clear that any successful socialist politics of the future is likely to have to be built upon a quite changed institutional basis. Recognition of these changed circumstances has helped to sponsor a continuing process of 'programmatic renewal' among many Western European socialist and social democratic parties and a 're-thinking of socialism' amongst some social and political theorists.[1] Given the profound disillusion with both the record of planned economies and state interventions more generally, and facing a rapidly changing international economic environment, both parties and theorists have been driven towards a much more enthusiastic embrace of the market. For many, embracing the market may be making a virtue of the necessity of tailoring party programmes to a changing electoral base. But for some socialists and social democrats, particularly those whose concerns are principally theoretical rather than electoral, the transfer of allegiance seems much more fundamental. Some, indeed, have sought 'to steal the ideological clothes of the neo-liberals', offering a 'principled' rather than a purely 'pragmatic' defence of market institutions and seeking to 'capture' the market for a revived socialist political project. It is with this belief that the traditional ambitions of socialists and social democrats may be recast under the rubric of markets, and that this represents a way out of the difficulties indicated in the first part of the book, that I am principally concerned in the rest of this study. In part II, I outline the case for a market-based form of socialism. In part III, I assess the claim that this offers a promising way out of socialism's present practical and theoretical impasse.

Markets under Socialism

As we shall see in the coming chapters, it has traditionally been a commonplace of both the political left and right to argue that socialism and the market are antithetical principles. Markets have commonly been identified with capitalism, private property and the economic sovereignty of the individual, whilst socialism has been seen to be premised upon social ownership of property and the planned and communal use of economic resources. For many traditionalists, socialism stopped where the market began. While this has undoubtedly been the predominant understanding of the relationship between socialism and markets, in practice, the divergence between the two has never been so clear-cut. Almost all *practical* experience of socialism, aside from a few short-lived utopian experiments, has entailed the use of markets. Even the most centralized command economies had recourse to (albeit grossly distorted) markets in labour and consumer goods and if social democracy is admitted as a form of socialism, it is clearly a form in which markets have a central place. Indeed, the German Social Democrats at Bad Godesburg opted for 'the market wherever possible; planning wherever necessary' (see Hodge, 1993; Padgett, 1993). In addition, there is the long-standing, if often marginalized, experience of producer and consumer co-operatives, which has attempted to set the social ownership of economic assets within a market context (Oakeshott, 1978; Lambert, 1963; Jones and Svejnar, 1982). Whilst the co-operative movement has often been regarded with considerable suspicion by the mainstream of the labour movement, it has also been described as 'the oldest and purest form of economic democracy' (Potter, 1891; Lambert, 1963, p. 177).

There is also a small and sometimes obscure theoretical tradition which has sought explicitly to construct a more general account of a market-based form of socialism. In Britain, for example, Noel Thompson has identified a 'thin strand of nineteenth century socialist thinking which may be labelled the political economy of market socialism' (1988, p. 158). But the evolution of a distinctive concern with 'market socialism' is largely a product of that twentieth-century era in which there were real world *planned* economies (and their problems) with which to contrast it. Nuti (1992) attributes the first usage of *Marktsozialismus* to Eduard Heimann in 1922, but its origins are most widely identified with the work of the Polish economist Oskar Lange and a number of like-minded theorists in the inter-war period.

Langean Market Socialism

Lange's model of market socialism was itself a response to an earlier article published in the formative years of the Soviet Union by the Austrian economist Ludwig von Mises. Reproduced in 1935, with an amplifying endorsement by Friedrich von Hayek, von Mises' article denied the possibility of rational economic decision-making under socialism (von Mises 1935; originally published in German in 1920). Rational economic calculation under socialism would be impossible, he argued, because 'where there is no free market, there is no pricing mechanism; without a pricing mechanism, there is no economic calculation'. For him, 'Socialism is the abolition of rational economy' (1935, pp. 110–11). The institutional details of Lange's response need not concern us here. The essence of his reply was to insist that rational calculation was indeed possible under socialism because the state's Central Planning Board could act as a surrogate for the market by setting prices (and the institutional context for socialist enterprises), and then adjusting these prices through a repeated 'trial and error' procedure, so as to respond to fluctuations in supply and demand. Indeed, Lange insisted that a similar *theoretical* resolution of the problem of prices under socialism, worked out by Vilfredo Pareto and Enrico Barone, *predated* von Mises' criticisms (Lange, 1938, p. 59; Barone, 1935; see also Lavoie, 1985; Taylor, 1929; Dickinson, 1933; Lerner, 1937 and 1944).

Although there is no universally endorsed judgement upon what came to be called the 'Socialist Calculation Debate', many analysts have followed the position outlined in Abram Bergson's well-known commentary (Bergson, 1966 and 1967; see e.g. Leeman, 1977). Bergson's view was that, while *technically* Lange's argument represented a successful reply to von Mises' criticisms of the economic irrationality of socialism, there were other aspects of the market, such as the promotion of motivation and innovation, which only *real* markets could secure (Bergson, 1967). A revival of interest in the 'Socialist Calculation Debate' in the 1980s saw a still more critical judgement of Lange's position. In an influential study, Don Lavoie argued that, while the Langean scheme was almost 'unanswerable' as a simulation of the price-setting process as it was described in neo-classical economics, the Austrian school of economics, to which both von Mises and Hayek belonged, also rejected this equilibrium theory of the neo-classicists as static and unrealistic (Lavoie, 1985, p. 168 n. 2; Lavoie, 1981; see also Murrell, 1983; Shapiro, 1989; Keizer, 1989). In practice, the market did not just disclose equilibrium prices. Indeed, it was the existence of *dis*equilibrium in the market, and the possibility of profiting from it, that called forth entrepreneurial innovation and sponsored economic dynamism. Still more importantly, the market was 'a procedure for the discovery and conveyance of inarticulate knowledge', and this was a function which a socialist market, even one that built in managerial and entrepreneurial incentives, could not fulfil (Lavoie, 1985).

We shall have to return to some of these important criticisms of the market socialist model later. At this point, however, it is perhaps more important to note that Lange's central concern in proffering a model of market socialism was with the rationality of resource allocation (by a centralized state) and not with the democratization or decentralization of economic decision-taking. He did assume 'that freedom of choice in consumption and freedom of choice in occupation are maintained and that the preferences of consumers, as expressed by their demand prices, are the guiding criteria in production and in the allocation of resources' (Lange, 1938, p. 72). Yet he did not seek to limit the (extremely extensive) powers of the (one-party) state, but rather to secure a market-mimicking device which would permit the rational calculation of the prices of capital and production goods. In this sense, Lange's model belongs more properly to the category of 'decentralization procedures in central planning' than to the promotion of an authentically market-based form of socialism (Nuti, 1992, p. 20).

Indeed, the *political* context of one-party Communist rule within which Lange's model is set is quite central to understanding the way in which the theory of market socialism has subsequently developed. Many of the most distinguished advocates of market socialism are Eastern European economists (including Brus in Poland, Kornai in Hungary and Sik in Czechoslovakia), and much of their advocacy was focused upon the internal reform of existing communist regimes. In general, the theorists of market socialism were concerned with both the improvement of economic efficiency through the promotion of markets and, of necessity less explicitly, with the extension of economic and political freedom. Indeed, Ota Sik was both a leading advocate of economic reform and deputy Prime Minister in Alexander Dubcek's brief and ill-fated Reform Administration in the Prague Spring of 1968. However, the leadership of the Communist Parties of Eastern Europe and the Soviet Union, as in contemporary China, were generally interested in strictly limited reforms which would improve overall economic efficiency without compromising the leading role of the Communist Party and its ideology, that is, without sponsoring an accompanying process of political reform. In practice, even more than in theory, the absence of accompanying *political* reform tended to undermine the possibility of effective *economic* reform. Even in those countries such as Hungary and Yugoslavia, in which economic reform was most 'successful' (and even here 'success' was highly qualified), efficiency and growth were constantly compromised by a largely unreformed political system (see Hankiss, 1990; Swain, 1992).

As a consequence, much of the existing literature of market socialism, while of a technically and intellectually high order, has a strictly limited applicability to the revival of interest in the market as an institutional basis for socialist politics in the West. Many of the technical arguments about the conditions for achieving efficiency through markets or discussion about the incentive structure for management in the absence of the private ownership of capital may apply equally in both East and West. But there are important differences in the institutional context within which such discussions take place. Certainly, market socialists in the West are seeking a system that is in some respects *more* economically efficient than contemporary welfare capitalism (for example, in its aspiration to make use of all available labour), but they do not proceed, as have the market socialists in Eastern Europe, on the basis of reforming an existing highly centralized command economy. Again, advocates of market socialism in the West seek an enhancement of democracy; indeed, they are probably more concerned with the possibilities of increasing economic *democracy* than with the prospects for improved economic *efficiency*. But this is generally to be achieved on the basis of an *extension* of existing and well-established liberal democratic institutions (representative democracy, civil liberties, party pluralism), rather than by either their inauguration or their replacement. At the same time, while discussions in the East were almost exclusively debates with or even within the Marxist heritage, many of the most significant arguments against the market which market socialists in the West confront rely not upon Marx's expectations of the transcendence of the law of value, but upon the morally undesirable consequences of reliance upon the market (whether or not circumstances of scarcity apply). Finally, the revolutions of 1989 following upon half a lifetime of frustrated reform persuaded some former market socialists in the East to abandon the 'half-way house' of market socialism in favour of an uninhibited embrace of free market capitalism (most spectacularly in the case of Janos Kornai, 1990b). Yet it is not clear that the same logic can be applied to the (as yet) largely untried models developed in the West. Overall, whilst the established literature developed under the old order in Eastern Europe is important, much of the case for market socialism in the West must rest upon different and

independent arguments. This does mean, however, that the failures of
market socialism in Eastern Europe and beyond are not just so damning as critics of its Western invocation very readily suppose.

Market Socialism: The Western Model

In the rest of this chapter, I want to establish the case for a market form
of socialism as it has been developed primarily amongst Western
economists and political theorists over the past decade. I draw principally upon the work of Robin Blackburn, Jon Elster, Saul Estrin, Julian
Le Grand, Michael Harrington, David Miller, Alec Nove, Adam
Przeworski, John Roemer, Radoslav Selucky, Ota Sik, Leland Stauber
and James Yunker. Some of these sources are quite skeletal, others
represent fully worked out models of a market socialist economy and
polity. My intention is not to give exhaustive coverage to every position, but to construct a composite which highlights the most prominent
and widely agreed elements of a model for market socialism in the
West. Even so, there is substantial internal variation in these accounts.
Some see a very limited direct role for the state (Le Grand), while others
see the state in a position of economic predominance (Nove). Some see
market socialism as a system of workers co-operatives (Miller), while
others see a much more traditional method of economic management
(Yunker, Stauber, Roemer). There is considerable variation in judging
just how much of the economy should remain under capitalist ownership, and upon what terms (see e.g. the contrast between Nove and
Yunker). Where essential, I shall give an indication of these differences,
though it remains my principal ambition to construct an 'optimal'
account of a market form of socialism, whose strengths and weaknesses
we shall be able to investigate in the third section of the book.

Socialism and the Market

The core principle of the market socialist position is easily stated. At its
simplest, market socialism describes an economic and political system
which combines the principles of social ownership of the economy with
the continuing allocation of commodities (including labour) through
the mechanism of markets. For market socialists, it is not markets but
capitalist markets, that is, markets which inscribe the social and economic power of private capital, that are objectionable. They offer an
alternative model in which markets are combined with varying forms
of the *social* ownership of capital. Amongst its supporters, the market is

recommended not only as a way of attaining greater economic *efficiency* under socialism, but also as a way of securing greater individual *liberty* or a more *equal value of liberty*, of increasing *democracy* and of enhancing *social justice*.

Why Socialism?

It might seem that the first or most fundamental question to be asked about market socialism is 'why socialism?' Whilst some market socialists do make an explicit attempt to answer this question (Nove 1991, pp. 1–11; Plant, 1989), the general case for socialism is more or less taken for granted. This is understandable. What is (intended to be) distinctive and original about the market socialists' position is not their defence of the values of socialism – which is, with some notable exceptions, quite conventional – but their assertion that these values are best redeemed through the agency of the market – a radically unconventional claim. In fact, the contemporary advocacy of market socialism is best understood in terms of the historical and institutional context outlined in part I. While not itself 'defeatist', it is a form of socialism which has clearly been tutored by (an often painful) experience, representing 'an attempt to come to terms with [the] defects in state socialism and social democracy while still holding on to certain core socialist ideals' (Miller, 1989, p. 9). Some attempt is made to depict market socialism as an optimal realization of socialist ambitions, but it is more characteristically defended as 'feasible', 'pragmatic' and 'a compromise' (Nove 1987 and 1989 and 1991; Yunker, 1988 and 1990a; Miller, 1989). Indeed, it is probably most sensibly understood as a 'second-order' concept, showing how the best real-world approximation of certain established and cherished socialist values – equality, fairness, liberty, autonomy, 'social justice', 'full employment' and so on – can be secured in a system that also offers optimal economic efficiency and enhanced democracy. In the preface to his outline of a market socialist polity, Radoslav Selucky approvingly quotes Keynes's claim that 'the political problem of mankind is to combine three things: economic efficiency, social justice and individual liberty' (Keynes quoted in Selucky, 1979, p. vi). It is this reconciliation which the market socialists strive to realize.

As with most socialist advocacy, much of the case for market socialism rests upon a rejection of existing forms of capitalism, and much depends upon the rather delicate task of uncoupling what is essential to capitalism from what is essential to the market. Typically, it is argued that 'there is nothing specifically capitalist about the market'

(Selucky, 1979, p. 181). Nonetheless, the market socialists' critique is unusually and varyingly cautious. Whilst happy to condemn capitalist invocations of the market, market socialists are quite equivocal about the claimed inefficiency of markets under capitalism, particularly when these are compared with the efficiency gains promised by a planned economy. Yunker, for example, insists that, given 'the apparently high level of economic efficiency presently witnessed in such advanced market capitalist nations as the United States, it seems evident that *the proposed market socialist economy should very closely parallel the existing features of the present market capitalist economy*' (Yunker, 1990, p. 113; emphasis added; see also Sik, 1976, p. 24).

This ambivalence towards the market is quite clearly incompatible with some (quite central) elements of a more traditional and radical advocacy of socialism. The sort of role that is envisaged for the market seems quite incompatible with even an approximate equality of condition or with the distribution of goods according to need or with a communitarian regime in which we do not regard unfamiliar others as a means to achieving our market-determined ends. To understand why market socialists are willing to abandon so much traditional socialist baggage, we need to understand why they recommend this much closer embrace of the market.

Why Markets?

As we shall see in chapter 5, socialism and the market are frequently presented by their respective supporters as antithetical principles. In the Marxist tradition, for example, markets were synonymous with alienation, the dictatorial power of private capital, wasteful and irrational production for profit and the exploitation of workers. As Selucky has it, 'a traditional Marxist critique of capitalism is, at the same time, a critique of the market' (1979, p. 7). Interestingly, amongst neo-liberals, we find a parallel claim that the liberty-enhancing organization of the market is quite irreconcilable with socialist institutions. Given the authority of this traditional view, we need to consider the arguments for combining markets and socialism in some detail.

'There is No Alternative'

The first, most basic and rather negative premise of the market socialist position is that, in developed societies which value social heterogeneity and economic efficiency, *there is no alternative* to the market. Certain forms of the market are undesirable and all markets need intervention to address their inevitable failures (see Bardhan and Roemer, 1993a). But traditional socialists are seen generally to have been quite mistaken about the circumstances in which it would be possible to move 'beyond the market'. By far the most authoritative and systematic source for this traditional belief is to be found in the work of Marx. Despite Michael Harrington's ingenious attempt to depict Marx's position on markets as 'ambivalent', it seems clear that the essence of his theory implied 'the incompatibility of the market with . . . a rational socialist economy' (Harrington, 1989; Brus and Laski, 1989a, pp. 5–6). Thus Marx wrote of 'united cooperative societies [regulating] national production upon a common plan, thus taking it under their own control and putting an end to the constant anarchy and periodical convulsions which are the fatality of capitalist production'. Engels insisted that 'with the seizing of the means of production by society, production of commodities is done away with, and . . . Anarchy in social production is replaced by systematic, definite organization' (Marx, 1974, p. 213; Engels, 1987, p. 270; see also Lavoie, 1985, pp. 28–47).

In some accounts, the core problem with Marx's position is that he envisaged socialism as a society approaching abundance, in which the law of value (indeed, all the laws of economics insofar as these were premised upon the need to allocate *scarce* means and resources), would no longer apply. Attention is often drawn to the difficulties of those pursuing Marx's ambition in the Soviet Union, where an ideological aspiration to transcend the law of value was repeatedly frustrated by the need to reintroduce market mechanisms in order to avoid catastrophic economic collapse (Nove, 1991, pp. 12–72). Ota Sik is typical of the Eastern European reformers in insisting that 'at the existing level of development, products cannot be distributed directly in kind among all workers, but must be distributed indirectly by means of commodity relationships and currency' (Sik, 1967, p. 29; Sik, 1985).

Radoslav Selucky is particularly rigorous in arguing that Marx and his followers were mistaken in supposing that the abolition of capitalism could bring in its wake the abolition of the market. In order to abolish the market, Selucky argues, 'it would be necessary to abolish some of its prerequisites: social division of labour, scarcity and autonomy of producers' (1979, p. 10). But, he insists, the social division of labour cannot be abolished in complex and developed societies, nor can there be any (envisageable) expectation of reaching global conditions of abundance. Under these circumstances, Marx's aspiration to abolish the autonomy of producers by ordering the entire economy as if it were the internal division of labour within a single enterprise (the 'one nation, one factory' model), is bound to be pernicious.

Selucky concedes that, since an uncontrolled market is likely to lead to the steady concentration of wealth in the hands of a minority, whilst relegating the majority to the category of wage labour, 'it seems to be quite logical to suggest, as *the* socialist remedy, the abolition of the market':

> But here lies the main problem for the Marxist approach: the abolition of the market is, at the same time, the abolition of the economic base for equality and freedom . . . any non-market socially-planned economy resting on the division of labour and scarcity would create a structure of vertical relations of personal dependence, superiority and sub-ordination . . . the concept of a non-market socialist system cannot turn the formal and partial equality and freedom of the capitalist market into real and universal equality and freedom. By abolishing the market without destroying its roots, especially the division of labour and scarcity, the social foundation of equality and freedom disappears. (Selucky, 1979, p. 21)

Marx recognized this problem, so Selucky argues, but 'the evils of the capitalist market bothered him much more than the virtues of the market as such'. As a consequence, 'instead of trying to construct a socialist market, which would eliminate inequality while preserving the general foundation of equality and freedom, he decided in favour of a non-market socialist system', with fateful consequences (Selucky, 1979, p. 21).

This largely theoretical judgement is reinforced by what is perceived to be the sheer awfulness of the alternative represented by existing planned economies. Elster and Moene are particularly straightforward in their assessment:

> Capitalism – actually existing capitalism – appears in many respects to be an ugly, irrational, wasteful way of organising the production and dis-tribution of goods and services. [This ugliness] makes us look to central planning for a possible remedy, but the irrationality of central planning sends us back to capitalism as, probably, the lesser evil. (Elster and Moene, 1989b, p. 1; see also Sik, 1985, pp. 193–8)

The core premise of the market socialist position is then a largely negative one. The market is indispensable, not as an *optimal* way of arranging society's political and economic affairs, but rather as the *least worst* form of such organization under prevailing conditions.[2]

Efficiency

However, the market socialists do more than recommend the market as a regrettable necessity, and they find in it many positive qualities, especially when contrasted with the possibilities afforded by existing non-market forms of socialism. Perhaps the most prominent of these virtues is the capacity of markets to maximize economic efficiency. In the accounts offered by Estrin, Le Grand and Winter, markets offer 'the most efficient way of co-ordinating decentralized economic decision-making'. They are 'an excellent way of processing information, while simultaneously providing incentives to act upon it'. They 'encourage innovation both in production techniques and in the goods themselves' and 'disperse economic power'. The market 'can provide incentives for people to act in a way that is socially desirable, without further central direction', so that, 'assuming competitiveness, and that prices are a true reflection of scarcity, pursuit of individual interest is . . . in harmony with pursuit of the social interest' (Le Grand and Estrin, 1989, pp. 1, 3; Estrin and Winter, 1989, p. 107). John Roemer is less up-beat, but no less unequivocal: 'profit maximization under the right conditions (which include a competitive environment for the firm) leads to an efficient allocation of resources [and] we have no example of a large economy that has operated successfully without profit maximization as a goal of firms'. Differential wages are a regrettable necessity under market socialism: 'they are a by-product of using a labor market to allocate labor, and there is no known way to allocate labor more efficiently in a large complex economy than by use of a labor market' (Roemer, 1991, pp. 564, 567).

This is a controversial position for socialists to maintain. It has traditionally been seen as one of socialism's greatest strengths that it promised to replace the irrationality and anarchy of the market – with its orientation around profit rather than need and its periodic underutilization of both capital and labour – with a more efficient (rational and planned) employment of all available resources. The market socialists generally accept, with Meade, that 'prices used for . . . efficiency purposes may result in a very undesirable distribution of income and wealth' (Meade, 1964, p. 13), but they also insist that, given scarce means and resources, markets remain the most efficient mechanism for directing economic effort. Existing market outcomes are vexatious either because of their (chronic but not necessary) coincidence with the institutions of capitalism and/or because of a lack of outside interventions to 'rig' markets or to redistribute their products.

Liberty

If it is a little unusual to find socialists endorsing the market because of its capacity to promote efficiency, it is perhaps even more odd to find them arguing that the market promotes liberty. After all, it was one of

Marx's central ambitions in *Capital* to show how the *surface* relationships of freedom and equality in the capitalist market masked an *underlying* reality of inequality and unfreedom (Marx, 1973a). In fact, defining liberty is acutely problematic, (see e.g. Berlin, 1969; Miller, 1989, pp. 23–46; Rawls, 1972; Hayek, 1982; Gray, 1984). But many discussions still proceed from the (far from unambiguous) distinction between 'negative liberty' (crudely described as the absence of coercion) and 'positive liberty' (connoting, at its simplest, the capacity to make effective choices). Just as crudely, it is argued that liberals confine their interest to 'negative' liberty, whilst socialists are more concerned with 'positive' liberty. Whilst the market socialists' argument for liberty is often advanced with a sophistication that defies this simple dichotomy, their position may be distinguished from the classical neo-liberal defence of the market under capitalism by their greater concern with the *capacity* to exercise freedom. Thus Miller, while denying that there is a straightforward opposition between negative and positive liberty, argues that the neo-liberals' stipulations of the conditions of liberty are too narrow. He insists that 'the central ideal of the new socialism [is] equality of effective choice' (1988, p. 52). He maintains that 'constraints on freedom are those obstacles for which one or more agents can be held to be morally responsible' and this opens the way for the argument 'that economic impediments such as unemployment may indeed restrict my freedom, so that a freedom-maximizing order must remove such obstacles' (Miller, 1989, pp. 35, 45). Similarly, Hoover and Plant confront Hayek's limitations upon the claims of liberty, insisting that 'I value liberty because freedom enables me to advance my ends and purposes and it is surely the case that to do this means that I need resources, powers, and opportunities' (Hoover and Plant, 1989, pp. 208–9). Thus the *value* of liberty rests upon the circumstances for effective agency and these cannot be secured by the operation of an unconstrained capitalist market. Indeed, under market socialism there must be a 'redistribution of resources in order to give to individuals the capacity to act as effective and free agents in market transactions' (Hoover and Plant, 1989, p. 212).

However, once such redistribution of resources and opportunities as are required to furnish an approximately equal worth of liberty have been put in place, there are a number of reasons to believe that the market may be the best institutional guarantee of the freedom of individual actors. First, markets are seen to optimize *choice*, both for consumers and for sellers of labour power. The dissatisfied customer may shift her patronage and the dissatisfied employee may (though with rather more difficulty) change her employer. However imperfect, both of these freedoms compare favourably with the situation in a centrally planned economy where both workers and consumers are seen to face the (more or less) monopolistic authority of the state. An especially crucial aspect of this freedom of choice under the market, according to Miller, is its status as an essential precondition for freedom of expression. Again, it may be necessary to intervene in this market to improve opportunities for access to the means of communication, and to avoid the concentrations of mass media control which typify contemporary capitalism. Yet this is to be preferred to a situation in which these media are controlled by a public agency, however democratic the latter may be.

Finally, Selucky insists that both negative and positive liberty under socialism can only be secured through the agency of the market. Recasting Milton Friedman's favourable judgement on the market and freedom to make it compatible with socialism, he argues that negative liberty can only be secured through the market:

> The only known voluntary (non-coercive) way of macroeconomic co-ordination is the technique of the market-place. Since only certain combinations of political and economic arrangements are possible, the market technique is a necessary (though not sufficient) economic condition for negative political freedom defined as an absence of coercion by men. (Selucky, 1979, p. 137)

At the same time, he posits a necessary link between the market, 'self-managed' socialism and positive freedom:

> Since self-management is undoubtedly a very important aspect of positive liberty; since no self-management is conceivable without an autonomy of work-places; and since no real autonomy of work-places could be guaranteed without the market – [there is a] *structural link between the market and positive freedom.* (Selucky, 1979, p. 154)

Democracy

Neo-liberals have always made much of the empirical connection between market capitalism and liberal democracy and Selucky, for example, accepts Friedman's judgement that 'we know of no example in time and place that universal political freedom has been in existence except in capitalist societies' (Friedman, 1962; Selucky, 1979, p. 136). But, as before, market socialists insist that it is not capitalism but rather markets that are essential to democracy. They present a series of arguments to show that the scope and intensity of this democracy could be much enhanced if the market under capitalism were replaced with markets under socialism.

First, socialists of very varying persuasions have argued that the democratic process in capitalist societies is distorted by the concentrated ownership of private capital. Such arguments range from the disproportionate control of the media of mass communication by capitalist corporations to the capacity of private investors to place socialist governments under irresistible forms of economic duress. At its most radical, market socialism would simply eliminate this barrier to effective democracy by abolishing large-scale holdings of private capital. We may anticipate that, as a part of the legitimate process of political bargaining, enterprises and organized interests would continue to seek to represent their interests before government. However, the *undue* influence which derives from concentrated and coercive economic power would be eliminated by the general socialization of capital ownership. According to Roemer, politics under market socialism 'would be more democratic than in capitalist democracies because a class of capitalists who have the economic power enabling them to affect and to a great extent control state policy, both through the electoral process and by other means, would not exist' (Roemer, 1991, p. 567).

Secondly, while market socialists reject the belief that economic life can be effectively subjected to detailed planning by a democratically controlled state, they do argue that representative democratic institutions under market socialism would yield *some* form of general democratic control over the management of the economy. Just how much control government can exercise depends upon how extensive planning is to be under market socialism. For some market socialists, the state will still have a leading role, with 'conscious planning by an authority responsible to an elected assembly of major investments of structural significance' (Nove, 1991, p. 245). Others recommend that the state largely confine itself to forms of *indicative* planning, giving general guidance to independent enterprises about its overall intentions for economic development. Roemer suggests a system in which the government will shape the overall pattern of economic investment by introducing differential interest rates for differing economic sectors. This interest rate policy would be a part of political parties' electoral programmes, and in this way it would enable people to 'exercise some collective control, through democratic politics, over the use of savings in society' (Roemer, 1991, p. 563). Though the institutional arrangements vary, market socialists argue that where government was no longer subject to the disproportionate influence of capitalist interests, its actions as custodian of the public interest and overseer of general economic management could be more authentically the expression of institutionally articulated democratic sentiment.

Thirdly, (at least some) market socialists endorse the criticism that in market capitalist societies 'democracy stops at the factory gates'. Economic decision-making *within* existing economic enterprises, even where these are in public ownership, is seen to be explicitly hierarchical and authoritarian. Yet, Dahl, for example, argues that 'if democracy is justified in governing the state, then it must also be justified in governing economic enterprises' (1985, p. 111). According to Joshua Cohen, 'the extension of self-government into the traditionally undemocratic sphere of work contributes to both the formation of an active character and to the development of a sense of the common good, and thus contributes to a more fully democratic state' (1988, p. 29). Virtually all market socialists insist, in an argument whose socialist pedigree is often retraced to Rosa Luxemburg (1961), that no large-scale, developed society can afford to abandon the institutions of representative democracy. Yet, at least some of them also argue that market socialism offers a way of securing a limited sphere of more direct democracy without abandoning the necessary institutional framework of representative forms. This is to be achieved through workers' self-management in an economy of interacting co-operative enterprises (see e.g. Miller, 1989; Selucky, 1979). In practice, many co-operatives would choose internally to operate a mixture of representative and direct democracy and might well hire in management from outside their membership. Yet workers' co-operatives are seen to offer an institutional form in which many of the demanding criteria of direct democracy (small scale, permanent involvement of all members of the *demos*, no division between legislative and executive functions) may be reconciled with the 'necessity' of representative democracy at the national (and increasingly the supra-national) level.

Not all market socialists support this initiative. Some fear that efficiency may be undermined by the abandonment of more traditional managerial structures, whilst others believe that workplace democracy may reproduce the vices of syndicalism or of a kind of workers' 'collective capitalism' conspiring against the more general public interest (Potter, 1891; Roemer, 1991). Even supporters are fearful of the consequences of introducing *party* politics into workplace democracy (see Selucky, 1979, pp. 179–89). Yet enthusiasts for the co-operative principle insist that it is the one way of delivering real economic control into the hands of workers rather than surrendering it either to the controllers of private capital or to the planning agencies of a command economy.

Social Justice

Finally, we may deal with the issue of the justice of the market. The attainment of social justice has often been considered, by both its proponents and its opponents, to be one of the defining ambitions of the socialist project, and injustice has frequently been described by the opponents of market capitalism as one of its most characteristic vices. Of course, the nature of justice and what would count as a just distribution are vigorously contested and Hayek famously insisted (1982) that the idea of 'social justice' was both 'meaningless' and pernicious. In fact, some market socialists make very limited claims for the 'justice' of market institutions. John Roemer, for example, insists that 'it is wrong . . . to maintain that any market system, with or without capitalists, allocates resources and incomes justly' (1991, p. 566). In his account, the market is justified, not by the legitimacy of the allocations to which it gives rise, but solely by the beneficial *consequences* that follow from it (principally gains in overall efficiency).

Amongst those market socialists who do wish to sustain a rather bolder claim for the justice of market allocations, the contrast between capitalist markets and the market under socialism is once again crucial. In the most sustained defence of this position, David Miller argues that whilst it may be appropriate to criticize markets under capitalism for allocating benefits in ways that are unjust or unrelated to merit or effort, such a claim is much less effective when levelled against markets under socialism. For, Miller argues, without the private ownership of capital, differential returns to individuals and enterprises will tend to reflect the greater marketability (or capacity for want-satisfaction) of their assets. Such unequal returns in the marketplace will tend to be a (deserved) reward for greater efficiency, harder work, entrepreneurial skill and natural ability. Though some windfall gains on the market will still be attributable to (morally arbitrary) luck, such luck will tend to be dispersed and occasional, rather than cumulative as it is under capitalism.

A similar argument applies to the overcoming of exploitation. In a variety of forms (most famously in Marx's labour theory of value) socialists have argued that the appearance of equal exchange in the marketplace in fact conceals the forced expropriation of surplus value from workers by the owners of capital. The owners of capital are in a position to exploit workers because of their systematically privileged position within the market. The dissolution of the private ownership of capital is seen to dissolve this condition for the systematic exploitation of waged workers (though, of course, it does nothing to change the position of unwaged workers within the domestic sphere). Thus, according to Miller, market exchanges without the private ownership of capital will not be exploitative so long as they take place at equilibrium prices, and each individual's holdings depend solely upon '(a) natural facts about the world – the availability of resources, their physical properties, human tastes and aptitudes etc.: and (b) personal facts about him – the choices he makes, the skills he possesses, the effort he expends' (Miller, 1989, p. 194).

Exploitation could arise under market socialism, where these criteria were not satisfied, if, for example, a successful co-operative enterprise was able to achieve monopolistic power within a particular market. But there would not be the chronic and *systematic* circumstances of exploitation which prevail under capitalism and such breaches of the equilibria conditions as did occur (as in the case of monopoly) could be righted by the state. Indeed, the state under market socialism would have a substantial role to play in securing the circumstances for 'social justice'. Thus, Miller recommends that under market socialism 'we must adopt a distributive policy which ensures that everyone has adequate resources to satisfy their needs, in advance of other resources being made available to meet non-basic desires'. This is not

an argument for abandoning markets, but rather for framing the market in such a way that primary income is more equally distributed, with special supplements for those who are unable to earn an adequate income in the labour market ... With market socialist institutions in place people will be able to meet most of their needs through normal market purchases. (Miller, 1989, 148–9)

Even then, it will still be appropriate for certain needs, for example medical provision, to be met outside the marketplace. Finally, while this mixture of markets without private capital plus state intervention could not secure perfectly just and equitable outcomes, it is recommended as the best 'real-world' approximation of that substantive equality which planned economies are quite unable to deliver.

MARKET SOCIALISM: THE BASIC STRUCTURE

The essence of the market socialist model, as we have seen, is that 'the market mechanism is retained as a means of providing most goods and services, whilst the ownership of capital is socialized', (Miller, 1989, p. 10). In the final section of this chapter, I want to sketch in outline the institutional arrangements through which this simple formula could be realized. Disputes about the feasibility and desirability of this market socialist agenda are the subject of discussion in the subsequent evaluative chapters.

Social Ownership

At the heart of the market socialist model is the abolition of the large-scale private ownership of capital and its replacement by some form of 'social ownership'. Even the most conservative accounts of market socialism (e.g. those of Yunker and Stauber) insist that this abolition of large-scale holdings of private capital is essential. This requirement is fully consistent with the market socialists' general claim that the vices of market capitalism lie not with the institutions of the market but with (the consequences of) the private ownership of capital and it is this, if anything, which redeems the claim of its authors that their model is 'socialist'. As we shall see, it may also have profound consequences for the political feasibility of transition to even a quite modest form of market socialism.

The nature of that new form of ownership (be it 'public', 'co-operative', 'collective' or 'social') which is to replace private holdings of capital is, however, quite unclear. Critics, identifying 'social ownership' with 'ownership by society', insist that it is impossible for 'society', as opposed to individuals or corporations, to exercise many of the ordinary rights of ownership. They suspect that, in the end, social ownership will come to mean ownership by the centralized state, with all its associated vices. In fact, market socialists give quite varying accounts of what social ownership will mean. Nove, for example (1991, p. 213), identifies three types of social ownership:

1 State enterprises, centrally controlled and administered . . . *centralised state corporations.*
2 Publicly owned (or socially owned) enterprises with full autonomy and a management responsible to the workforce . . . *socialised enterprises.*
3 Enterprises owned and/or administered by the workforce . . . [including] *co-operatives.*

Nove is actually rather exceptional amongst the market socialists in the prominence he is still willing to allow to institutions in the first of these categories, that is to centralized state corporations, although John Roemer is also happy to describe market socialism as 'a politico-economic system in which firms are publicly owned [and] the state has considerable control of the "commanding heights" of the economy' (Roemer, 1991, p. 562; Roemer, 1992a). Given their acute awareness of the twin failures of state socialism and existing forms of social democracy, market socialists are for the most part very reluctant to promote any strategy which removes significant areas of economic activity (with the exception of some natural monopolies and certain social services) from the domain of the market. To this extent, they are unsympathetic to traditional forms of state ownership, represented by strategies of nationalization or the promotion of public corporations. In general, they tend to favour some more decentralized version of social ownership. As we shall see, many market socialists have a strong preference for co-operatives as a prefigurative enterprise form. However, it is not clear that the category of enterprises owned by their workers offers an attractive and *socialist* alternative form of ownership. As Estrin observes, whilst existing co-operatives may represent 'islands of socialism' in a wider capitalist sea, an economy of worker-owned co-operatives would be 'workers' capitalism, not socialism' (1989, p. 185).

Selucky finds a partial answer to this problem in the admittedly flawed experience of the Yugoslav model, exploiting an ambivalence over *ownership* and *control* more normally found in discussions of the rise of corporate capitalism. Whether it be a capitalist or the state, 'it is the *owner* of capital who dominates labour'.

> In order to eliminate any external domination over labour, the workers themselves have to become owners of capital . . . Consequently, the ownership of the means of production ought to be separated from the state and put under the direct control of the employees by virtue of self-management. [However] this does not necessarily mean that the social means of production would be *formally* owned by direct producers. Though they are still *owned* by the society as a whole, they are *controlled* by those who work with them. (Selucky, 1979, p. 111)

In Estrin's account, the theory of the Yugoslav model offers a slightly different way of resolving the problem of social ownership. In essence, rights of ownership are *split* between workers and the state.

> Workers are granted the right to use the capital, to extend it and to adapt it. They earn their incomes as the fruit of it. However they do *not* own it, and are *not* permitted to sell it off or run it down. The capital stock is owned collectively by the society and is merely administered by particular groups of workers. (Estrin, 1989, p. 173)

Other market socialists seem less troubled by the question of ownership. They look to the institutional form of the individual enterprise (generally organized along co-operative lines), and to a structure of intermediary financial structures between the state (as ultimate lender) and enterprise to check the overweening economic power of the central state (see e.g. Miller, 1989, pp. 10–11). Yet, despite these explanations and given the undoubted centrality of the elimination of large-scale private holdings of capital to the market socialist model, the appropriate forms of social ownership of capital with which this can be replaced remain rather unclear.

The Capitalist under Socialism

Almost all the market socialists, whilst advocating a more or less radical elimination of large-scale holdings of private capital, envisage the retention of a small capitalist sector under market socialism. To this extent, their recommendation is for a form of 'mixed economy'. Inasmuch as this is not simply a concession of convenience to deal with agricultural smallholdings or the personal services sector, this conclusion may rest upon the question of civil liberties. Given that it is primarily corporate capital which market socialists wish to unseat, it may be better to countenance small-scale capitalist acts between consenting adults than to endorse the levels of state surveillance and discretion that would be required to prevent them (Nove, 1991, pp. 204–5). More important, however, is the *positive* role which is envisaged for the genuinely *entrepreneurial* capitalist under market socialism. One of the most frequent arguments deployed against the economic efficiency of socialism (especially of actually existing socialism), is its inability to foster innovation. Indeed, the Austrian school's response to Lange's model of market socialism went at least some way towards conceding that Langean state socialism might be able to mimic the *static* allocative function of the market (see Lavoie, 1985). However, it could not provide the incentives (or the information) for dynamic interventions in the market or for innovation. Critics of socialism insist that it is the promise of a property gain that persuades the private capitalist investor to undertake the risk entailed in economic innovation. Under socialism, no one has the incentive to innovate and the consequence will be economic entropy.

Market socialists go some way towards accepting this criticism. Whilst insisting that the great bulk of current investment in corporate capitalism is neither 'heroic' nor entrepreneurial, they do accept that 'the death of the entrepreneur', anticipated by both Marx and Schumpeter (1976), has been exaggerated. They stress that socialist objections to capitalism have always focused upon *unearned* income, the rentier element in capitalism, whilst recognizing that some of the work done by the capitalist (in the management and co-ordination of the production process) represents the discharge of essential economic functions which would have to be carried out under any system of ownership. With more or less regret, the *genuine* entrepreneur (s/he who introduces a new product or service or initiates a new method of production), must be encouraged. In an economy where labour is intended to be the sole source of income, the entrepreneur performs especially valuable work for which there has to be a corresponding incentive and reward. In Yunker's model of 'pragmatic market socialism', there would be 'material incentives to personal entrepreneurial endeavour almost as strong as those which currently exist under capitalism' (Yunker, 1988, p. 76). However, in tolerating or even encouraging the private firm, and the *entrepreneurial* capitalist, most market socialists also make provision for bringing such companies (upon reaching a certain size or upon the death or retirement of their founder) into social ownership (see, e.g. Roemer, 1991, p. 566). The intention seems to be to sever a (perhaps generous) reward for the scarce skill of the genuine entrepreneur (in an economy of significant income inequality), from an unearned return to the owner of private capital.

Enterprise Structure and Governance

Whilst the elimination of large-scale holdings of capital furnishes a point of consensus for almost all advocates of market socialism, questions of enterprise structure and governance reveal considerable diversity. From Miller and Estrin (1985, p. 6) we may derive the following fourfold classification of socialist attitudes to enterprise governance under market socialism:

1 *The Libertarian position* socialism implies no more than equal entitlement to the means of production, with the question of how people choose to use their endowments left entirely open.
2 *The Social Democratic position* capitalist forms are an acceptable component of socialism provided that the state uses its powers of taxation and regulation to correct income deficiencies and so forth.
3 *The Codetermination position* the respective rights of capital and labour in the enterprise should be redefined in the form of a capital – labour partnership, with each party being allocated a pre-determined share of profit.

4 *The Workers' Co-operative position*   enterprises in market socialism
should normally take the form of workers' co-operatives, with capital supplied externally and entitled only to earn interest.

Miller and Estrin themselves describe the co-operative position as 'the
most congenial from a socialist point of view' and in Miller's subsequent outline of a 'pure' model of market socialism, 'all productive
enterprises are constituted as workers' co-operatives' (Miller and
Estrin, 1985, p. 6; Miller, 1989, p. 10). A significant number of market
socialists advocate workers' self-management as an optimal and, in
some cases, necessary component of a market socialist economy. Thus,
in his *Preface to Economic Democracy*, Dahl argues that

> none of the reasoned arguments for private property as a right success-
> fully justifies private ownership of corporate enterprises . . . Conse-
> quently, the demos and its representatives are entitled to decide by
> means of the democratic process how economic enterprises should be
> owned and controlled in order to achieve . . . such values as democracy,
> fairness, efficiency, the cultivation of desirable human qualities, and an
> entitlement to such minimal personal resources as may be necessary to a
> good life. (Dahl, 1985, p. 83)

Within the parameters set by economic markets and a law-upholding
state, these ambitions may be best achieved through the promotion of
self-governing enterprises, 'a system of economic enterprises collectively
owned and democratically governed by all the people who work in
them' (Dahl, 1985, p. 91).

Returning to the argument of Radoslav Selucky, we find that his
advocacy of a similar position rests upon the contrast he finds between
'Marx's perception of the economic and the political liberation of man':

> While Marx's *economic* concept of socialism consists of a single social-
> wide factory based on vertical (hierarchical) relations of superiority and
> subordination, his *political* concept of socialism consists of a free associ-
> ation of self-managed work and social communities based on horizontal
> relations of equality. (Selucky, 1979, p. xi; emphasis added)

We have already seen that Selucky rejects Marx's economic case for the
abolition of the market. In supporting his political image of socialism,
Selucky endorses a model of '*labour* self management' in which 'labour
is the sole source of income [and] the means of production are owned
and socially managed by those who make use of them' (1979, pp. 179–
80). For both Dahl and Selucky, the internal democratization of the
enterprise is at least as important a reason for endorsing market socialism as the distributional consequences of eliminating corporate capital.

There remain, however, considerable disagreements amongst these advocates of labour self-management about the ownership of capital, the status of worker/owners, the internal structure of enterprise governance and the right to appropriate the enterprises' profit (and these are taken up below in chapter 6).

Whilst a number of commentators follow Jon Elster in arguing that 'market socialism [simply is] a system of labour cooperatives', there are also those who resist the idea that market socialism should ideally be made up of enterprises under workers' self-management.[3] The more conservative market socialists, such as Stauber and Yunker, prefer a model of 'capitalism without the capitalists' in which the essentials of the existing hierarchical relationship between labour and management within the enterprise are retained. Stauber, whilst favouring a range of institutional arrangements under market socialism, expresses a preference for what he calls 'the full market model' which 'fully duplicates the characteristics of a competitive private capitalism, excepting only the replacement of private ownership by public ownership and the use of tax measures that remove large individual and family wealth and other extreme economic inequalities' (Stauber, 1987, p. 187). Whilst he favours some sort of co-determination along the lines of West German or Swedish experience, he is sceptical of the efficiency claims of 'too great' workers' control, and his review of the Yugoslav experience stresses the weaknesses of workers' self-management (1987, pp. 300–11). Meanwhile, under Yunker's 'pragmatic market socialism', 'executives of the publicly owned, large-scale, established business corporations would enjoy the same discretionary authority that they do under capitalism', including control over 'production levels, prices, marketing and advertising expenditures . . . hiring and firing of labor [and] the allocation of after-tax profits' (Yunker, 1988, p. 76). In addition to this rather conservative scepticism about the capacity of workers for efficient self-management, there is also an argument that the economic product under market socialism does not belong to the workers of any particular enterprise, but to the community as a whole. These views are combined in John Roemer's model. Roemer is 'somewhat leery' of workers' control, fearing that 'it may impede profit maximization and its concomitant efficiency' (though he also argues that it may be a 'lesser evil' than the overweening authority of a semi-autonomous managerial class; Roemer, 1991, p. 567). He further argues that workers under market socialism do not own the firms in which they work and that consequently, whilst they will continue to receive (varying) wages from these firms, any enterprise profits should be distributed amongst the owners of capital (i.e. everyone), in the form of a social dividend (1991, p. 563).

The Distribution of Income

Roemer's comments bring us to a further central consideration in the market socialist model – the distribution of income. Socialists have characteristically voiced at least three objections to the distribution of income under capitalism. First, the income which capitalists derive from their profits is unearned and/or expropriated from its rightful owners, the workers who created it. Secondly, the final distribution of incomes under capitalism, in part because of the maldistribution of profits, is unacceptably disparate, offending against socialist principles of distributive justice and undermining the circumstances under which a genuine and universal community of societal interests could develop. Thirdly, income is related to (paid) labour rather than to need. The market socialist response to these objections is a partial one. Generally, it proceeds from what Selucky describes as the first principle of democratic socialism, that is that [waged] 'labour is the sole source of income' (1979, p. 179).

For the most part, market socialists are happy to accept the inevitability of some disparity of incomes arising from the varying market value of labour. According to Nove, 'income differentials (a species of labour market) are the only known alternative to the [unacceptable] direction of labour' (1991, p. 231). In general, the *absolute* equality of incomes (what Selucky calls 'crude egalitarianism') is rejected as utopian because, short of conditions of abundance, it must yield an uneconomic use of labour resources and exact an unacceptably high cost in terms of the authoritarian allocation of work. However, under market socialism, existing differentials in income could be much reduced. First, the principal source of large-scale wealth through private capital holding would be abolished. Secondly, within co-operatives at least, wages would be determined (more or less democratically) by the entire workforce. Whilst the need to attract skilled labour would dissuade co-operators from instituting an equality of wages, it is argued that differentials could be reduced to the order of 3:1 or 4:1. The experience of the large-scale co-operative venture at Mondragon in northern Spain is taken as partial evidence of the probability of narrowing wage differentials under a co-operative system (Thomas and Logan, 1982; Nove, 1991; Estrin, 1989). Thirdly, with the elimination of private capital holdings, such differences as remained would simply reflect differential purchasing power, not differential power over economic decision-taking. Fourthly, income differentials at the societal level could be checked by the state's imposition of a wages policy and compensated by the provision of certain essential needs and public goods, (health care and education, for example), outside the market (as in Nove, 1991). The market socialists' sense of compromise is neatly summarized by Selucky: 'Any realistic socialist programme relies on the distributive principle according to one's work. Although this principle is less appealing than the ideal distribution according to one's needs, it is still more appealing than the capitalist distributive principle according to one's capital' (Selucky, 1979, p. 155).

Given these broadly shared parameters, there is considerable variation in market socialists' institutional models for the distribution of income. It is clear that most commentators would still allow some space under market socialism for returns to private capital. This would clearly apply to those small or entrepreneurial firms which remained in private hands and also to those co-operative enterprises in which working capital was largely furnished by the co-operators themselves. But, of course, capital under market socialism would more generally be under social ownership. It is widely argued that under the socialist market, co-operatives (or other socially owned enterprises) should normally be externally financed, borrowing capital at a fixed rate of interest from the guardians of social capital (the state, public investment agencies, public holding companies or whatever). The enterprise would be responsible for sustaining the value of this capital and servicing its interest debt.

Since capital is socially owned, it may not form a part of anyone's income. In some models (e.g. Miller, 1989), net enterprise profits, after servicing the debt on borrowed capital, 'form a pool out of which incomes are paid'. In Miller's co-operative economy, 'each enterprise is democratically controlled by those who work for it, and among the issues they must decide is how to distribute income within the co-operative' (1989, p. 10). In other versions, profits form the basis for a 'social dividend income' (Yunker, 1990b, p. 118). This, in turn, may be paid out either as 'an across-the-board, proportional wage and salary increase for all working members of the population' (Yunker) or as 'a form of guaranteed income [paid] more or less equally among all households', being 'that part of the national income which . . . belongs to the people as owners of the means of production' (Roemer, 1991, p. 563). In the latter account, there is a return to (social) capital, but it is one which is to be distributed more or less equally amongst the whole of the population.

Finally, there may be an income to be derived from household savings. Some market socialists, most notably James Yunker (1990a), have doubted the necessity of interest payments on private savings under market socialism. Others take a more conventional view of the need to 'reward' savers for their deferred consumption. It should be clear, however, that such private savings would be placed in (some form of) public investment and should not constitute a surrogate 'restoration of capitalism'.

In Roemer's account, this would leave the typical citizen under market socialism with three sources of income: *'wage income*, which will vary depending upon the worker's skill and amount of time worked; *interest forthcoming from savings*, which will also vary across households; and *a social dividend* that will be, in principle, approximately equal across households.' (Roemer, 1991, p. 563)

The State under Market Socialism

Finally, we need to give some brief consideration to the envisaged nature of the state under market socialism. Of course, it is one of the principal ambitions of the market socialists to rid socialism of its pejorative association with the domineering state and the failures of centralized state planning, and to show that the economic efficiency promised by the market is fully reconcilable with socialist forms of ownership. There are some market socialists, such as Yunker, who do genuinely confine their (still very radical) reforms to the decentralized socialization of capital ownership. He insists that 'the question of "capitalism versus socialism" is almost entirely independent of the question of "market versus plan"'. His central ambition is to establish a socially owned 'analogue' which would 'duplicate the market characteristics of market capitalism' (1988, p. 72). Yunker's 'pragmatic market socialism ... would have no obvious predisposition toward either planning or regulation' (1990, p. 136). Even this 'fully marketized' socialism is condemned by the neo-liberals who insist that, however market-oriented a socialized economy may appear to be, private ownership of capital assets is essential if economic control is not, in practice, to fall under the tutelage of the centralizing state. Nonetheless, as neo-liberal critics have been quick to observe, most of its advocates in fact recommend a much more substantial role for the state and some (amended) form of economic planning under market socialism.

Thus, for most of it supporters, social ownership is a necessary but not a sufficient condition for the realization of market socialism. Just as their hostility is directed not against markets but against *capitalist* markets, so is their criticism not so much of all forms of planning but of regimes of *centralized, directive* and *comprehensive* planning. In Selucky's account a socialist economy should be directed towards 'the maximisation of social welfare'.

While the most efficient instrument of rational economic allocation and use of scarce resources, goods and services is the market, the most efficient device for adjusting market regulation to welfare priorities is macroeconomic (central) planning. A synthesis of the plan and the market is indispensable. Of all known types of planning, *only an indirect (indicative) social planning is compatible with both the market and labour self-management*. (Selucky, 1979, p. 208; emphasis added)

Similarly, Estrin and Winter, whilst finding 'strong arguments related to decentralization and efficiency [which] lead us to favour markets as the primary mechanism of resource allocation', still insist upon the necessity of a form of *indicative planning*, 'a decentralized, and preferably democratic, process of consultation and discussion concerned exclusively with plan construction and elaboration' (Estrin and Winter 1989, pp. 115–16; Brada and Estrin, 1990; Estrin and Holmes, 1990). For Estrin and Winter, the non-binding and consultative quality of indicative planning makes it essentially different from the classical model of mandatory centralized planning, which they reject. In Roemer's model of market socialism, 'the government will have the power to intervene in the economy to direct the pattern and level of investment'. But this 'will not be implemented through a command system but by manipulating the interest rates at which different industrial sectors can borrow funds from state banks' (Roemer, 1991, p. 563).

Other market socialists, whilst quite explicitly rejecting the possibility of a planned economy without markets), give a still more prominent place to both planning and state ownership in a new form of 'mixed economy'. Sik's model for a 'humane economic democracy' includes an elaborate mechanism for 'macro-economic planning (1985, pp. 133–229). Under Sik's ambitious plans:

> Long-term programs and middle-range plans will determine the macro-structure of the desired development of the quality of life. This includes the determination of the pace of growth . . . the necessary continuous and harmonious development of investments . . . the planned determination of wage increases, wage differentials, and profit-sharing quotas. (1985, p. 320)

This is to be realized through 'planned economic policy, income policy, fiscal policy, credit policy' (1985, p. 321).

Nove's planning ambitions are perhaps more modest, but little less extensive. Under his *feasible socialism*, 'the centre' would perform 'a number of vital functions':

> First, major investments would be its responsibility. Secondly . . . the planners would endeavour to monitor decentralised investments . . . Thirdly, the centre would play a direct and major role in administering

such 'naturally' central productive activities as electricity, oil, railways. Fourthly, there would be the vital task of setting the ground-rules for the autonomous and free sectors, with reserve powers of intervention when things get out of balance. There would plainly also be functions connected with foreign trade. There would be drafts of longer-term plans (Nove, 1991, pp. 220–1)

In addition, Nove envisages a category of 'centralised state corporations' which would be both owned and managed by the state. These would be likely to embrace 'the "commanding heights" of large-scale industry and public utilities' and at least some of the institutions of 'banking and finance' (Nove, 1991, pp. 213–14). As Nove himself concedes, 'the role of the state will be very great, as owner, as planner, as enforcer of social and economic priorities' (1991, p. 247).

Finally, many of those goods and services which are identified with existing welfare states (in the areas of health, education, income maintenance, personal social services and housing), would continue under market socialism to be the responsibility of the state. Selucky devotes considerable space to demonstrating that in the cases of provision for health and education the principle of 'distribution according to work' should give way to the principle of 'distribution according to need' (1979, pp. 163–8). Similarly, Nove argues that under his feasible socialism 'some sectors (education, health, etc.) would naturally be exempt from market-type criteria' (1991, p. 246). Miller insists that 'socialists should not be dogmatic about the form of welfare provision'. But on balance

in the case of medicine and education (surely the key welfare goods), the balance of argument tips in favour of a public system incorporating a substantial element of consumer choice; in other cases . . . it seems more appropriate to rely primarily on markets, with public authorities playing a subsidiary financial role where necessary, (Miller, 1989, p. 317).

In a rather unconventional contribution, Julian Le Grand argues that it may be appropriate for the state to withdraw from some areas of welfare provision but to reallocate the capacity to purchase welfare so as to favour those with fewest assets and opportunities (Le Grand, 1989). Under his system of 'left-wing vouchers', the state would allocate earmarked vouchers for purchasing welfare services, with a disproportionate value given to those with the fewest existing resources. Consumers could then purchase their welfare goods and services from competing providers in a welfare market (subject to certain state criteria and monitoring). This echoes the view, which Le Grand has himself done much to substantiate, that under prevailing welfare states it is those with greater resources who are able to derive most benefit from the provision of 'free' services (Goodin and Le Grand, 1987). The most effective way of redistributing wealth and opportunities may not be to offer services free, but directly to reallocate primary income. Clearly, Le Grand's scheme represents a significant increase in the competence of the market for welfare, but it is, as yet, the exception rather than the rule amongst market socialists.

Conclusion

It is clear that we can understand the contemporary advocacy of market socialism by those in Western Europe and North America as at least in part a response to the sorts of difficulties for the socialist project laid out in part I. Thus, market socialists concern themselves with the inefficiency of existing models of socialism, with the impossibility of highly-centralized planning, with the unpopularity and limited effectiveness of state intervention and with the opportunities for enhancing economic democracy. Above all, they seek to reorientate our thinking about markets, so that these may be rehabilitated as a central organizing element in a revived socialist political intitiative. In part III I want to consider just how compelling this new revisionism might prove to be and I begin in chapter five by addressing the fundamental counter-claim that the market and socialism are simply incompatible.

PART III

Market Socialism Assessed

5

Market Socialism: A 'Contradiction in Terms'?

The most fundamental and simple objection to the model outlined in part II is that socialism and the market are simply irreconcilable. Traditionally, this was common ground for both supporters and opponents of the socialist cause. Thus, market socialism is condemned simultaneously as 'not socialist', by those who insist that the market is a pernicious institution incompatible with 'real' socialism, and as 'not truly a market order', by those on the liberal and neo-liberal right, who maintain that 'genuine' markets cannot be reconciled with the prerequisites of a socialist society. For both sets of critics, market socialism is 'a contradiction in terms', (see e.g. de Jasay, 1990; Mandel, 1986). In this chapter, I consider the weight of both of these fundamental arguments against market socialism.

AGAINST MARKET SOCIALISM I:
THE TRADITIONAL SOCIALIST CASE

It seems clear that, even if we do not wholeheartedly endorse the relativism of the postmodernists and the post-Marxists, we cannot hope to establish unequivocally *the* essential and defining propositions of socialism (whether 'traditional' or otherwise). In this section, I seek to circumvent this problem by identifying certain core claims about the nature of the market which, if not quite ubiquitous, can be found routinely amongst socialist writers in a range of quite diverse periods and traditions and which I think convey a sense of the most profound objections that socialists of very varying kinds have raised against the market. I do not mean to suggest that, taken together, these propositions add up to a programmatic alternative to the market project of the market socialists (or anyone else). Yet, this more orthodox socialist tradition still furnishes the most systematic and comprehensive statement of the limitations of markets. Given the ever more universal and heroic claims made for the market, if this socialist critique did not exist, we should have to invent it. Even if we choose to dismiss most of the positive claims made for 'traditional socialism', it is still useful in sounding out a programme which subscribes simultaneously to markets and socialism, and correspondingly, the discussion that follows is organized around seven more or less axiomatic claims summarizing this traditional position.

Proposition 1

Markets generate inequality The market generates a radically unequal distribution of resources and opportunities which offends against (even quite modest forms of) the aspiration to equality.

Whilst I have forsworn any identification of *the* essential defining criteria of socialism, it is clear that the aspiration to equality lies close to the heart of much socialist thinking. Indeed, Berki described egalitarianism as 'the *classical* principle of socialism' (1975, p. 25). Unfortunately (at least for the purposes of our analysis), equality is a principle which is also very broadly endorsed throughout much of modern social and political theory, including at least some variants of neo-liberalism. What is most keenly debated is not so much the desirability of equality itself, but the *type* of equality which is endorsed (equality of *condition*, equality of *opportunity*, equality of *respect* and so on), and the legitimate forms of *in*equality to which this equality (and other favoured principles, such as need, desert and individual liberty) may properly give rise.[1] The picture is further complicated by the diversity of views within the orthodox socialist camp. There is perhaps some measure of agreement that equality should be a substantive rather than a purely formal principle, and that, in some way, equality of *condition* is essential to its socialist invocation. However, the call for an *absolute* equality of condition is rather exceptional and most socialists have viewed this aspiration as, at best, utopian and often (given the institutional arrangements needed to sustain it) dystopian. Equality may also be qualified by other valued socialist principles, such as an equitable (but unequal) response to (unequal) needs. Nonetheless, it has been very widely argued that the market, with its radical disparities of wealth (and of status and opportunity), has generated forms and levels of inequality which are unacceptable to socialists.

Whilst the traditional socialist view of equality is then complex and qualified, it seems clear that there are some variants of market socialism with which it cannot be reconciled. Raymond Plant, for example, argues (somewhat equivocally) that while the radical market socialist will embrace a more positive view of liberty than the neo-liberal, s/he will also see this as 'a starting-gate rather than an end-state principle' (Plant, 1989). According to this radical version of market socialism, the market needs socialism in order to make its starting-points fairer and more free, but it would neglect the outcomes of the transactions and exchanges which were then undertaken in the market. There are difficulties with this formulation; not least, the infinitely recurring problem that what appears from one perspective to be an *acceptably unequal end-state* will appear from a different position to be an *unacceptably unequal starting-point* in a new set of transactions. It is also evident that a concern with 'end-states' is one of the principles that has most frequently been taken to distinguish socialists from liberals. While the radical market socialist solution may be preferred (on grounds of liberty, efficiency or even of equity), it is not clear that it can be called 'socialist' without severely straining our understanding of what has normally passed for socialism.

Whether or not a less 'radical' market socialist position can be reconciled with traditional socialist thinking on equality is not so clear. Certainly few market socialists would contest the claim that the existing distribution of wealth and opportunities through capitalist markets inscribes levels and forms of inequality which are unacceptable to socialists. Their contention is that, under market socialism, with the abolition of large-scale private holdings of capital, inequalities would be radically reduced to that (acceptable) level required to achieve the optimization of general social welfare. Evidence is drawn from existing co-operative enterprises to show that, while some inequalities of income would remain (though not inequalities through the differential ownership of private capital), these would be radically lessened and could be limited by law. Given that the traditional socialist commitment to equality of condition is qualified, such an arrangement might well satisfy some socialist critics of the market. However, whether inequalities would be so drastically reduced under a co-operative market economy must be uncertain. One can imagine particularly successful co-operatives or even individuals with especially marketable skills (such as the basketball player Wilt Chamberlain in Nozick's celebrated example), commanding a price which would challenge the limiting of income differentials to proportions of, say, 3 : 1 or 4 : 1. The restraint or regulation of such markets would surely require substantial intervention by the state (which it is a part of the market socialist ambition to minimize).

Proposition 2

Markets generate inequity The market distribution of resources and opportunities is unfair. Not only is it unresponsive to *need*, it is also often insensitive to *merit* and *effort*. The allocation of goods and opportunities is systematically class-biased.

Here again, a part of the market socialist response is to insist that it is *capitalist* markets that are inequitable, not markets in themselves; and it is indeed the case that socialists have traditionally been concerned above all with the inequitable outcome of exchanges between privately owned capital and labour. Marxist (and other) theories of exploitation focus centrally upon the unequal exchange that takes place within the capitalist labour contract and one must assume that the elimination of private holdings of capital would remove this important source of inequity through the market (though, of course, it cannot rule out the possibility of some other and perhaps more exploitative basis for the application of labour power). Elimination of private capital must also, by definition, have a substantial impact upon the *class* allocation of goods and opportunities where classes are defined around the axis of ownership and non-ownership of private capital. But this would not entirely answer the objections of the traditionalists. For there remain the arguments that markets are insensitive to need and that they fail to reward merit and effort.

Both of these issues are addressed by David Miller. On the first of these questions, he properly points out that there are very considerable difficulties in identifying what would count as 'basic human needs' (though it is surely clear that on a global scale the most basic human need does go unmet, while others satisfy their patently non-essential wants). He is also right to point out that creating a non-market institution which would allocate goods to satisfy these needs is extremely difficult (see, e.g. the proposals of Mandel, 1986, pp. 14–25 and Martell, 1992, p. 159). Yet this does not really meet the underlying intuitive core of the traditional socialist position. To put it in suitably lurid terms, the argument is that because the market responds to marketable assets ('the ability to pay'), rather than to needs, the millionaire may winter over in the south of France, while the pensioner dies of hypothermia for want of the money to heat her flat.

As we saw in chapter 4, Miller has an answer for this problem. That is, under market socialism, 'we must adopt a distributive policy which ensures that everyone has adequate resources to satisfy their needs, in advance of other resources being made available to meet non-basic desires' whilst certain fundamental needs (for example, medical provision and education), should be met outside the market (Miller, 1989, pp. 148–9). This seems to me to be a substantial (if perfectly proper) 'concession' to the traditional socialist position. But it does put in doubt the distinctively 'market' quality of Miller's market socialism. Only the most enthusiastic proponents of the most centralized planning have ever called for non-market provision of what Miller calls 'mundane private goods – food, clothing, household items and so forth'; and Miller's model might be thought to describe arrangements which look remarkably similar to existing (if radicalized) welfare states. While some welfare state provision is 'in kind' (notably in health and education), pensions and income maintenance payments, for example, already redistribute cash to their beneficiaries to enable them to meet their needs through purchases in the market. What is an appropriate level for this redistribution, to what extent the needs of all are to be met in preference to satisfying the desires of existing asset-holders is a decision taken (more or less democratically) through the state. It is not a decision reached through the market. Miller insists that 'with market socialist institutions in place, people will be able to meet most of their needs through normal market purchases', but this rather begs the question of how socialists are *previously* to have attained a (re)distribution of income which is sufficiently equitable to allow of this happy outcome (Miller, 1989, p. 128). What this suggests is that any form of market society which is to be consistent with the aspirations of the market socialists will require a strong and interventionist state, indeed a state whose interventions would almost certainly be *more* extensive than those that we find in existing welfare states.

Miller also addresses the traditional socialist claim that markets distribute benefits in ways that are unrelated to merit or effort. Such arguments may be effective against *capitalist* markets, Miller agrees, but they will not for the most part be true of markets under socialism. For, Miller argues, without the private ownership of capital, differential returns to individuals and enterprises will tend to reflect the greater marketability (or capacity for want-satisfaction) of their assets. Such unequal returns in the marketplace will tend to be a (deserved) reward for greater efficiency, harder work, entrepreneurial skill and natural ability. Though some windfall gains on the market will still be attributable to (morally arbitrary) luck, such luck will tend to be dispersed and occasional, rather than cumulative as it is under capitalism.

Once again, a substantial part of the traditional socialist argument against an unjust distribution by the market is seemingly undermined by the presumed elimination of private capital. Certainly, the most caustic socialist criticism has always been reserved for the 'unearned' wealth of 'rentier' capitalists and the unwarranted impoverishment of the 'real' producers of wealth. But the elimination of private holdings of capital does not exhaust traditional socialist objections to the idea that market distributions are 'deserved' in any morally compelling sense. Clearly, some traditional socialists will want to resist Miller's equation of (morally deserving) value with market price. Is, for example, the work of Madonna several hundred times more valuable than that of a practising midwife? John Christman (1988) argues that, given the presence of luck and disequilibria in real world markets, the connection which Miller presumes between the price of a commodity and the deservingness of its producer cannot be defended. Again, while Miller suggests that under market socialism 'each factor of production receives the equivalent of the value it creates', Sen has criticized such a 'personal production view' of the market as 'deeply problematic', because the process of production is irretrievably social and the calculation of the marginal contribution of any one factor of production to eventual output is 'essentially a fiction' (Miller, 1989, p. 172; Sen, 1985, p. 16). Such marginal calculations may be a proper and useful tool in the allocation of productive resources, but they cannot form the basis for calculating comparative weightings of moral desert. Even if one accepts Miller's premise on value there are other difficulties. As I have noted, Miller acknowledges that there is a problem with his account for all those (such as Rawls or, to take a fellow market socialist, John Roemer) who do not accept that rewards deriving from differential natural talents can be said to be 'deserved' (Rawls, 1973; Roemer, 1982 and 1991). Finally, as Miller also recognizes, his account assumes 'that markets gravitate towards a competitive equilibrium' (1989, p. 172). But as both traditional socialists and their Austrian opponents have in their differing ways argued, this is precisely something that we cannot assume about markets. Miller's response to this criticism is perhaps best considered in our next section.

Proposition 3

Markets generate injustice Classically, the vulnerability of the propertyless (or capital-less) worker is used to coerce him/her into an *exploitative* sale of labour power to an employer. The source of profit which makes the market work is the unpaid labour power of workers.

It is clearly the case that, for traditional socialists, the core of exploitation in the marketplace is to be found in the labour contract. In a variety of forms (most famously in Marx's labour theory of value), it has been argued that the appearance of equal exchange between capital and labour in the market in fact conceals the forced expropriation of surplus value from the workers by the owners of capital. The owners of capital are in a position to exploit workers because of their systematically privileged position within the market. Clearly, dissolution of the private ownership of capital (unless this is replaced by some form of state capitalism) dissolves this condition for the systematic exploitation of waged workers (though, of course, it does nothing to change the position of unwaged workers within the domestic sphere or to alleviate the disadvantages of the unemployed). Miller's claim (see pp. 115–16 above) was that, whilst exploitation could arise under market socialism, there would not be the chronic and *systematic* circumstances of exploitation which prevail under capitalism and such breaches of the equilibria conditions as did occur (as in the case of monopoly) could be righted by the intervention of the state.

Without entering into the recent and complex literature about what would count as 'exploitation' (and indeed whether it is a category with which socialists should properly be concerned), I confine myself here to three points.[2] First, the removal of private control over capital clearly removes the principal agency of exploitation under capitalism as this was identified by traditional socialists. It does, however, also raise the immensely important practical and theoretical question of who is to control the still scarce factor of capital once ownership is socialized. There is a critical view, on both right and left, that socialized ownership (especially under the control of the state) will create more opportunities for the exploitation of the workers than exist under prevailing arrangements within capitalist markets. Secondly, we may question whether Miller's criteria for non-exploitation (based upon unforced exchange at equilibrium prices) are sufficiently stringent. For example, there are some socialists who would argue that certain forms of exchange between those in the First and Third Worlds, even if taking place at equilibrium prices and satisfying the other conditions for Miller's fair exchange, would be exploitative. If a satisfactory response to this claim rests upon further manipulation of the parameters within which 'fair exchanges' may take place, this clearly places great weight upon the *non-market* conditions for equitable market exchange. This is a question I return to below. Thirdly, there is the issue of whether Miller's conditions for a non-exploitative market are in any envisageable circumstances capable of realization. It is certainly possible to imagine exchanges between individuals (and corporations?) which are unconstrained by differential market power. But it is much more difficult to imagine an economy, outside the textbooks of neo-classical economics, in which such a relationship could be sustained for any length of time. Marx's economics have not fared universally well over the last 150 years, particularly in their identification of the process of exploitation under capitalism. Nonetheless, one of the least discredited elements of the Marxian schema is the tendency of markets to generate monopoly. This is fairly common ground among traditional Marxists, Austrian neo-liberals and conventional economics (in which the formation of monopolies is often identified as a chronic form of market failure). If we take it that the principal form of injustice under markets is the existence of exploitation, the real challenge to Miller's position is not whether we can imagine a market that did not entail exploitation, but whether we can imagine the historical and institutional circumstances in which such a market could operate. Of course, it is possible that Miller's criteria for non-exploitative exchange should be read not as an empirical approximation of relationships under market socialism, but rather as a bench-mark against which the deficiencies of *any* actually existing form of exchange may be measured. However, if such a position is adopted, it seems clear that much greater weight must fall upon the ways in which the limiting conditions for market exchange are to be established outside the market itself.

Proposition 4

Markets generate inefficiency In a variety of ways, the anarchic allocation of goods and opportunities through the market is economically inefficient. The over-exploitation of scarce resources, the overproduction of certain goods, overconsumption by certain market actors and the cyclical under-utilization of capital and labour indicate the inefficiency of the market as an allocative mechanism.

The claim that markets are inefficient has long been at the heart of the traditional socialist case against capitalism, and characteristically it has been argued that the *socialist* economy with which capitalism is to be replaced must be a *planned* economy. More recently, this argument has been reformulated to challenge the claims made for the market under socialism (Mandel, 1986 and 1988; Elson, 1988; Devine, 1988; for an earlier defence of the planned economy against the market socialist alternative, see Dobb, 1955). In Devine's formulation, 'the case for planning is that it enables the conscious shaping of economic activity, in accordance with individually and collectively determined needs, and it overcomes the instability that is an endemic empirical characteristic of market-based economies' (1988, p. 5). The great strength of a socialist planned economy is that 'it substitutes the conscious planned coordination of decisions *ex ante* for the blind, anarchic coordination of the market mechanism *ex post*' (Devine, 1988, p. 18; see also O'Neill, 1988). It is precisely this 'greatest strength' of the traditional planned economy that the market socialists propose to abandon.

Of course, the force of this objection depends crucially upon the plausibility of the claims made for the planned economy. Many market socialists would acknowledge that, *under very favourable conditions* (transparency of social needs, nil information costs, a perfectly operating democratic planning system), planned production might be preferred to allocation through the market. Their argument is that real-world economics are so far from satisfying these optimal circumstances that markets are generally to be preferred, not because they offer a perfectly rational allocation of goods and services, but simply because they are *less inefficient* than central planning. In the light of the record of 'real-world' planned economies, there is surely an onus upon the defenders of planning to offer more compelling evidence of its practicability as a counter-weight to the perceived 'defeatism' of the market socialists (for models of varying plausibility, see Mandel, 1986; Elson, 1988; Devine, 1988). Yet if we have reservations about the claims made for the planned economy, it is also important to acknowledge the critical weight that lies behind traditional socialist objections to the market. We have already addressed the issue of maldistribution of resources in discussing the inequality and inequity generated by markets and it is certainly possible to argue that the tendency of the market to over-exploit scarce resources opens the way for an extensive repoliticization of economic decision-making (see Pierson, 1991a, p. 218). Anyone who has been travelling on the roller-coaster of the British economy in the last decade, with two major recessions and seemingly permanent mass unemployment, does not need reminding that markets do not always optimize the utilization of capital and labour. Any endorsement on the left of the gains in efficiency promised by the market is thus likely to be heavily qualified.

Furthermore, as all the market socialists recognize, markets can only be allowed to operate within a given regulatory framework. This is, in some sense, common ground with all but the most anarchistic of neo-liberals. The crucial issue is how extensive this framework should be. For neo-liberals it is to be as small as possible. But market *socialists* set much more stringent criteria for their regulated market and they would wish to see even socialist markets substantially modified by regulatory

institutions. Thus, we can find among the market socialists a commitment to securing full employment, to a minimum wage, to the promotion of an income and prices policy and to extensive government
economic planning (Nove, 1983, pp. 172–3, 207–8, 227; Miller, 1989, pp.
295–8; Estrin and Winter, 1989, pp. 100–38). Many of them would
undoubtedly be sympathetic to interventions in the market to rectify
inequalities arising from cleavages of race and gender. These may well
be perfectly appropriate policies for a socialist to want to pursue. However, we may wonder (1) to what extent such an arrangement may
properly be called *market* socialism (given that *all* forms of socialism
embrace the market to some degree) and, perhaps more importantly,
(2) whether such an arrangement really offers an institutional *alternative* to those forms of interventionist social democracy in the West,
whose perceived failures were a source of the search for market-based
reform. Though this is not always acknowledged, the market socialists
are likely to require a regulatory and planning framework which is still
more extensive than the interventions of a Keynesian Welfare State
strategy which has had to be abandoned precisely because it was institutionally over-extended. If the role of the state cannot readily be minimized under market socialism, much greater consideration needs to be
given to the ways in which state interventions can be made more
accountable, more democratic and more effective.

Proposition 5

> *The market is hostile to democracy*   While its defenders argue that
> the market economy is the *sine qua non* of democratic life, its critics
> insist that the market is a radically anti-democratic institution.
> Only by confining democratic practices to the less influential
> sphere of the formally political – and allowing authoritarian
> powers to private capital within the market – can the illusion of
> democracy within the market economies be sustained.

It is clearly essential to the market socialists' case that they should be
able to answer this claim that the market is irretrievably anti-democratic. Since they reject central planning as an effective way of democ-
ratizing the economy, they must be able to show that a market system,
stripped of its capitalist integuments, can deliver the democratization
of economic decision-taking. This is also a pivotal point in adjudicating
the claim that market socialism offers a viable alternative to liberal
democracy. It is a definitive feature of liberal democratic arrangements
that there should be some sort of institutional division between the

political sphere (in which democratic procedures are appropriate) and the economic sphere (in which generally they are not). This is a division which the market socialists reject.

Yet again, for market socialists, it is not markets but *capitalist* markets that are undemocratic. There are two principal elements in defending this claim. First, where economic power is concentrated in the hands of private capitalist concerns, the controllers of this capital will be able to exercise an undue influence upon democratically elected governments. In this way, political life, which within the rubric of liberal democracy should properly be under democratic control, is usurped by the dominant power of capital (Lindblom, 1977, pp. 172–84). A second market socialist objection to capitalist market societies is that 'democracy stops at the factory gates'. Thus decision-taking *within* economic enterprises, even where these are in public ownership, is explicitly hierarchical and authoritarian. Market socialists claim to be able to resolve both of these weaknesses within a transformed market system. First, the undue influence which derives from concentrated and coercive economic power will be eliminated by the general socialization of capital ownership. Secondly, the lack of democracy *within* economic enterprises is to be addressed by the similarly bold strategy of replacing the capitalist enterprise with worker's co-operatives. While the precise form of this internal democracy may be unspecific, and does not necessarily mean the elimination of a (now elected) managerial authority, the overall intention, which is to deliver control over the conduct of the enterprise to all its workers, is clear.

If we ignore, for the moment, the legion difficulties which might be thought in practice to militate against the socialization of capital and its replacement with an economy of workers' co-operatives, to what extent would the market socialists' model satisfy traditional socialist objections to the impossibility of democracy under market arrangements? Certainly, the projected socialization of capital and the inauguration of a co-operative economy do, in principle, meet several of the major objections that socialists have traditionally voiced against the anti-democratic element in capitalist markets. The objection to the unwarranted power of private capital must, by definition, be removed, where capital is no longer in private hands and enterprises which are democratically controlled by all those who work for them are likely to recommend themselves to most socialists in preference to a system that entrenches the unqualified powers of capitalist management.

Yet, while this model promises a much more extensive democratic determination of economic decision-taking than the neo-liberals are ready to allow, it is still quite clearly a *limited* form of democratization that is on offer. Market socialism promises a form of economic democracy *within* the enterprise but not *between* enterprises, where market competition will still apply. It promises economic enfranchisement to those who are *employed*, but not to the growing numbers in all advanced societies who find themselves (for all sorts of reasons) *outside* the paid/employed population. It promises greater democratic control over *micro*-economic decision-taking, but little prospect of greater democratic control over the economy *as a whole*. Those who see the rational and democratic management of social and economic life *in general* as central to the realization of democracy will be disappointed by the market socialists' mixture of (a measure of) direct democracy within the enterprise and (a largely unreformed) representative democracy at the level of the state. Again, the market socialist model does offer some encouragement to enthusiasts of more direct forms of democracy. Workers' co-operatives do offer an institutional context in which at least some of the demanding criteria may be satisfied. But once again there is a 'trade-off', in the insistence that at the *societal* level, governance will still be through representative forms, and that, within the enterprise, certain forms of authority and decision-making are likely to be devolved to (albeit accountable) professional managers. At the same time, comparatively little has been written about the potential clash between differing layers of democratic governance *within* a market socialist polity. Yet it is clear that there may well be clashes between a democratically elected government and democratically self-managed co-operatives and, as a number of commentators have recognized, this tension is likely to be most acute over the allocation of scarce capital. This relationship between democracy at different levels remains theoretically underdeveloped.

Proposition 6

The Market is hostile to liberty   Although the market's underwriting of liberty is seen by advocates as one of its greatest strengths, for detractors its (largely negative) freedoms in fact allow discretion only to those with existing power and resources. The *capacity to exercise freedom* is effectively denied to those made dependent by market relationships.

For its traditional socialist critics, the defence of freedom under market capitalism has always had a faintly mocking tone. It is the freedom of everyone to dine out at the Ritz or to publish a national newspaper. No one is prohibited from doing these things. It is just that only those with substantial capital holdings have the necessary resources. In practice, the liberties celebrated under market capitalism are often seen to guarantee little more than the freedom of the strong to impose themselves upon the weak.

In fact, many market socialists show considerable sympathy with this traditional socialist view and, as we have seen, they devote considerable energy to rejecting the circumscribed definition of freedom (as *the absence of coercion*) of the neo-liberals. They insist that a more adequate account of liberty must include (ensuring) the *capacity to exercise freedom* and that the claims of freedom justify 'the redistribution of resources in order to give to individuals the capacity to act as effective and free agents in market transactions' (Hoover and Plant, 1989, p. 212). However, with this redistribution accomplished, the operation of the market may most effectively secure the freedom of individual economic actors, since markets are seen to be maximally responsive to the requirements of consumers, to allow a diversity of lifestyles and 'workstyles' and to promote a sense of 'developed individualism' (Miller, 1989, pp. 213–19).

It is important to stress that the account of liberty developed by the market socialists is significantly different from that of the neo-liberals and, once again, it would justify a much more extensive process of intervention in the conduct of the market. Yet even given a much more equal distribution of resources, and the elimination of private ownership of capital, there are still a number of reasons why more traditional socialists might remain sceptical about the sorts of liberty that the market can guarantee. First, they express an apprehension that 'in the real world', markets can never achieve the sorts of equality of access and treatment which both the neo-classical and market socialist models presume. Any redistribution short of (an iterated) equality will deliver effective market power into the hands of certain privileged economic actors. Secondly, consumers are not truly sovereign, given the manipulation of their preferences, the countervailing powers of producers and the limited number of choices offered by the market (particularly for those with unusual or eccentric needs). Thirdly, consumer sovereignty in the market is seen to afford an impoverished conception of human freedom. For some traditional socialists, this formulation gives an unmerited status to the freedom to consume, at the expense of other valued liberties, whilst others have followed the early Marx in insisting that the freedom of the individual in a market-based society can only be the freedom of alienated, egoistic and atomized individuals. For them, 'truly human emancipation' is premised upon 'overcoming' the market (Marx, 1975; for a commentary, see Pierson, 1986). It is also suggested that while the market is promoted as a 'value-free' device for making choices, the market as an institution actually tends to favour particular substantive outcomes. Indeed, markets are seen to disadvantage precisely those forms of collective and co-operative behaviour which might most commend themselves to socialists. The more general claim that markets promote forms of freedom and individualism which are inconsistent with socialist ambitions is considered in the next section.

Proposition 7

The market is 'anti-social' The atomizing individualism and 'war of all against all' of the market economy denies us the possibility of fully realizing our innately social selves. The possibility of a communal, supportive, co-operative human nature and society is effectively excluded by a system in which we see each other as means to achieving our ends, or as obstacles to such a realization. The best form of society of which we are capable is excluded by reliance upon markets.

For traditional socialists, this is a central claim. Where interaction in society is premised upon markets this is necessarily corrosive of those forms of sociability and communality upon which a truly socialist society could be built (see e.g. Devine, 1988; Martell, 1992). Traditional socialists have always denied that this means the suppression of individuality. It is the atomizing and alienating individualism of a market society which they challenge, and they often argue that release from the dictates of the market is a precondition for 'true' individuality to flourish. But they have frequently argued that overcoming the market will lead to the 'discovery' of a generally shared morality and to a broad and informed consensus about the premises of socialist social organization.

Market socialism sits rather uneasily with this tradition. Raymond Plant is quite explicit that 'in its most radical form market socialism will go a long way towards accepting the neo-liberal critique of traditional socialism, based as it is upon end states and a conception of the good' (1989, p. 63). While Plant's own view is more measured, it is clear that he too sees advantage in the diversity of lifestyles and personal choices which the market offers, and market socialists more generally are clearly ambivalent about the idea that there could be a particular 'socialist morality' to which socialism corresponds.

Perhaps the most skilful attempt to reconcile the traditional perspective with the parameters of market socialism is that offered by David Miller. Familiarly, a first move is to argue that some of the alienating features that socialists have identified with the market should more properly be attributed to *capitalist* markets. Yet it is clear that this must be a much more partial response to this particular socialist claim. For much of the socialist argument here does indeed appear to be directed against markets *in any form*. Miller isolates three such claims in Marx's criticism of the alienating consequences of the market: 'Under the market economy, the relationship between production and human need is distorted by the intervention of exchange value; human interactions take on a detached and potentially hostile character; and the whole economic system slips out of people's theoretical and practical grasp' (Miller, 1989, p. 207). Miller's response is to argue that the sort of developed individuality to which Marx aspired under communism can only effectively be secured through the mechanism of a market economy. But how is this to avoid the attendant problem of alienation? Miller's answer is that where the use of a market mechanism is itself the result of a reasoned and collective choice, much of its alienating quality is dissipated. Thus, for example, it may be true that in a market *particular* outcomes are unintended and to that extent outside the control of human agency. Nonetheless, we may choose the market (with its unanticipated outcomes) as the best available means of attaining some particular aim (maximizing output or choice, for example). As developed individuals, we are capable of living with relationships that have the dual character of being in part competitive and in part co-operative (Miller employs the analogy of a game of tennis between friends). 'Under market socialism . . . work would appear to be merely instrumental . . . but at an underlying level would be seen to be communal, because everyone would understand that the system of exchange led to beneficial results' (Miller, 1989, pp. 220–3). Inasmuch as the use of the market process is itself a conscious and deliberate choice of the community, its outcomes need not be seen as lying outside the (non-alienating) control of human agency.

This is an ingenious argument and Miller may well be right to suppose that what he proposes is the closest to a communal form of economy that those concerned with developed individualism might wish to come. However, I doubt that it is a view that is so readily reconciled with traditional socialism. First, there are some elements of alienation which 'choosing the market' cannot overcome. For example, there is little reason to believe that having chosen the competitive market would make the intensive division of labour any less alienating. Secondly, and however unsatisfactory one may take it to be, the Marxist view of alienation (with which Miller is principally concerned) is not easily reconciled with its resolution through 'choosing'. The classical Marxist tradition cleaves to the view that alienation may be overcome in a much more radical sense – that is, that the quality of human relationships and institutions may be transformed in such a way that traditional forms of competition, of the division of labour and of exchange may be eliminated. I think it is better to argue that this view is wrong (or utopian) than to insist that it can be rewritten in the way that Miller describes.

Our discussion of the contrast between traditional and market forms of socialism certainly suggests that there are important respects in which the typical features of a market socialist model are incompatible with some of the core claims of more traditional socialist advocacy. But before we consider the consequences of this judgement, I want to examine the challenge that is presented to market socialists by critics on the liberal and neo-liberal right.

AGAINST MARKET SOCIALISM II: THE CASE FROM THE RIGHT

At the heart of the neo-liberal project, and of the essence in their condemnation of socialism in all its forms, has been the ubiquitous appeal to the omnicompetence of the market. In both East and West, the apparently 'world-historical' collapse of socialism rested upon the baleful consequences of socialists' attempt to displace the market with the state direction of social and economic life. Correspondingly, the neo-liberal case against socialism has been built principally upon the contrast between the optimizing capacity of the market and the universal ineptitude of planning and state intervention. Much of this traditional criticism will seem irrelevant in attacking a variant of socialism which is so unashamedly in favour of the market, and market socialism clearly presents a much narrower target than socialism *per se*. Nonetheless, for its neo-liberal critics in particular, market socialism turns out to be no less flawed than its more traditional forerunners. That it should seek to shroud itself (misleadingly) in the mantle of the market simply makes market socialism still *more* pernicious (and incoherent) than 'genuine socialism' (de Jasay, 1990, pp. 33–5). Accordingly, I shall concentrate here not upon the (oft-rehearsed) liberal and neo-liberal argument against socialism *in general*, but upon the rather more specific grounds used to condemn *marketized* forms of socialism.

Markets: True and False

Amongst its opponents, there is sometimes a suggestion that the advocacy of the market by socialists must be disingenuous, in part reflecting the Eastern European or Chinese experience, in which the introduction of market-style reforms is seen to have been an attempt to improve economic efficiency without loosening the stranglehold of one-party rule. But even where the good intentions of reformers are acknowledged, the core argument of the neo-liberals (in some ways mirroring the argument of the traditional socialists) is that the logic of the market is simply incompatible with the requirements of (any) socialist political practice. Even though market socialists would allow much greater latitude to market outcomes than their more traditional forerunners, they would still tamper with the market order in ways which would eventually negate all of its advantages.

Hayek's Catallaxy: The Universal Market Order

The definitive and most sophisticated source for this position is to be found in the work of Friedrich Hayek (see especially Hayek 1982 and 1990). Undoubtedly, the principal target of Hayek's criticism was socialism premised upon a centrally planned economy. Insofar as he did address the specific claims of market socialism, this was generally in the form advocated by Lange and his collaborators, which we have already seen attributed more persuasively to the category of 'decentralization procedures in central planning' than to the promotion of an authentically market-based form of socialism. There is even some (rather ambiguous) evidence that Hayek's strictures upon socialism might have been a little less severe where the market was given a much more extensive role (see Lavoie, 1985). Nonetheless, it seems clear that the fundamental grounds for his condemnation of the claims of traditional socialism may also be applied to its more marketized forms.

At the heart of Hayek's rejection of socialism lies his understanding of the nature of the market order. A free and just society, he insists, can only be secured on the basis of 'catallaxy', the neologism used to describe 'the special kind of spontaneous order produced by the market through people acting within the rules of the laws of property, tort and contract', (Hayek, 1982, vol. 2, p. 109). Interestingly, Hayek acknowledges that

> if socialist analyses of the operation of the existing economic order, and of possible alternatives, were factually correct we might be obliged to ensure that the distribution of incomes conforms to certain moral principles, and that this distribution might be possible only by giving central authority the power to direct the use of available resources, and might presuppose the abolition of individual ownership of means of production. (Hayek, 1990, p. 6)

But this is *not* the situation that we face, since 'there is no known way other than by the distribution of products in a competitive market, to inform individuals in what direction their several efforts must aim so as to contribute as much as possible to the total product' (1990, p. 7). It follows that:

> the conflict between, on the one hand, advocates of the spontaneous extended human order created by a competitive market, and on the other hand those who demand a deliberate arrangement of human interaction by central authority based on collective command over available resources is due to a factual error by the latter about how knowledge of these resources is and can be generated and utilised . . . by following the spontaneously generated moral traditions underlying the competitive market order . . . we generate and garner greater knowledge and wealth than could ever be obtained or utilised in a centrally-directed economy whose adherents claimed to proceed strictly in accordance with 'reason'. (1990, p. 7)

This fundamental epistemological fault in the socialist position is compounded by a number of more specific programmatic errors. First, socialists use the powers of the state to try to 'improve' upon the spontaneous order generated by market transactions. But, in Hayek's view, these interventions in the market will *always* have sub-optimal outcomes and *always* lessen general social welfare. Secondly, socialists' sponsorship of the welfare state and of particularistic legislation, most notably to confer privileges upon its allies in the organized labour movement, break with Hayek's insistence that the law must be confined to rules of 'just conduct of universal application'. Thirdly, socialists intervene in the market and its outcomes to promote *social* justice, but Hayek insists that justice is strictly *procedural* and can only refer to the proper enforcement of general rules of universal application without regard to its particular results. 'The mirage of social justice' which the socialists pursue is, at best, a nonsense and, at worst, pernicious and itself unjust. It means undermining the justice of the market, confiscating the wealth of the more successful, prolonging the dependency of the needy, entrenching the special powers of organized interests and overriding individual freedom.

Catallaxy and Market Socialism

As we have seen, some of the more radical market socialists go a considerable distance towards meeting this Hayekian critique of traditional socialism. They too deny the coherence and efficiency of a centrally planned economy and they accept much of the argument about the indispensable epistemological function of the market. Does this mean that market socialism can avoid the strictures that Hayek and his followers direct against socialism more generally? Whilst some critics to the left do indeed suggest that market socialism has become little more than 'a gloss upon Hayek', neo-liberal commentators have tended to argue that the market socialists' commitment to the market is subverted by a continuing attachment to socialist goals (Tomlinson, 1990; de Jasay, 1990; Gray, 1992). For Hayek himself, it was not enough that socialists should be willing to replace centralized planning with the allocation of commodities through markets or that the market should be used in particular (even if very extensive) areas of social and economic life to deliver maximally efficient outcomes or to optimize consumer choice. The central requirement of catallaxy is not that the market should be used in this or that context, but that the entire moral order should be premised upon market-like exchanges between freely choosing individuals.

SOCIAL OWNERSHIP:
THE ACHILLES HEEL OF MARKET SOCIALISM

In defending themselves against the criticisms of a more traditional left, we have seen that market socialists redeem their claim to be presenting a *socialist* programme by stressing their commitment to the *social ownership* of the means of production. Indeed, market socialism may be summarily described as 'social ownership plus markets' and it is certainly this commitment (if anything) that distinguishes market socialism from traditional forms of social democracy and justifies its claim to constitute a 'radical' alternative. By contrast, neo-liberals are more or less unanimous in identifying private property or, in Hayek's preferred usage, *several property*, as the indispensable core institution of a free, fair and just society. Hayek argues that 'men [sic] can use their own knowledge in the pursuit of their own ends without colliding with each other only if clear boundaries can be drawn between their respective domains of free action' and there must be rules which make it possible 'to ascertain the boundary of the protected domain of each and thus to distinguish the *meum* from the *tuum*'. This is 'the basis on which all known civilization has grown' (Hayek, 1982, vol. 1, p. 107). While the *precise* form taken by private property may vary, Hayek is clear that justice 'cannot exist without the recognition of private property' (1990, p. 34). It is in its contrary commitment to *social* ownership that the neo-liberals identify the source of market socialism's most debilitating economic, political, epistemological and moral weaknesses.

Private Property as the Basis of Freedom and Autonomy

Of course, neo-liberals deny the core socialist claim (to which market socialists still subscribe) that private property is an institution which overwhelmingly (and unjustly) serves *particular* interests, most notably the interests of those with the power of disposal over accumulated capital (Hayek, 1990, pp. 77–8). But, whilst they denounce the 'inevitable' inefficiency of the socialist economy, the more philosophically-minded neo-liberals at least do not generally argue that the greatest strength of the market order lies in its capacity to secure economic well-being. Indeed, for many neo-liberals the productivity of the market economy is rather a benign *side-effect* of a system which is to be recommended for quite other reasons. For them, the *principal* virtue of the market with several property is its contribution to securing individual freedom and individual autonomy. Thus, both Hayek and the English political philosopher John Gray are agreed that the extended market order is not to be justified by some sort of 'hedonistic' or utilitarian ethic, in which 'we can make moral judgements simply by considering the greatest foreseeable gratification' (Hayek, 1990, p. 8). It is, rather, 'in its indispensable role as one of the chief preconditions of the autonomy of the individual that the ethical justification of the market lies' (Gray, 1992, p. 19). According to Gray: 'The free market enables the individual to act upon his own goals and values, his objectives and his plan of life, without subordination to any other individual or subjection to any collective decision procedure' (1992, p. 19).

Hayek and Gray belong within a long-standing liberal tradition in holding that private property is essential to the development of the human personality (see Reeve, 1986, especially pp. 136–43; Waldron, 1988). In Hayek's account, 'to have something of one's own, however little, is . . . the foundation on which a distinctive personality can be formed and a distinctive environment created within which particular individual aims can be pursued' (Hayek, 1990, p. 63). For Gray, 'it is from its role as *an enabling device* for the protection and enhancement of human autonomy that the ethical justification of the market is ultimately derived' (1992, p. 19). Thus, the most *primitive* line of argument against the market socialists is that the development of human personality and the securing of individual freedom and autonomy can only be assured under a regime of private property.

'Social Ownership is State Ownership'

At the same time, neo-liberals are profoundly sceptical that 'social ownership', as a third form of property-holding lying between private and state ownership, can really exist.[3] In the most robust neo-liberal accounts, it is suggested that the usage 'social ownership' is a meaningless 'camouflage', designed to conceal what is the (only available) real-world choice between *private* ownership and *state* ownership. According to de Jasay, 'social ownership' is invoked because the record of 'state ownership' is so dire, but, in reality, ' "social ownership" . . . is clearly state ownership' (1990, p. 19). Much the same position was adopted by Hayek. 'Social ownership' evokes the image of a benign, non-coercive and sociable property regime, whereas in practice it can mean little other than the compulsory control of economic assets by the state. In essence, ownership resides in that legal entity which exercises rights of disposal over a given property. These ownership rights may be exercised by an individual, a corporation or the state, but not by 'society'. Such ownership rights as 'society' enjoys must, in practice, be held and exercised 'on its behalf' by the state. Market socialism is seen to face an irresoluble dilemma. It advocates the market, (in labour, in consumer and production goods) as a way of avoiding the statism and inefficiency that has bedevilled more traditional forms of socialism; but, in the view of the neo-liberals, all of the gains that might follow from this embrace of the market are vitiated by the unwillingness to accept a market in capital. Yet, market socialists are prevented from taking this final and decisive step by their own recognition (endorsed in turn by many of the neo-liberals) that it is precisely the absence of a capital market that makes their programme socialist.

The Epistemological and Incentive Problems of Social Ownership

This same unwillingness to embrace the capital market, which makes market socialism socialist, is also seen to make it vulnerable to many of those other weaknesses which undermine more traditional forms of socialism. First, the absence of private ownership of capital assets leaves market socialism exposed to the long-standing claim, retraceable at least to the work of von Mises, that socialism lacks the *incentive* structure necessary for the efficient use of limited resources.[4] Only private ownership of capital, and the return of investment gains (and losses) to private owners will induce that entrepreneurial behaviour upon which economic growth depends. According to Alfred Schuller:

> The nature, extent and use costs of the economic potential of entrepre-neurial authority depend decisively on the property system. If there is no adequate personal link between disposal rights and liability, there is a continuous incentive to divide authority in such a way that the conse-quences of decisions for the value of resources do not adequately fall on those responsible for the decisions. In contrast, the more exclusive and linked to persons the disposal rights are, and the more freely they can be used in accordance with the principle of unity between disposal and liability, the stronger is the incentive to acquire and use *entrepreneurial rights*. (1988, p. 62)

Still more fundamental, according to John Gray, is 'the epistemic argument' which effectively disqualifies 'all forms of socialism, includ-ing market socialism' (1992, p. 47). We have seen the market presented, in Lavoie's paraphrase, as a 'procedure for discovery and conveyance of inarticulate knowledge' (Lavoie, 1985). In this process, competing private capitals have an indispensable role to play. 'Incomes from property ownership are information-carrying money flows' and 're-placing the dialogical process of interacting private owners with a single, monological social owner, would only eliminate the very give-and-take process that generates . . . price information' (Lavoie, 1990, p. 78). Gray pursues the same point:

> It is a fundamental objection to central planning that the planners will in the absence of market pricing inevitably lack the knowledge of relative scarcities needed for rational resource-allocation. The question now arises: . . . without a capital market how can the state investment banks know what are the most productive uses of the investment capital at their disposal? (1992, p. 46)

There is, Gray suggests, no satisfactory socialist response to this ques-tion, and the 'policy implication is a radical one . . . there must be a market in capital – which is to say, private or several ownership of capital'. But this conclusion is, in its turn, fatal to the market socialist project. For, with the restoration of the capital market, 'we are at least half-way towards the reinvention of one of the key institutions of market capitalism' (Gray, 1992, pp. 46–7). For Gray, at least, there seems little reason to stop short of 'the real thing'.

Social Ownership and the Co-operative Economy

These several vices of the market socialist economy are seen with particular clarity in its preferred enterprise form of the workers' co-operative. First, the co-operative economy is presented as a surrogate form of state socialism which 'dares not speak its name'. Since rights of ownership are not to be vested in the individual co-operators themselves (for this would be 'workers' capitalism not socialism'), they must be exercised by 'society's representative', that is, by the state. Ownership may be devolved amongst a number of 'competing' state investment banks, but this cannot undo the damaging consequences for both freedom and efficiency that come from concentrating all capital ownership in the hands of the state. Secondly, the absence of a genuine market in capital means that state investment banks will 'inevitably lack the knowledge of relative scarcities needed for rational resource-allocation' (Gray, 1992, p. 46). An economy under social ownership will lack the multiple sites of capital allocation which are said to be essential to rational economic decision-taking. Thirdly, the lack of private holdings of capital sets up all sorts of perverse economic incentives. The absence of the incentive of capital gains will tend to discourage the formation of new enterprises and suppress entrepreneurial initiative more generally. As under centralized planning, the allocation of capital within a co-operative economy will tend to 'favour entrenched producer groups, exhibit a high degree of risk aversion and a tendency to seek to conceal mal-investments' (Gray, 1992, p. 47). Within the co-operative enterprise itself, there will be perverse incentives for workers, encouraging them to underinvest, to fail to take up new market opportunities, to restrict the expansion of employment and to dissipate the enterprise's working capital.

Market Socialism, Social Justice and Redistribution

Finally, neo-liberals enter a number of objections against the market socialists' continuing commitment to some form of 'social justice' and some measure of redistribution of wealth. We saw in chapter 4 that most market socialists are tolerant of *some* level of inequality of income and wealth, on grounds of individual freedom and economic efficiency, but also that they believe that *some* level of intervention by the state to redistribute resources and opportunities is justified by an appeal to social justice. The rejection of such a view is at the heart of Hayek's condemnation of socialism. 'In a society of free men' [*sic*], he contends, 'the concept of social justice is strictly empty and meaningless'. For, in such a free society, 'nobody's will can determine the relative incomes of the different people, or prevent that they be partly dependent on accident' (Hayek, 1982, vol. 2, pp. 68–9). The rules and procedures of the catallaxy can and should be just, but the *outcome* of particular market exchanges, and the pattern of distribution to which they may give rise, is without moral content. While there are legitimate ends for which the state may raise taxation, these do not include the promotion of equality (or any other distributive pattern) through the compulsory redistribution of assets from some citizens to others. Similarly, Gray argues that redistribution has no sound moral basis. Principles of distribution are always addressed to the position of groups or individuals *in relation to* other groups or individuals. 'What is wrong with every form of distributionism [is] its fixation on relational qualities that have no moral status' (Gray, 1992, p. 40). The only *real* premise of political morality – the well-being of individuals – requires that we meet the (satiable) *basic needs* of all citizens, but not a concern with the *relative* distribution of incomes. For Gray, this may justify quite extensive state action (for example, to promote an enabling welfare state and to subsidize the opera), but *not* government intervention to favour a particular and patterned distribution of goods and resources.

Conclusion

It is clear that the contemporary forms of market socialism which were outlined in chapter 4 face a substantial and systematic challenge from both right and left. Market socialism stands condemned by its several critics as incoherent, inefficient, unjust, undemocratic and anti-libertarian and, in the light of the responses offered by the market socialists themselves, it has to be said that some of these criticisms carry considerable weight. But they are not quite so damning of the market socialist project as its critics suppose. Thus, criticism from the left would be fatally damaging to the market socialist case only if we thought that the traditional socialist position were 'true', feasible and exhaustive of what 'really' counts as socialism. Since none of these claims is especially convincing, it seems mistaken to argue that market socialism must be abandoned because of its incompatibility with the demands of this tradition. At the same time, the criticism of the neo-liberal right might seem compelling, if we believed that the market order was truly as Hayek and his followers have described it. Yet while the Hayekian challenge is profound and will be thought by some to justify rejection of the market socialist project, it cannot be seen incontestably to carry the day. This is more especially the case when we move from the realm of the catallaxy to real-world market societies in which many of the justifying preconditions for Hayek's market order simply do not exist. Since market socialism is recommended by its followers above all as a pragmatic or feasible strategy, it is above all in terms of its real-world plausibility that it should be judged. Finally, whilst the combined challenge from right and left is substantial, it cannot be the case that *all* the arguments of *both* tendencies can be simultaneously effective against market socialism. It seems perverse to condemn market socialism *simultaneously* for both abandoning social ownership *and* nationalizing all economic assets, or for both pursuing social justice and at the same time abandoning it. (However, it is of course possible that, in trying to bridge the gap between socialism and markets, market socialism ends up embracing the worst, rather than the best, of both worlds.)

Interestingly, despite their enormous differences, critics from right and left tend to identify the same areas of the market socialist programme as the most problematic. Thus particular attention has been directed towards the forms of social ownership and the nature of the co-operative economy and I consider these critical elements of the market socialist apparatus in some detail in chapter 6. At the same time, whilst critics to both left and right say something (rather conventional) about the nature of politics under market socialism, both wings (along with many of the market socialists themselves) fail to give sufficient attention to the nature of the state and democratization under market socialism.[5] Yet it is clear that if market socialism were to be a guide to action it would require as much a rethinking of the *political* regime (of state and democracy), as of the economic arrangements, of a transformed market order. I discuss these underconsidered political problems of market socialism in chapter 7. Finally, we have observed that market socialism's greatest claim (said to offset many of its theoretical imperfections and inconsistencies) is its *feasibility*. In the final chapter, I consider this claim to feasibility, judging not simply whether market socialism offers a coherent and workable model, but more importantly, whether it can contribute to a viable political programme in the actual context of left-of-centre political forces in a changing environment, the context discussed in part I. In short, does anybody want it, and, if they did, could it be done?

6

The Political Economy of Labour Management

We have already seen that what is in many ways most distinctive about the advocates of market socialism is their desire to retain much of the allocative apparatus of the market economy, whilst divorcing this economy from its familiar association with a regime of privately owned capital. For many (though far from all) of these market socialists, the producer co-operative and/or the labour-managed economy are essential in distancing socialism from an over-mighty state and attaching it to the imperatives of a reconstituted market economy.[1] At the level of the individual enterprise, the producer co-operative run by its own workers, who now cease to be employees and become 'members of the firm', is seen as a form in which the many advantages of the market in terms of efficiency, innovation, consumer choice, decentralization of power, pluralism, and so on, can be combined with a property system which breaks with the domineering and exploitative power of private capital. At the macro-economic level, the labour-managed economy promises the efficiency and decentralization of markets without tutelage to a regime of private capital. It is the competence of the co-operative and the labour-managed economy to fulfil this central role in the market socialist schema, and the consequent and difficult questions about the nature of 'social ownership' which this raises, that are considered in this chapter.

The Co-operative Tradition

The co-operative movement has a long and distinguished, if rather chequered, history. In its modern form, it is frequently retraced to the

1820s and 1830s, to the writing and advocacy of, most famously, Robert Owen and the Christian Socialists in Britain, and of Fourier, Buchez and Blanc in France (Potter, 1891; Cole, 1953; Lambert, 1963). As a social movement, it owes quite as much to generations of practical-minded men and women, of whom the Rochdale Pioneers are perhaps only the most celebrated (Cole, 1945; Pollard, 1967; Oakeshott, 1978). Some enthusiasts have suggested that down to the end of the nineteenth century, the co-operative principle represented an active alternative form for the transition to socialism, an alternative which was only lost when socialism became (fatally) identified with trade unionism, collective bargaining and the interventionist state (see Luard, 1991; Hirst, 1993b). Certainly, there was an important historical tradition of working-class mutualism which was in some circumstances simply overwhelmed by the intervention of the state. In Britain, the marginalization of friendly societies by the introduction of statutory welfare provision affords a good example (Gilbert, 1966; Pierson, 1991a). But it is rather fanciful to project producers' co-operatives as an alternative path for the twentieth-century labour movement. Whilst there was a time when *consumer* co-operatives might have been said to constitute a mass organization (though not perhaps a mass movement), *producer* co-operatives have always represented a small and, at times, a tiny sector of industrial activity (Estrin and Perotin, 1987). In many continental European economies (and despite the oppressive interlude of fascism), producer co-operatives have long had a significant niche. They enjoy privileged constitutional status in both Italy and Spain. In 1951, Italy already had more than two thousand producer co-operatives, employing more than 55,000 workers (Zevi, 1982, p. 241). By 1970, the famous Mondragon complex in the Basque region of northern Spain had expanded to incorporate no fewer than 40 industrial co-operatives with a total workforce of 8,500 (H. Thomas, 1982, p. 131). But this still represented a tiny proportion of economic activity within these countries and in the larger Anglo-American economies the role of producer co-operatives has been still more marginal. Derek Jones records that by 1968 there were just 30 long-established producer co-operatives in Britain, employing fewer than 4,000 workers (1982a, p. 181; 1983, p. 36). In the giant US economy, he estimates that in the 1950s there were fewer than 500 producer co-operatives, and these were heavily concentrated in particular industries and regions, (Jones, 1982b, p. 54).

The last twenty years have seen a remarkable rate of growth in the number of these producer co-operatives (albeit expanding from a very modest baseline). Bartlett and his colleagues (Bartlett and Pridham, 1991; Bartlett, Cable, Estrin, Jones and Smith, 1992) indicate that by the mid-1980s the number of producer co-operatives had reached 20,000 in

Italy, 6,000 in Spain and in excess of 2,000 in Portugal. Thomas estimates the UK producer co-operatives to have expanded by 1990 to
include more than 1,400 enterprises, with as many as 10,000 workers
(A. Thomas, 1990; see also Hobbs and Jefferis, 1990). By the mid-1980s,
employment in this sector in Italy stood in excess of 300,000. The *rate* of
growth in the co-operative sector remained impressive throughout the
1980s, in a period in which many more traditional sectors faced severe
retrenchment, and this, allied to the difficulties of the more traditional
political vehicles of the left (trade unions and socialist and social democratic parties), led to a renewal of academic and political interest in the
co-operative form. Yet, with the partial exception of Italy, this rapid
expansion still left producer co-operatives as a tiny proportion of most
OECD economies (even by 1990 British producer co-operatives, for
example, still accounted for less than 0.001 per cent of the nation's
employed workforce).[2]

The Labour-managed Economy in Theory and Practice

Despite their rather marginal status in practice, there is a substantial
literature on the co-operative enterprise and the labour-managed
economy, stretching back into the nineteenth century (for the earlier
period, see e.g. Jones, 1968; Potter, 1891; Fay, 1908). Modern discussions
have been dominated by the theoretical work of Jaroslav Vanek,
Benjamin Ward and, to a rather lesser extent, James Meade, Branko
Horvat and Evsey Domar.[3] While much of this work is highly abstract
and not readily accessible to the reader without a background in the
formal techniques of economics, the broad *theoretical* arguments for
and against labour management can be summarized (with some loss
of precision) in a largely non-technical vocabulary. For a number of
reasons, discussion of the *practical* experience of labour management is
more difficult. Although the recent period of expansion has allowed for
a growth in comparative and empirical studies of the co-operative firm,
there are still relatively few real-world cases to be assessed (especially
if we are interested in enterprises which have persisted over any length
of time). There is a further difficulty in that what we discover about the
economic conduct of a small number of co-operative firms *under capitalism* may give little indication of the likely conduct of such firms within
an economy dominated by the co-operative form. Thus, what applies to
co-operatives as a wholly untypical enterprise form under capitalism
(often established with an atypical workforce under atypical circumstances) may not apply to the co-operative as a 'normal' firm within a
labour-managed economy. It may be that *co-operative firms* are pecu-

liarly disadvantaged (and perhaps prone to degeneration) in a broadly capitalist economy (where they are dwarfed by a largely hostile economic and legal environment), generating a set of problems which simply would not arise within a broadly *co-operative economy* (Horvat, 1982, pp. 456–61; Elster, 1988). Even the empirically established weaknesses of co-operatives under capitalism may thus be irrelevant in assessing the desirability of the co-operative form under marketized socialism.

Given these considerations, it is a grave disadvantage that there should be no 'real-world' model of a labour-managed *economy* from which to derive predictions about the potential of a marketized form of socialism. There were, of course, co-operatives within the socialized economies of the Soviet Union and Eastern Europe, but these were for the most part so deeply implicated in the statist administration of the economy as to afford little or no indication of the likely conduct of co-operatives within a socialized market.[4] To some extent this experiential gap has been filled by the example of the former Yugoslav economy. As is well known, the breach of Yugoslavia under Tito from the Soviet Union under Stalin was consummated with the inauguration of a new politico-economic system of 'workers' self-management' (Broekmeyer, 1970; Comisso, 1979; Djordjevic et al., 1982; Estrin, 1983; Lydall, 1984; Ben-Ner and Neuberger, 1990; Dyker, 1990; Prout, 1985). Formally, at least, Yugoslavia appeared to offer a testing ground for economy-wide hypotheses about a labour-managed economy and we might justifiably describe Yugoslavia after 1950 as the closest we have yet come to a real market socialist *economy*. Yet, in reality, it is far from clear that Yugoslavia offers a satisfactory testing-ground for the workings of a labour-managed economy. According to Bonin and Putterman,

> it may be misleading to think of Yugoslavia as a model of independent worker-run economic units competing in a true market environment. Instead, workers' control is observed in the context of a socialist economy that lacks both planners' and market discipline, and that is hostage to an ideology enshrining both workers' self-management and worker income security. (Bonin and Putterman, 1987, p. 112)

In Yugoslav practice, workers' self-management and the logic of the market were consistently undermined by the political considerations of the League of Communists and the delicate task of maintaining the nation's federal structure. Furthermore, the system was subject to almost continuous reform. Ben-Ner and Neuberger identify no fewer than six separate economic systems which operated between the end of the Second World War and the effective dissolution of the country in 1990–1, and it is only perhaps in the decade 1965–1974 that the Yugo-

slav system could be sensibly described as one of 'market self-management' (Ben-Ner and Neuberger, 1990; Estrin, 1983, pp. 58–77;
Flakierski, 1989, pp. 3–17; Prout, 1985).

Given its status as the only (but deeply-flawed) model of a socialist
market economy, Yugoslavia has attracted considerable attention.[5] In
the face of a rather messy economic and political reality, however, most
commentators (both critics and admirers) have tended to extrapolate
from actual Yugoslav experience their own rather stylized models of
an ideal-typical, Yugoslav-style economy. This tendency is neatly
captured in Benjamin Ward's classic critique of the labour-managed
enterprise, widely adopted by later commentators, as 'the firm in
Illyria' (Ward, 1958). Illyria is, of course, an imaginary and idealized
land, but shares its name with a peninsula in north-eastern Slovenia, a
part of what once was Yugoslavia. Ward's own treatment is itself
largely theoretical, but is seen to have implications for those who
advocate a Yugoslav-style economy of workers' self-management.
Those who are more sympathetic to the idea of a labour-managed
economy, such as Horvat and Vanek, see in the flawed Yugoslav experience an indication of the possibilities of self-management, whilst
attributing its failures in practice to the political and economic peculiarities of the Yugoslav situation rather than to weaknesses in the
overall conception of a market under workers' self-administration
(Vanek, 1972; Horvat, 1982).

This background makes it clear that we are unlikely to be able to
reach some definitive judgement upon the practicability or desirability
of an economy of workers' self-management. Nonetheless, there is
much in the existing literature that should enable us to make some
provisional judgements about the plausibility of the producer co-operative as a central element in a future market socialism. It will also, I
believe, point us towards a fundamental problem in the configuration
of market socialism, that is, the nature of social ownership.

An Outline of the Labour-managed Economy

There are, of course, a number of quite different ways of characterizing
the worker-owned enterprise and the labour-managed economy.[6] In
this section, I furnish a summary account of what I take to be the most
widely adopted model of the labour-managed economy, drawing out
some of the more important deviations from this model in the subsequent critical discussion. I consider assessments of the co-operative
enterprise under capitalism principally as a way of increasing our
understanding of a more general system of workers' self-management.

At its simplest, a labour-managed economy is one in which 'the means of production are owned socially and managed by those who make use of them', a system in which 'labour hires capital rather than capital hiring labour' (Selucky, 1979, p. 179; Estrin, 1983, p. 12). In Meade's summary, the labour-managed economy is one

> in which workers get together and form collectives or partnerships to run firms; they hire capital and purchase other inputs and they sell the products of the firm at the best prices they can obtain in the markets for inputs and outputs, they themselves bear the risk of any unexpected gain or loss and distribute the resulting surplus among themselves (1988a, p. 158).

In its 'pure' form, the labour-managed enterprise is one in which 'the ultimate decision-making rights . . . are held by worker-members, on the basis of equality of those rights regardless of job, skill grade, or capital contribution' and in which 'no non-workers have a direct say in enterprise decisions' and 'no workers are denied an equal say in those decisions' (Bonin and Putterman, 1987, p. 1). Thus, all members of the labour-managed enterprise, but only they, should have an (equal) say in its governance (although day-to-day administration may be devolved upon professional managers). The pattern of income distribution within the firm need not be egalitarian (though it should be collectively agreed and 'just'). Whilst workers should remain free to choose the nature and place of their work, there would be no wage labour in the conventional sense (Vanek, 1970; Steinherr, 1983; Horvat, 1982). In Scott Arnold's account, such a system differs from market capitalism in two fundamental respects: 'First, the workers collectively control the means of production. Secondly, workers' labor power is not a commodity they sell to the firm for a wage. Because the workers are the residual claimants they are working for a share of the firm's income and not a wage' (Arnold, 1992, p. 9).

Amongst its advocates, this system is seen to enjoy many advantages over traditional capitalist market economies. On the one hand, it is seen to rectify many of the gravest moral and political weaknesses of such economies. Exploitation, when this is understood as 'command over the labor of others [plus] appropriation of nonlabor income', is eliminated (Horvat, 1982, p. 239). Alienation, where this is identified above all with the worker selling his/her labour power to an employer, may also be drastically reduced (Horvat, 1982, p. 90). Opportunities for democratic involvement and individual autonomy in the workplace, which are severely constrained by the structures of corporate capitalism, would be greatly extended by the new participative structures of labour management (Pateman, 1970; Dahl, 1985; Cohen, 1988). Inequalities of wealth and income should be greatly reduced. At the same time, and given the appropriate institutional structure, labour-management may also improve upon the purely *economic* efficiency of existing market economies. Participation is seen by its supporters to be likely to improve motivation and morale amongst the workforce. It should eliminate many of the costs that arise from the traditional hostility between managers/owners and employees. It should lessen the need for supervision, curb absenteeism and reduce the number of work stoppages and strikes. It should encourage greater flexibility and innovation in work practices, and a freer flow of technical and organizational information within the firm. Since average labour tenure is likely to increase in the labour-managed enterprise, there should also be improvements in the incentives for training and an augmentation of general and firm-specific human capital (Vanek, 1970; Pateman, 1970; Jones and Svejnar, 1985; Estrin, Jones and Svejnar, 1987; Elster and Moene, 1989a).

The Case against Labour Management

Of course, these arguments for worker self-management are far from universally endorsed and in this section I consider the (principally theoretical) case against the viability and/or the desirability of a labour-managed economy. At this stage, I shall generally ignore those arguments which are concerned *exclusively* with the difficulties of the labour-managed enterprise under capitalism (for example, the reluctance of commercial banks to lend to co-operatives or the tendency for co-operative enterprises to 'degenerate' into conventional capitalist concerns through the hiring of labour).[7] I shall concentrate upon the case against labour management within the context of market socialism, that is, where capital is under some form of 'social ownership'.

A common starting-point for much of this discussion is to be found in the work of Benjamin Ward (1958 and 1967) and Jaroslav Vanek (1970 and 1972). Whilst Ward and Vanek disagree about the prospects for workers' self-management, they do so on the basis of a broadly similar model of the labour-managed economy and this model has set the terms for much of the subsequent debate. Most significantly, they are agreed that what is distinctive about the market economy under labour self-management is that the economic objective of the enterprise is no longer (as under capitalism) the maximization of profit, but rather the maximization of income per worker. Working with a simple model and under conventional neo-classical assumptions, Ward argues that *in the short term* pursuing the distinctive maximand of income per worker within a labour-managed economy will have perverse effects. In brief, a co-operative firm (in contrast to its capitalist counterpart) will respond to an increase (decrease) in the price of its product with a decrease (increase) in output and (if possible) employment. Ward also suggests that the labour-managed enterprise would respond perversely to changes in fiscal policy and would tend to produce less than a corresponding capitalist firm under monopoly conditions. *In the long run*, the self-managed economy should reach the same Pareto-optimality as the capitalist economy, through the equilibrating effect of the free entry and exit of new enterprises. However, if these considerations are at all relevant to the anticipated working of real-world economies, this would clearly place enormous reliance upon the institutional mechanisms for the free entry (and exit) of firms.

Despite the very considerable attention devoted to Ward's hypothesis (and to the range of derivative models of a 'modified' Illyrian economy), its real salience for labour management remains unclear.[8] Some have argued that the perverse outcomes which Ward predicts may be theoretically robust, but insist that they are a consequence of unrealistic assumptions or tend to disappear once a less simplified economic model is adopted (Pfouts and Rosefielde, 1986; Mygind, 1986; Miyazaki and Neary, 1983; Fleurbaey, 1993). Others, such as Branko Horvat, insist that the limited empirical evidence which we already have about the actual behaviour of enterprises in a labour-managed economy shows that their response to market signals is not as Ward describes it, but is essentially the same as that of the traditional capitalist firm (Horvat, 1982, pp. 339–44). It may be that Ward's overall case is simply too general and abstract to count compellingly against the possibility of an effective labour-managed economy. Yet there are a number of other and more specific reservations, drawn both from economic theory and the actual experience of the co-operative economy, which are likely to trouble advocates of labour self-management.

Many of these criticisms focus upon the *economic* viability of self-management. Of these, perhaps the most long-standing and frequently stated objection is that co-operative enterprises will lack systems for effective management and worker discipline.[9] It is suggested that an elected management will always lack the authority to impose discipline upon their 'constituents' and that, in a worker-run shop, no one has either the authority to direct production or the incentive to impose work discipline. Mutual worker supervision might work in very small groups, but even this is not without its costs (see Demsetz, 1967; Chiplin and Coyne, 1977; Potter, 1891). Co-operatives are also perceived by their critics to be much less well equipped than their capitalist counterparts to respond to changes in the marketplace. In part, this criticism refers to what are presumed to be the cumbersome features of democratic decision-taking and the inability to act quickly and decisively in response to rapid changes in market conditions (even if, given sufficient time, workers might arrive at the right decisions). In part, it refers to workers' lack of the technical and financial skills to cope in a complex and constantly changing market environment. Critics also insist that there are structural features in a worker-managed economy which militate against innovation and optimal growth. The entrepreneurial function is often presented as essentially individualistic and the incentive to innovate and its attendant risk is seen to rest principally upon the expectation of a commensurate capital return (see Fanning and McCarthy, 1986). Even if a worker-managed enterprise acts entrepreneurially, it may be that the perverse incentives of maximizing worker income (rather than profits) will lead to a failure fully to exploit technical innovations (Brewer, 1988). Furthermore, given the nature of the worker's stake in a particular firm (even where none of the capital is provided by workers themselves), there is a likelihood of heightened risk-aversion amongst member-workers as opposed to capitalist entrepreneurs (who are able to disperse their risks across a portfolio of investments). Similarly, it may be that the set-up costs of a new enterprise are much greater for a collective of worker-members (who have amongst other things to find each other) than it is for the founding (and perhaps lone) capitalist entrepreneur. Finally, and despite Ward's expectations, co-operatives might in practice be extremely reluctant to shed labour. Indeed, it is sometimes taken to be a strength of co-operatives under capitalism that they are able to deal with periods of economic downturn by cutting income rather than reducing employment. However, this is sometimes redescribed by critics as the incapacity of labour co-operatives to survive without subjecting themselves to chronic self-exploitation. All of these weaknesses of the labour-managed economy may add up to a significant misallocation of resources at the macro-economic level, with neither capital nor labour applied where they will yield the maximum return, and with economic efficiency and growth correspondingly reduced.

A second set of criticisms relate to the *political* character of worker self-management. Perhaps the most primitive point is that market socialism lacks any credible political support. John Gray records that whilst 'in Western societies there is an absence of any political force in its favour . . . in the former Soviet bloc . . . it is rejected with derision' (1992, p. 53). But there are also a number of more theoretical objections to the market socialist model, many of which confront the claimed virtues of the self-managed system. Scott Arnold, for example, challenges the widely voiced claim that market socialism will eliminate exploitation. In an economy of worker co-operatives, he argues, workers' incomes within a given firm would be determined by a democratic decision of the whole workforce. In the medium term, there would be a tendency for a majoritarian coalition of less skilled workers to drive down the income of skilled workers below a level which reflected the latter's 'real' contribution to the enterprise, whilst rewarding themselves with incomes that were higher than their own 'real' contribution. Within the firm, the less skilled would thus exploit the more skilled and, in an economy of such workers' co-operatives and with the banning of private capital, these more skilled workers would have little option but to allow themselves to be subjected to such exploitation by those with less valuable labour (Arnold, 1992).

A parallel argument is developed by John Gray. We have already seen that co-operatives are frequently recommended as a way of freeing workers from subjection to the dictates of private capital. Yet the empirical evidence shows a very considerable reluctance on the part of ordinary workers to opt for the co-operative form. According to Gray, there is 'not a shred of empirical evidence that most workers prefer self-managed worker-cooperatives to capitalist corporations, or that they would not choose to exit from the former to the latter if they had the choice' (1992, p. 49). David Miller and Jon Elster both seek to explain this reluctance in terms of the systemic prejudice which small enclaves of co-operation are seen to face within a more broadly capitalist economic order (Miller, 1981; Elster, 1989). For Gray, the explanation is rather more straightforward. His judgement is that workers actually enjoy greater freedom under capitalism than they would under any form of socialism, including the market socialism of worker's co-operatives (Gray, 1988 and 1992). The worker's hostility to the co-operative form is well founded. It seems that a co-operative economy could be established only by denying the worker the right to sell his/her labour power to an employer, that is by proscribing traditional forms of wage-labour. Yet this proscription cannot be justified by the claim that it will make workers generally more free. Gray's argument is that with capital socialized, workers will face not a plurality of capital owners but a monopoly supplier (in the shape of the state or its surrogates). The allocation of capital will become increasingly a *political* decision, with unfavoured minorities finding it increasingly difficult to gain access to productive resources. With alternative forms forbidden, workers will be 'imprison[ed] in their worker-cooperatives, where they may be subject to exploitative interference by central government' and, in Scott Arnold's account, by coalitions of less skilled workers (Gray, 1992, p. 51; Arnold, 1992; see also Arnold, 1987a, 1987b and 1989). Workers may indeed face restrictions upon their freedom under existing forms of corporate capitalism. Yet 'capitalist institutions may [still] be defended as institutions that promote workers' freedom better than any realizable alternative', including market socialism (Gray, 1988, p. 109).

A further challenge is offered to the central claim that market socialism encourages (a more participatory form of) democracy. The objection here is twofold. First, it is argued that while the co-operative form appears to promise enhanced democracy within enterprises, this expectation will be disappointed in practice as self-management is 'diluted by the inevitable emergence of managerial elites and curtailed by frequent episodes of authoritarian intervention . . . by central government' (Gray, 1992, p. 49). Still more fundamentally, whilst the utopian expectation of democracy at plant level is certain to be disappointed, the consequences of market socialism for really existing democracy, that is, representative democracy at the level of the nation state, will be disastrous. We have already seen, in the work of Hayek and Friedman for example, that democracy is seen to be conditional upon the existence of private and voluntary exchange. The argument of market socialism's opponents is that, in practice, the elusive category of 'social ownership' will mean effective ownership by the state and the testament of all twentieth-century experience is that such a concentration of economic power in the hands of the state will foster more authoritarian forms of governance.

The threads of both the economic and political arguments against workers' self-management converge in dealing with the contentious issues of ownership and capital allocation. It is clear that many of these problems would apply principally to co-operatives working within a capitalist environment. For example, in raising external finance, the co-operative, in which self-management precluded external holdings of equity, would be likely to find itself at a disadvantage compared with a capitalist competitor. The co-operative that is entirely funded by its own workforce but also collectively owned (with no alienable rights in the assets of the firm for its individual members) faces the difficulty of reconciling the competing claims of 'old' and 'new' members and dealing with the incentive problems of workers who can expect no return on the principal they have invested within the firm (Furubotn and Pejovich, 1970; Pejovich, 1990). In any case, such internal investment has extremely poor risk properties for individual worker-members. As Meade has it, 'while property owners can spread their risks by putting small bits of their property into a large number of concerns, a worker cannot easily put small bits of effort into a large number of different jobs' (1988a, p. 181). The worker who has both employment and capital tied up in one concern faces disaster in the event of that firm's failure, and has a corresponding incentive to be peculiarly risk-averse.

Many of these problems should simply not apply within market socialism under the Ward–Vanek definition, that is where the means of production are in social ownership (Ward, 1967, p. 7). Indeed, Vanek, whilst an enthusiastic promoter of the co-operative form, is so persuaded of the degenerative qualities of the combination of collective ownership and self-finance that he insists upon the labour-managed economy being one in which all firms are entirely externally financed. In a 'mixed economy', the costs of raising finance on these terms might seem to make the worker-managed firm a non-starter (and this may indeed help to explain why co-operatives within such an economy are so frequently chronically under-financed). This competitive disadvantage should not, of course, apply where the co-operative is the only legitimate, or at least a legally privileged, enterprise form. Yet there remain a number of deep-seated objections to labour management in this externally funded form. Milenkovitch cites the neo-classical principle that 'risk-bearing will not be efficient unless the recipient of the gains is also the bearer of the losses' (1984, p. 87). She insists that under a system of wholly external capital financing enterprises will tend to be excessively capital-intensive. Whether through the pursuit of high-risk investment strategies or illicit disinvestment through excess wages, workers will simply not be mindful of the real cost of capital. Chiplin and Coyne (1977) make a similar point, insisting that where workers control their enterprises without owning them, they will tend to disinvest through taking excessive wages at the expense of the 'social owners' of capital. Of course, capital would not be a 'free' resource for worker-managed enterprises. The expectation is that enterprises would pay a scarcity-reflecting rent for capital and that an inability to (continue to) meet these costs would issue in bankruptcy. But this raises two further problems. One is an echo of von Mises' argument on the general irrationality of socialism: without a market in capital, how can we know what would constitute a scarcity-reflecting rent? It is not clear (to me at least) just how damning this claim must prove to be given the neo-classical framework within which the labour-managed economy is generally discussed. We saw in chapter 4 that several commentators feel von Mises' objection to Oskar Lange fails, if we remain within the realm of neo-classical assumptions. A second and perhaps more damaging claim is that, in practice, 'social ownership' will mean effective ownership (and control) by the state. It may (just) be possible to imagine a system of state investment banks lending to independent worker-owned enterprises at market-clearing rates. But if the rights of the owners of this capital (that is, 'society') are to be properly protected, these banks should surely take an active interest in the running of worker enterprises. Indeed, we would not normally commend a financial system in which banks simply lent out their assets and then took no further interest in the conduct of a firm's business, short of foreclosing in the event of debt. However, if (even a plurality of) state banks are to be the sole source of capital, there is a real danger of an excessive concentration of economic power in the hands of the state (one of the principal vices which market socialism is supposed to overcome). Under these circumstances, it is easy to imagine political pressure being brought to bear to prevent free entry and exit of firms (especially to avert bankruptcies), to prevent enterprises being charged the full market price for their capital, to soften budget constraints and perhaps to favour the interests of large and well-established co-operatives. For the critics, all of this (and more) can be seen in the experience of the former Yugoslavia, which proves to be not a perversion of labour-management, but rather its natural fulfilment.

Labour Management Assessed

It is difficult to draw definitive conclusions about the prospects of a labour-managed economy. There is a suspicion in some quarters that the theoretical work (whether Ward's 'Illyrian firm' or Vanek's 'general theory') yields conclusions which, while analytically 'robust' and interesting in themselves, tell us comparatively little about the practicability of labour self-management (Elster and Moene, 1989a; Milenkovitch, 1984; Bonin and Fukuda, 1986). Some critics insist that this theoretical literature is positively misleading. In theory, enterprises under labour management would be more capital-intensive than their capitalist counterparts and more inclined to shed labour in response to success. In practice, co-operatives under capitalism are frequently under-funded and extremely reluctant to shed labour even under the most adverse circumstances. Of course, this may simply reflect quite understandable behavioural differences between a small number of co-operatives under capitalism and an economy of labour-managed enterprises. But there remains a suspicion that in practice the labour-managed economy would look quite different from these neo-classical projections and at least some commentators are persuaded that 'the more realistic the assumptions are, the more efficient the self-managed firm will be compared to its capitalist "twin"' (Mygind, 1986, p. 74). Whilst the body of *empirical* work is growing, it is still very limited and mostly drawn from the experience of co-operatives located in broadly capitalist economies. The relevence of this evidence for the behaviour of enterprises within a prevalently labour-managed economy with social ownership of capital is quite unclear. At the same time, evidence of the *macro*-economic consequences of labour management is largely confined to the extremely contentious case of the former Yugoslavia. Nonetheless, there are some rather qualified conclusions about labour self-management which I think we can legitimately draw.

First, the most apocalyptic judgements about the incapacity of workers to manage their own enterprises are rather poorly vindicated. Certainly, many new co-operatives fail to survive their first few years. But this is a fate which they share with fledgling small businesses of a more traditionally capitalist kind, and there is some evidence to suggest that their survival rate is at least as good as, if not rather better than, that of their capitalist counterparts (Estrin and Perotin, 1987, 167). Co-operatives may also be subject to internal dissent and vulnerable to fraud. But the last decade has shown corporate capitalism, especially under circumstances of financial deregulation, to have its own quite impressive catalogue of fraud, embezzlement and internal division. Controlling financial irregularities under labour management, as under capitalism, may depend upon company law, auditing practices and policing, rather than upon the incentive properties of ownership. In fact, the lengthy historical record of working-class mutualism, despite inevitable episodes of dishonesty, may be quite encouraging for those who advocate an extension of self-management.

Some encouragement for the supporters of self-management may also be found in the growing body of empirical material on co-operatives in developed Western economies. In his studies of the plywood industry in the north-western United States, Greenberg (1984) found evidence of higher productivity amongst co-operatives than their capitalist counterparts. In their survey of Mondragon in a period of recession, Bradley and Gelb (1986) found that the co-operative complex outperformed the surrounding capitalist economy in terms of pay, profitability and employment. In a comparative study of capitalist and co-operative enterprises in North Central Italy, Bartlett and his colleagues (1992), found that co-operatives not only had more egalitarian pay structures, more stable employment patterns and better industrial relations, they also consistently outperformed their capitalist counterparts in terms of productivity. Estrin, Jones and Svejnar (1987), found across a range of Western producer co-operatives evidence that worker participation has a positive effect upon productivity (see also Jones, 1985). Not all the evidence, however, is quite so encouraging for supporters of labour management. Berman and Berman (1989), for example, are rather more ambivalent than Greenberg about the record of the US plywood co-operatives. In the UK, Hobbs and Jefferis (1990) have challenged the scale and nature of expansion in the co-operative sector over the last decade. Nonetheless, I think we have sufficient evidence of the success of individual and interconnected co-operative ventures to refute the belief that the labour-managed enterprise is *necessarily* unstable.

A number of substantial problems remain, however, for the supporters of self-management. One is the tricky issue of political support. Many would accept the claim that there is amongst employees a (sometimes undisclosed) aspiration for greater self-direction. Yet there is also amongst the more thoughtful supporters of self-management a recognition that transformation to a labour-managed economy does not present itself to many people as a realizable or even an especially desirable political goal. Given Elster's logic of 'adaptive preferences', it may be that employees under capitalism would never express a preference for a labour-managed economy. It may also be that an incremental transition to labour management is impossible, because of the adverse circumstances that co-operatives face in a prevalently capitalist economic order.[10] Yet at the end of the twentieth century, surely no one will want to argue that the will of the majority ought to be set aside for the policy of an enlightened elite which knows where the majority's 'real' interests lie. The problem of political support and the politics of transition is addressed in chapter 8.

There is also quite clearly a range of economic problems in the structure of a labour-managed economy which remain unresolved. Some of these are technical questions which are best left to professional economists (though it is not clear that in this area economists, any more than political theorists, can be expected to reach an unambiguous consensus). In the face of a range of theoretical expectations about the labour-managed economy, it seems that much must turn upon empirical evidence and this, for reasons already discussed, is itself comparatively sparse and rather indeterminate. The precise consequences of labour management for productivity, employment, growth, savings, inflation and so on remain to some extent in doubt. Yet we have seen repeatedly that, important as these considerations certainly are, at the core of the case against labour management is an argument about the nature of ownership. Of course, virtually all market socialists allow of a more or less broad margin of private capitalist ownership on the fringes of their socialized economies, and most also retain a significant economic role for the state, if not as owner then as indicative planner or provider of last resort. Yet, it is clear that the defence of a distinctively 'social' form of ownership, that is, neither private nor state, is quite essential to the redemption of the market socialists' claim to be presenting a theory which is both radical and, indeed, socialist. At the same time, the consequences of social ownership lie at the heart of critics' condemnation of market socialism and we have seen these objections developed with particular vehemence in discussion of the labour-managed economy and the worker's co-operative. If the market socialists are to be able to defend their position, it seems clear that they need above all to furnish a compelling and workable definition of social ownership.

Social Ownership: Yugoslavia and Beyond

In the quest for a coherent definition of social ownership, it is perhaps natural to turn first to the theoretical tradition of Yugoslav self-management. After all, at the heart of the Yugoslav communists' self-definition lay the claim to have founded a new form of socialist regime based upon a new form of social property. In fact, Yugoslav sources are of some use in establishing what social ownership is *not*. Social ownership is said *not* to be a system of communal ownership, in which all of society's goods are available without exclusion to all citizens at all times. To this extent, it may escape the harshest judgements of those critics (from Aristotle to Demsetz), who have argued that what is available to all will tend to enjoy the stewardship of no one (Aristotle, 1946, p. 44; Demsetz, 1967).[11] Social property is also said *not* to be the same as state property. State ownership may (particularly in less developed societies) be an essential stage in the transition towards a more fully socialist form of ownership (Kardelj, 1979, p. 47). But it is consistently represented as a developmentally 'lower' form of socialism, required only in the earliest stages of the transition from capitalism and liable to degenerate (as in the Soviet Union) into a new species of domination in which an all-powerful bureaucracy commands the surplus labour of what remains 'a materially dependent and politically and ideologically subordinated . . . working class' (Djordjevic, 1966, pp. 79–80).[12]

Turning to the more positive task of establishing what social property *is* (rather than identifying what it is not), the Yugoslav doctrine of self-management is remarkably *un*helpful. The leading theorist Edvard Kardelj cites approvingly a number of passages in which Marx sought to distinguish the forms of social property which will succeed capitalism from the undifferentiated collectivism of an imagined 'primitive communism'. In *Capital*, for example, Marx insists that the regime which replaces the capitalist mode of appropriation 'does not re-establish private property for the producer but gives him [sic] individual property based . . . on co-operation and the possession in common of the land and of the means of production produced by labour itself' (Marx, 1973a). Yet the institutional form for this 'individual property based on co-operation' remains quite unclear. A number of Yugoslav commentators have insisted (following Marx, so they suggest) that social property is not so much 'a legal institution' (which might seem to require a rather precise definition), but rather 'a socio-economic relationship' (Caresvic, 1974, pp. 3–5). According to Kardelj, 'the form and substance of social ownership keeps changing'; it is 'an historical process', not a 'static social phenomenon' (1979, p. 47). The few substantive definitions of social property that we can find in this literature are themselves largely negative. In Djordjevic's account, social property defines 'not a property right but a form of *de-propertising* the means of production' (Djordjevic, 1966, p. 87), and much the same emphasis can be found in the Yugoslav Federal Constitution:

> Since *no one has the right of ownership of the social means of production*, no one – either the socio-political community, or the work organization or individual working men – may appropriate on any property-legal ground the product of social labour, or manage and dispose of the social means of production and labour (Constitution of the Socialist Federal Republic of Yugoslavia; quoted in Caresvic, 1974; emphasis amended)

In Kardelj's paraphrase, 'social ownership really means – in the positive sense of the term – nobody's and everybody's, that is collective and personal ownership' (Kardelj, 1979, p. 49). It is little wonder that Djordjevic rather coyly describes social property as 'semantically ambivalent', nor that Milenkovitch should dismiss it less charitably as 'vacuous' (Djordjevic, 1966, p. 83; Milenkovitch, 1971, p. 266).

Under these circumstances, it is unfortunate that contemporary Western advocates of market socialism should have had so little to say about the forms of social ownership. Saul Estrin (1989) broadly endorses the aspiration underpinning the Yugoslav conception of social ownership, where this is understood to describe a system in which 'the capital stock is owned collectively by the society and is merely administered by particular groups of workers': 'Workers are granted the right to use the capital, to extend it and to adapt it. They earn their incomes as the fruit of it. However, they do *not* own it, and are *not* permitted to sell it off or run it down' (Estrin, 1989, p. 173). Whilst the principle and intention of this division of the rights of ownership may be plain enough, Estrin's elaboration of the institutional forms in which it might be embedded and the consequences of these forms for the overall constitution of market socialism remain a little unclear. On the one hand, he is bitterly condemned by de Jasay for seeking to conceal the fact that, in practice, 'social ownership' can mean nothing other than 'nationalization' (de Jasay, 1990, pp. 19–20). Initially, this judgement appears to be countermanded by the leading role attributed in Estrin's model to a series of 'competing holding companies . . . whose primary task would be to manage social capital' and which, he judges, should, on balance, be under 'private ownership' (Estrin, 1989, pp. 186–90). But the picture is further clouded by Estrin's own subsequent suggestion that 'since the state has the task of creating the holding companies, it might choose to retain ownership itself' (1989, p. 192).

Other advocates of market socialism are similarly ambivalent on the question of ownership. Sometimes, John Roemer opts for a market socialism in which 'firms are publicly owned [and] the state has considerable control of the "commanding heights" of the economy' (Roemer, 1991, p. 562). At other times (Roemer, 1992a, 270–1), he seems to prefer a species of voucher-based market socialism in which all citizens would enjoy an individual though non-alienable stake in the profits of a country's largest corporations. Given his commitment to an economy of externally funded co-operatives, David Miller recognizes the importance of new investment capital and of the existence of a number of competing sources of funding, 'so that a cooperative can switch away from an investment agency that tries to dictate the terms of a loan in an unduly narrow way' (Miller, 1991, p. 412). But he is uncertain whether this capital is best furnished 'by a set of private banks or through a devolved system of public funding' and, in the end, he argues that, given the right institutional and legal regime, 'it might not make much difference . . . what formal system of ownership was adopted for the investment banks' (1991, p. 412).

This brief review of the meanings attaching to 'social ownership' suggests that it is a term which is, at best, 'semantically ambivalent' and theoretically underdeveloped. Critics of market socialism wish to go further and suggest that 'social property' is necessarily incoherent and institutionally unstable. But there are, I think, good reasons to pause before drawing such a damning conclusion. For there are a range of more general problems in the identification and legitimation of property regimes, not least with the contrasting case made out for existing forms of private property – and these may persuade us to see social property in a less uniformly unfavourable light.

The Claims of Private Ownership

We are all aware of the distance that may exist between ordinary language and the terminology of legal and academic discourse. This distinction appears to be peculiarly stark in the treatment of private property. Seemingly unproblematic beliefs about private property – above all, the claim that what is mine is mine, to be done with as I choose – appear deeply embedded in popular sentiment. Defenders of the status quo have always played upon these popular feelings with great skill, suggesting that even quite modest reforms represent a threat to the entire order of established property and deftly identifying the secure possession of the humble householder with the interests of corporate capital.[13] But the certainty which has often seemed to attach to popular perceptions of the claims of property contrasts sharply with the uncertainty of property claims in legal and academic discourse. Thus much of the mundane business of the lawcourts, in probate and family law, for example, is concerned with the adjudication of competing or contested property rights. At a more abstract level, the literature of jurisprudence and much classical and contemporary political theory is replete with contrasting claims about the nature and status of private property (Reeve, 1991; Macpherson, 1977b; Ryan, 1982 and 1984).

A brief consideration of even a small fraction of this theoretical literature is enough to cast serious doubt upon many of the grander claims made for private property. Indeed, even amongst its defenders, it is now almost commonplace to find long-cherished justifications of the private appropriation of property (on the basis of first occupancy or inheritance, for example) routinely dismissed. Thus, in his essay on *Property Rights*, Lawrence Becker (1977) sets out a case for the greatest-possible private property acquisition. Yet, in the course of this defence, he substantially rejects classical justifications of property title deriving from first occupancy or 'mixing one's labour' and insists that, in practice, his 'maximalist' regime of property (grounded in a desert-based labour theory), will need to be heavily qualified:

> Alienability and transmissibility rights may . . . have to be substantially revised to scale down ownership to life tenancies . . . Ownership of vital depletable resources (fossil fuels, fresh water, mineral deposits) may have to be restricted to the rights of income, transfer, and limited transmissibility, with management, use, and actual possession effectively under public control . . . Assuming that the preservation of a democratic political system is a moral necessity, new measures will have to be devised to limit accumulations [since existing arrangements] are not capable of preventing the accumulation of vast wealth . . . which confers political power in quantities sufficient to undermine the democratic ideal (Becker, 977, pp. 116–17)

This an impressive array of 'qualifications' to find in an account which sets out to give the greatest possible scope to the claims of private property.

In a much more expansive treatment, Jeremy Waldron (1988) sets out his own defence of *The Right to Private Property*.[14] Yet, whilst Waldron defends the claims of individually held private property over against those of collective or common property, he does so upon a basis which has very radical consequences for actually existing regimes of private property. He rejects that line of argument (which he traces from Locke to Nozick) which holds that the right of individuals to property derives from 'special rights' deriving from 'what they happen to have done or what has happened to them' (1988, p. 3). Locke's defence of private property on the basis of 'mixing one's labour', he argues, is 'incoherent', whilst Nozick's claims for historical entitlement are 'indefensible' (1988, pp. 252, 278). Ironically, what *can* be defended in Locke's account is 'a general right to subsistence', a right which places a powerful welfarist *limitation* upon any legitimate system of private property. In fact, Waldron prefers to defend the general claims of private property by following a line developed from Hegel, in which property-owning is seen as essential to the full personal and moral development of the individual. The possession of private property helps to foster qualities such as 'individual self-assertion, mutual recognition, the stability of the will, and the establishment of a proper sense of prudence and responsibility' (1988, pp. 377–8, 4). Since the right to private property is a *necessary* condition of fully human development, Waldron insists that it is a right which should not just confer a *liberty* for the individual to acquire property (if s/he is so fortunate) but also furnishes for the individual a legitimate *claim* upon the community's resources.[15] In his paraphrase of Hegel, 'everyone must have property'. It follows that 'Just as a right-based argument for free speech establishes a duty to see to it that everyone can speak freely, so a general-right-based argument for private property establishes a duty to see to it that everyone becomes a property-owner' (1988, p. 4).

So for Waldron, defence of the right to private property is anything but a defence of the status quo. The right of *everyone* to private property, allied to the general background right to subsistence, is likely to justify serious curtailment of some of the rights of existing property-holders, substantial redistribution of existing assets, an extensive role for the state in guaranteeing welfare and redistribution, further restrictions upon the rights of inheritance, a fairly frontal assault on the claims of corporate capital and at least the possibility of some form of citizen's basic income. Of course, Waldron's position is still decisively separated from that of the market socialists because of the latter's commitment to some form of non-private ownership.[16] Nonetheless, Waldron's argument does imperil much of the traditional private property case against market socialism, shifting some of the burden of disproof away from the rights of property and towards practical and/ or utilitarian issues.

The arguments mobilized in James Grunebaum's *Private Ownership* (1987) offer even more solace to the advocates of social ownership. Grunebaum's ambition is to establish 'which of the many possible forms of ownership is morally justifiable' (1987, p. 1). His strategy is to move from what he takes to be at least 'a plausible first principle of morality' – the Principle of Autonomy – and then to elaborate the sort of property regime which the operationalization of such a principle requires – that is, to establish the forms of Autonomous Ownership (1987, p. 170). At its simplest, the Principle of Autonomy holds that: 'Each person has an equal right to decide upon his own good and how to pursue it while respecting others' autonomy, and a right to the necessary means of acting autonomously while never violating that right in others' (1987, p. 143). In Grunebaum's judgement, the Principle of Autonomy requires a 'mixed' property regime 'which excludes both private ownership of land or resources and social ownership of self or labour' (1987, p. 170). Respect for individual autonomy requires that individuals should have the rights to use and manage their labour, the right to whatever income can be earned from this labour and the right to give or to exchange portions of this labour with others, implying the existence of a 'free labor market' (1987, pp. 171–2). In this sense, ownership of self and labour would be 'private'. These private rights would, however, be constrained by the fact that 'the autonomy principle requires that individuals help others who are in genuine need' and that this affords prior authority to meeting the 'basic needs' of all members of the community. At the same time, and having rejected all arguments for original private appropriation as 'question begging and incoherent', Grunebaum insists that:

> the autonomy principle requires ownership rules for the domain of land and resources which respects each person's right to decide upon his [*sic*] own good, how to pursue it and to possess the well-being needed for autonomy . . . It follows that forms of ownership which do not permit each person to participate in decisions about how land and resources are to be used are incompatible with the autonomy principle. (Grunebaum, 1987, p. 174)

He concludes that 'the autonomy principle morally requires that rights over land and resources should ultimately vest in all members of the community' (1987, p. 173).

Grunebaum describes this regime as lying 'between private ownership capitalism and state ownership socialism' (1987, p. 197). Yet it is clear from his own discussion that the 'private' ownership of self and labour only, in fact, rules out those forms of socialism which proscribe a labour market. Whilst Grunebaum makes no explicit reference to the writings of the market socialists, it seems clear that an economy which combines a market for labour (and other commodities) with a guaranteed social minimum plus the social ownership of capital comes very close to describing the sorts of institutional arrangements which his model of 'autonomous ownership' requires.

Perhaps most encouraging for the supporters of market socialism is the position adopted in Robert Dahl's essay *A Preface to Economic Democracy*. Here, Dahl proposes a frontal challenge to the claims of private ownership as these have become institutionalized under corporate capitalism. In he US, so Dahl argues, rights to private property had once served as the underpinning of what was (for white males at least) a Jeffersonian agrarian democratic republicanism. But towards the end of the nineteenth century, these rights were successfully (and 'amazingly') translated into a defence of the unqualified property claims of 'the revolutionary new order of corporate capitalism'. But Dahl doubts that there could be 'any reasoned justification for private property . . . that would also justify a claim to private ownership of enterprises in existing corporate form' (1985, pp. 72, 77). Dismissing by turns the arguments for a prior right of private property in Locke, Nozick, J. S. Mill and Becker, he concludes that:

> None . . . of the reasoned arguments for private property justify a right to the unlimited acquisition of private property. If anything, they would justify a right to a minimum collection of resources, particularly the resources necessary to life, liberty, the pursuit of happiness, the democratic process, and primary rights. (1985, p. 83)

'We cannot', he memorably insists, 'leap from my entitlement to secure possession of the shirt on my back or the cash in my pocket to a fundamental moral right to acquire shares in IBM and therewith the standard rights of ownership that shareholdings legally convey' (1985, p. 75).

Conclusion

Clearly, drawing attention to uncertainties in the specification of property falls some way short of a ringing endorsement of the principle of social ownership. But, in fact, bringing shades of grey into the seemingly monotone contrast between private and social property has some interesting consequences. First, regimes of 'mixed property' of the kind that the market socialists endorse look rather less eccentric. As the more thoughtful critics of market socialism recognize, unconstrained private ownership is in the real world 'almost a limiting case' (see Gray, 1992, p. 54).[17] In this real world, it is not difficult to find fairly standard cases in which the rights of ownership (rights of use, income, alienation, control and so on), are split between several parties (though not generally in the ways to which market socialists aspire). Again, the more thoughtful critics of market socialism have tended to defend market institutions in terms of their tendency to promote values such as individual freedom or autonomy, seeing economic efficiency and growth as the adventitious benefits of an independently justifiable property regime (Gray, 1992; Hayek, 1982). Yet we have seen that the link between freedom, autonomy, the right to private property and existing forms of the market are keenly contested. This may require, in turn, that more justificatory work is done by the broadly utilitarian arguments from economic efficiency and security of expectations (and these are probably the arguments that have carried the greatest weight in popular justifications of private property). These arguments may still be very formidable, but they are also radically *conditional*. If the argument for private property is in whatever form basically one from utility, it is always liable to be reconsidered in the light of some new and possibly better institutional arrangement.

If we are willing to allow that social ownership need not be summarily dismissed, we can recast the leading elements of its critics' condemnation as *operational* problems of market socialism. I want finally and very briefly to draw attention to three of these problems. First, can the anticipated economic and incentive problems arising from the absence of capital ownership *within* the co-operative enterprise be overcome without leading to a 'restoration of capitalism'? Secondly, can social ownership be organized in ways which make possible the rational allocation of capital? Thirdly, can 'social ownership' really be something other than 'state ownership'?

The essence of the first problem is that without workers having some sort of capital stake in the enterprise within which they work, there will be (dis)incentive problems which will unseat the rational allocation of economic resources. It may be that the best way to meet this objection is, in fact, by establishing just such a capital stake for individual workers. This is essentially the practice adopted by the Mondragon co-operators, who invest an initial capital sum upon joining the co-operative and who, in addition to drawing a wage, have assets annually credited to a capital account which, however, can only be drawn upon when they leave the co-operative (for a general model, see Ellerman, 1990). While this entitlement falls well short of Honoré's full liberal ownership (the accumulated assets are not alienable), it is clear that it entails a compromise of the principle of no return to capital (Honoré, 1961). Yet it seems to me that it is really a definitional sleight of hand to insist that this constitutes an irresistible half-way house leading to the restoration of capitalism, if we are to understand by capitalism something like the institutional arrangements which now prevail in developed Western countries. Since the rights of ownership (and analogously forms and levels of equality) lie upon a continuum, it does not make sense to suggest that any incidence of private capital ownership identifies what would otherwise be market socialism as a surrogate form of corporate capitalism.[18]

The further issues of the rational allocation of capital and the distinction between social and state ownership may be taken together. The essence of the first of these arguments is that there can only be a rational use of capital resources where there are *multiple* and competing sites of capital allocation. But this is seen to be impossible under market socialism because a regime of social ownership will always be found to relapse into monolithic ownership by the state. It is worth observing that the contrast between corporate capitalism and market socialism may not be just so straightforward as its critics suggest. First, it is clearly the case that, in those capitalist economies with which market socialism is unfavourably compared, the state already has a very substantial role in the allocation of capital. In part, this occurs through its fiscal, regional and labour market policies, through its policy on public expenditure and its role as a large purchaser of capital goods. Through its central banking institutions, the state may also play a much more direct role in determining the allocation of capital, dictating monetary policy, controlling interest rates and policing the private banking sector. At the same time, market socialism would not involve the concentration of all financial assets in the hands of the state. Market socialists are generally concerned with proscribing holdings of equity in labour-employing corporations. For the most part, they recognize that, through whatever financial institutions they may pass, private savings (paid a fixed or variable rate of interest) would be essential to the economic development of a market socialist economy. As is well known, many of the existing capital assets of developed capitalist societies are not directly owned by individual investors, but are held in pension funds or by institutions that manage the aggregated resources of very many comparatively small savers. This may suggest that the sorts of financial instruments available in a market socialist economy (including a variety of forms of financial partnership falling short of equity ownership) need not be so wholly different from the sorts of effective choices that now face the great majority of smaller asset holders.

Having entered these qualifications, it remains central to the critics' case that market socialism, having forbidden a market in private capital, cannot furnish the multiple sites of capital resources without which the rational allocation of capital is impossible. This, in turn, rests upon the supposition that social ownership represents, in practice, the concentration of capital ownership in a unitary or monolithic state. There is formidable historical evidence to support this claim, not least that drawn from the unhappy experience of Yugoslavia, and critics may also draw succour from the terms of much traditional socialist debate, in which the state has often been seen as a unitary and directive social force, the capture of which by progressive forces would allow it to become the instrument of socialist politics. But things are not quite so straightforward. First, we have seen that the idea of mixed regimes of property, in which certain rights to benefits might belong to the state and others to actors in civil society, is not necessarily so bizarre as many critics of market socialism have supposed. Secondly, it is unclear that the state has always been, in practice, just as unitary as some constitutional lawyers and Hobbesian and Weberian social theorists have imagined (see e.g. Mann, 1993). Indeed, Yugoslav experience shows not only the relentless intervention of the federal state in the socialist market, but just as clearly the attempts (sometimes successful) of political forces in the individual republics to subvert the will and investment policy of the national/federal government. Such contests between differing levels of governance are a common feature of other and more established federal systems (as, for example, in the US). It may even occur in as unitary and autocratic a political system as that of the United Kingdom (where during the 1980s the challenge was only effectively confronted by eliminating much of the apparatus of local government). This suggests that social ownership of a kind consonant with the aspirations of market socialists might be possible, but only if the state which must help to constitute it were reformed along more democratic and constitutional lines. Both the possibility and the necessity of such democratic reform under market socialism are more fully assessed in chapter 7.

7

Democracy and State under
Market Socialism

We have seen that it is one of the principal aspirations of the market socialists to be able to construct a workable system of social ownership which can achieve levels of economic efficiency similar to those of conventional advanced capitalist economies. At the same time, they are seeking an order which, while socialist, avoids those forms of tutelage to the state which have been identified as a debilitating feature of previous socialist regimes in both East and West. Many market socialists have argued that realizing both of these ambitions should also contribute to a major extension of democracy. In this chapter, we shall consider the validity of this final claim.

Despite the significance which many market socialists have attached to democratization, it is a process to which they have devoted surprisingly scant and unsystematic attention. Their rather diffuse discussion does, however, yield at least three characteristic claims about the capacity of market socialism to enhance the quality and quantity of democracy. First, and perhaps most significantly, an economy of workers' co-operatives promises a major expansion of opportunities for the practice of a more *participatory* form of democracy. A second and complementary claim is that under market socialism the quality of the *representative* democratic process should be greatly improved, above all, by eliminating the distorting political influence of private capital ownership. Thirdly, there is an expectation that the introduction of social ownership in a radically devolved form, with much of the work of economic co-ordination and innovation allocated to market mechanisms, will decisively curtail the overweening powers of the centralized state. I shall consider each of these claims and their consequences in turn.

The Co-operative Economy as Participatory Democracy

In practice, the case for labour management as a form of democratization has been most persuasively developed not by the market socialists themselves, but by those more immediately concerned with the
extension and deepening of democracy. Since the early 1980s, (and
before), there has been a remarkable renewal of interest in the idea of
democracy amongst Western political theorists, and for many of these
theorists, the watchword has been 'participation'.[1] Dissatisfied with the
complacencies and half-truths of Western representative democracy,
mindful of the theoretical and practical failures of the 'people's democracies' and often inspired by the flawed but innovative experience of
new social movements, this broad strand of contemporary democratic
thought has been driven by the conviction that democracy is not a 'once
and for all' achievement, (realized in the West and aspired to everywhere else). Rather, democracy is a promise still very partially fulfilled.
At the end of the twentieth century, these thinkers are understandably
circumspect about the extent to which more direct or participatory
forms of democracy should be seen as a *replacement* for representative
institutions. Nonetheless, they generally proceed from the belief that
within a 'mixed' democratic regime (of multi-sited democratic spaces,
embracing both representative and direct forms) participation should
be much more broadly encouraged. Gould is characteristic in calling
for decision-making to be 'participatory to the extent feasible, and
representative otherwise' (Gould, 1988, p. 25). At the same time, many
of these thinkers insist that it is now economic life which stands in
greatest need of democratization, and it is the economic realm which is
seen to offer the widest opportunities for the development of new and
more participatory forms of democratic life.[2]

Amongst the most influential texts in the evolution of this present
concern with participation in economic contexts was Carole Pateman's
Participation and Democratic Theory (1970). Drawing explicitly upon the
Yugoslav experience of self-management as well as the theory and
practice of industrial democracy in the West, Pateman rejected what
she saw as the excessively narrow understanding of 'practicable' democracy which had become the orthodoxy of contemporary US political science. It was only, she argued, by constructing a largely mythical
(and unworkable) model of 'classical democracy' that the architects of
this orthodoxy were able to defend their own contrasting and elitist
alternative as the best 'real-world' version of democracy. For Pateman,
a reading of some of the *real* classics of democratic thought (including
Rousseau, J. S. Mill and G. D. H. Cole), revealed by contrast a still very

relevant emphasis upon the educative and participatory imperatives of democracy. On this basis, Pateman called for the extension of democracy into economic decision-taking both as an end in itself and as a means of enhancing individuals' sense of political effectiveness and competence, enabling them to participate more fully in the wider realm of national political life. She was, in her own words, an advocate of 'a modern viable theory of democracy which retains the notion of participation at its heart' (1970, p. 111).

It is a tribute to the longevity and open-mindedness of at least some political theorists that in recent years the most articulate spokesperson for the kind of economic democratization which Pateman canvassed at the turn of the 1970s has been Robert Dahl, at the time one of those who had given most convincing expression to the prevailing pluralist orthodoxy.[3] Dahl's 1985 essay, *A Preface to Economic Democracy*, makes out a bold and encompassing general case for workplace democracy or, in his preferred usage, *self-governing enterprises*. Dahl's argument proceeds from a prior specification of those general circumstances in which people have a right to democratic government.[4] A democratic form of governance is justified, he argues, wherever there is an association whose members 'need to reach at least some collective decisions that will be binding on all the members of the collectivity'. Where such binding collective decisions have to be made, he maintains, they ought only to be made 'by persons who are subject to the decisions – that is, by members of the association'. He goes on to identify a number of further 'democratic assumptions' which should apply to such associations: *a principle of liberty*, under which 'each adult person in the association is entitled to be the final judge of his or her own interest'; *weak* and *strong principles of equality*, establishing that 'the good of each person is entitled to equal consideration' and that all persons 'are roughly equally well qualified to decide which matters do or do not require binding collective decisions'; and 'an elementary *principle of fairness*', under which 'in general, scarce and valued things should be fairly allocated'. Accepting these premises, so Dahl insists, establishes for 'all the adult members of the association . . . an inalienable right to govern themselves by the democratic process' (1985, pp. 56–8).

According to Dahl, such criteria are frequently (and rightly) used to justify democratic governance of the state. But he insists that the economic enterprise should also be understood as an association reaching collective decisions which are binding on all its members. Consequently, people involved in an economic enterprise have the same right as citizens of the state to govern themselves by the democratic process. His provocative conclusion is that '*If* democracy is justified in governing the state, then it must *also* be justified in governing economic enterprises; and to say that it is *not* justified in governing economic enterprises is to imply that it is not justified in governing the state' (1985, p. 111).

Dahl does not fully specify the institutional arrangements under which an enterprise-based democracy would operate. He certainly does not assume that all self-governing enterprises will become direct democracies, with all members of the *demos* participating in the making of every decision. He clearly anticipates a 'mixed' regime in which, whilst the *demos* is sovereign, it will only normally be involved in deciding on broad issues of *policy*. In all but the very smallest firms, it seems likely that employees 'would elect a governing board or council, which in the typical case would probably be delegated the authority to select and remove the top executives' (1985, p. 118; 1989, pp. 330–1). Dahl is cautious about the sorts of economic and political benefits that might follow from having a more participatory workplace democracy. He is insistent that self-government in the economic enterprise is in any case a *right*, and not to be judged in terms of its valued *consequences* (enhancing the political efficacy of the citizen at the level of the nation state, for example). Yet, it is clear that Dahl does believe that 'a system of economic enterprises collectively owned and democratically governed by all those who work in them' represents a major extension of the democratic principle (1985, p. 91).

A similar argument (proceeding from a participatory democratic principle to the self-management form), is developed in Carol Gould's *Rethinking Democracy* (1988). Gould's 'rethinking' of democracy is based upon the twin premises of *equal positive freedom* (or 'equal rights to the conditions of self-development') and *reciprocity* (requiring that in collective decision-making 'each participant not only permit the others to express their views and offer their judgements but take the others' views seriously into account in arriving at his or her own judgement'; 1988, pp. 88–90). This forms the basis for Gould's general 'principle of democracy', establishing that 'every person who engages in a common activity with others has an equal right to participate in making decisions concerning such activity [establishing a] right to participate [which] applies not only to the domain of politics but to social and economic activities as well' (1988, p. 84). Within the realm of collective economic production, 'this equal right of agency . . . is, in effect, the right to workers' self-management' (1988, p. 143). Under this workers' self-management,

> the workers in a firm would have the right to decide jointly on questions of the planning and organization of production or the provision of services and the right to determine jointly how the firm's income is to be distributed. [Whilst] one would expect that they would delegate various

functions to directors and managers whom they appoint . . . ultimate authority and decision-making power remains with all those who work in the firm. (1988, pp. 144–5)

In a further echo of the market socialist case, both Dahl and Gould insist that these workers' self-managed enterprises are to operate within the context of (reformed) *market* economies. Dahl is ambivalent (and apparently unconcerned) about whether the democratic order he proposes is to be called socialism or capitalism (1985, pp. 150–2). He does, however, insist that 'to achieve both democratic values and tolerable efficiency would require most firms – whatever their ownership – to possess considerable autonomy and to orient their activities toward the market'. Consequently, 'the only general form of a socialist economic order consistent with democracy and efficiency would be a relatively decentralized system of market socialism' (1989, p. 328). Similarly, for Gould, self-managed enterprises would operate in an environment where 'the market functions as the locus for the exchange of commodities [though] what is excluded here is the market between capital and labor' (Gould, 1988, p. 251). Once again echoing the market socialists, Gould insists that the vices which socialists have traditionally mis-attributed to the market belong elsewhere. For 'it is not the market as such that produces pernicious outcomes, but rather the social relations of property, in which control by some over the productive activity of others leads to domination and exploitation' (1988, p. 252). In the absence of a market for labour power, and with the property rights of capital suitably restricted, these problems should not generally arise (1988, pp. 178–85).

Self-management as the Extension of Democracy

The institutional details of the proposals made by Dahl and Gould need not concern us here (though, of course, whether workers' self-management can be given a *practicable* institutional form is an important question). Rather, I want to consider whether *in principle* a model along the lines indicated by Gould and Dahl could redeem the market socialist claim that enterprise self-management constitutes a significant expansion of democracy. In brief, I shall suggest that, if we accept that the enterprise should legitimately constitute a political community (a supposition that most neo-liberals would not allow), there are good grounds for endorsing the claim that, if feasible, workers' self-management would bring about a major extension of democracy.[5]

We can develop this claim in the light of the position taken by the Italian democratic theorist Noberto Bobbio (see especially Bobbio

(1987a and 1987b). Bobbio is very properly considered one of the most cautious and subtle critics of the possibilities of extending democracy. He has long defended the institutions of *representative* democracy against its critics on the left. He is particularly sceptical of the claims made for the extension of more direct forms of democracy and fiercely critical of the aspiration to 'the self-government of the producers' where this is seen as an alternative at the national level to 'the classic parliamentary state' (1987b, pp. 83–4). Yet the agenda of workers' self-management fits surprisingly well with Bobbio's own account of the appropriate forms for democratization. His argument is that, under present circumstances, 'an indicator of democratic progress . . . cannot be provided by the number of people who have the right to vote, but the number of contexts outside politics where the right to vote is exercised' (and where 'the vote' is a shorthand expression for the more general right to participate in the political process). In the present era, democratization is less about finding *new forms* of democracy than about exercising (largely traditional) democratic rights in *new places*. It requires a movement 'from the democratization of the state to the democratization of society'. Democracy is not a principle that should be applied at all times and in all places, but it is appropriate wherever there are 'great blocks of descending and hierarchical power'. In all complex societies, the two most important sites of such power are 'big business and public administration'. It is upon these areas, so Bobbio concludes, that 'the process of democratization' should be focused, and where, he argues, the democratic process 'has not even begun to scratch the surface' (1987a, pp. 55–7).

If at first sight a little surprising, the tacit support to be found for the Gould–Dahl thesis in the work of Noberto Bobbio is not perhaps, on reflection, so remarkable. All three represent rather differing strands of social democratic opinion. All three favour democratization of the more 'public' social institutions, in a continuing context of representative government and market economies at the societal level. The implicit support that we can find in Bobbio for this position also helps to highlight the fact that 'extending participation' need not mean a more direct democracy. Participation is very much a matter of degree. Even a representative democracy which does no more than allow its constituent population a vote every fourth or fifth year is, to this extent, participative. Gould and Dahl are quite clear that greater opportunities for participation are desirable and, indeed, a necessary element in the extension of democracy. There are several ways in which the organizational principles of a self-managed enterprise (with frequent meetings, the entitlement of all members to contribute to decision-making, members' direct involvement in the implementation of policy and so on), offer forms of direct democratic involvement which do not exist at the level of the liberal democratic state. But the promise of workers' self-management is principally one of enhanced participation, not of the elimination of representation.

There is, of course, a long-standing and venerable view, classically identified with Rousseau, that only direct democracy is *real* democracy and, to the extent that this view is accepted, the democratic bona fides of the partially representative institutions of workers' self-management (along with 99 per cent of all other institutions claiming to be democratic), will be rejected.[6] Perhaps more importantly, it also means that the structures of workers' self-management are much less vulnerable to those standard arguments (about cumbersome procedures and limited scale, lack of expertise, lack of time, lack of citizen interest and so on) which are typically levelled against the advocates of a 'pure' direct democracy.

Nonetheless, for those who favour enterprise self-management as a participatory form to be valued in a 'mixed' regime of more and less representative democratic spaces, a number of problems remain. Perhaps the simplest objection, and one that retraces its parentage to Michels's classic work on German social democracy (1962), is that politics in this more participatory mode simply will not work. In characteristically polemical style, and extrapolating from Yugoslav experience, John Gray insists that, within market socialist worker-co-operatives, 'the institutions and practices of self-management are diluted by the inevitable emergence of managerial elites and curtailed by frequent episodes of authoritarian intervention ... by central government' (1992, p. 49). Dahl, whilst recognizing that 'organizational imperatives create a thrust toward oligarchy', resists this kind of conclusion by distancing his own model from Yugoslav experience and insisting 'that Michels's "iron law" is neither iron nor law'. He supposes that 'it is not unreasonable to expect that democratic structures in governing the workplace would satisfy the criteria of the democratic process neither markedly worse nor markedly better than democratic structures in the government of the state' (Dahl, 1985, p. 134). This is perhaps a question that can only be definitively resolved by practical experience (though, of course, critics such as Gray may well insist that we have had all the experience we need). But lacking the evidence of extensive workers' self-management under the more propitious circumstances that Dahl anticipates, we may well feel a little less sanguine than he does about its prospects.

Even amongst those who are generally much more sympathetic to an expansion of democracy into the economic sphere, we can also find reservations about the dynamics of increased worker participation.

Perhaps the most familiar issue here is the political economy of time. Participation takes time and for the good democratic citizen or the good worker-citizen, the costs of participation may be high. Since enhanced political participation is generally understood to be a *right* rather than a *duty*, this need not present an insuperable problem. However, there is a danger that should *actual* rates of participation fall below a certain minimum, decision-making would effectively pass into the hands of a comparatively small part of the citizen population. This in turn might not be too damaging if the participant population was broadly similar in composition to the overall citizen population. But if the social composition of the activists were not generally the same as that of the wider population, decision-making power might in practice pass into the hands of an unrepresentative minority. In fact, we have plenty of evidence from existing political movements, as well as the experience of self-management in Yugoslavia, to suggest that the more active are not representative and would, indeed, tend to over-represent those with greater existing resources (financial, organizational and informational), and greater input into the existing decision-making process. It is a well-made point of the contemporary feminist literature on democracy (which still tends to favour more participative models) that it is women who have the least pre-existing resources and the greatest pressures upon their time (see Phillips, 1991). Without wholesale changes in attendant social practices (in child-rearing, the provision of informal social care, employment opportunities and so on), a model of open participation is in fact likely to be very unequally available to women. Yet the changes that would render possible this effective equal participation make the extension of democratic procedures to the workplace look like a modest incremental reform.

A less pressing, though still important, problem lies in the belief that participation requires the average citizen to be unduly virtuous. The Ancients may have held in contempt the man (for such he was) who preferred to attend to his private affairs rather than contribute to the good government of the *polis*. But we are probably (and rightly) not so sure. Even those of us who spend much of our professional or personal lives deeply embedded in the political process want to do other things as well. A *reasonable* democratic political order will surely not place such demands upon the time and energies of its citizens as to preclude all the many other and diverse things they wish to do nor make the costs of participation a deterrent to all but the most determined activist. Once again, the issue is not just that of *permitting* inactivity, for this is simply to deliver effective decision-making power into the hands of a self-selecting population of the most active. What is required is a system which not only makes possible participation but also ensures that the demands of participation are such that they may be met under normal circumstances by a reasonably conscientious citizen (on the political rights of the 'half-virtuous', see Walzer, 1970).

These arguments are sometimes conflated into an argument against more participative forms of democracy *per se*. Representative government with minimal participation is recommended as a way of ensuring that a presumed-to-be uninterested majority are not put upon by an active minority of participators (see Sartori, 1987). But it is surely curious to argue that we should avoid the possibility of domination by activists in a devolved democracy by abandoning the conduct of political business to national-level governing elites. This seems to be but one more recommendation to avoid the nuisance of the pole-cats by allowing ourselves to be devoured by lions.[7] To use a less felicitous analogy, however many 'little Hitlers' we encounter in our day-to-day lives, they do not leave us craving the real thing! In any case, the recommendations for workers' self-government we have considered here are an unusually poor target for this sort of criticism. As both Dahl and Gould make clear, participation is not an alternative to representation and levels of participation would be variable and related to questions of size, technology, and the founding will of the *demos* itself. Presumably those who wanted enhanced participation might be drawn to the more participative (perhaps smaller and/or more labour-intensive) organizations. Those who wanted the quiet life (at least so far as their work was concerned), might be drawn to those enterprises where decision-making was more extensively devolved upon management. These organizational differences need not preclude the *demos* being sovereign in both sets of circumstances.

A further difficulty with the participative mode, to which liberals have been particularly sensitive, is its perceived tendency to encourage consensus to petrify into conformism. This is a matter of degree. Some level of consensus (if nothing else about the rules of the democratic game and the limits of the *demos*), is probably indispensable to the democratic process. But liberals, at least, have seen one of the great strengths of (representative) democracy lying in its tolerance of legitimately differing values and interests. Nearly all the advocates of a more participative politics envisage the possibility of arriving at a much more consensual view of what is to be done. The suggestion is that with open-minded (and open-ended) discussion and a modicum of public-spiritedness, citizens should be able to find much greater areas of mutual agreement than has been possible under existing representative (and largely adversarial) institutions (see e.g. Barber, 1984, Dryzek, 1990). The danger identified here is of a politics which becomes *too* consensual. This is not a close relation of the traditional problem of an over-assertive majoritarianism. Rather, it is the sense that, particularly in small groups, there will be a pressure to reach (unanimous) agreement which may deprecate and indeed suppress what are perfectly proper disagreements about appropriate ends and means.[8]

This is a real problem and anyone who has been involved in the politics of social movements, old or new, will know that dissenters from 'the next step forward' are not always welcome. Yet it is not just so acute in the context of worker's self-management as critics might suppose. First, whilst there may be internal disagreements about the *ends* of the enterprise (for example, choosing to maximize profits or introduce a less alienating labour process), some of the basic parameters of policy will be externally set (if profits are not at least *adequate*, bankruptcy and dissolution will follow). Secondly, whilst primary political beliefs (about the ecological limits to production or positive discrimination in hiring practices, for example), may well impinge upon enterprise decisions, many of those abstract elements of ideology which are most fiercely contested in the national political process should impinge much less upon day-to-day decision-making in the workplace. Indeed, there is a sense that, where citizens are actively involved in real decision-making with the consequences of which they must live (thus facing real choices and real resource constraints), there should be less opportunity and less incentive for 'ideological grandstanding'. Thirdly, consensus is actually a much more valuable and appropriate quality within an enterprise than it is in national politics. We should probably hesitate to describe a national political system which did not institutionalize a permanently organized opposition as democratic. But while dissenting opinion in the enterprise should be sanctioned, we might well think that a permanently organized 'opposition' was not a desirable feature of a workplace democracy. Enterprise self-government would surely demand, in a way that national liberal democratic politics does not, that once a decision is properly arrived at, *all* should commit themselves to its successful implementation. Fourthly (and despite Dahl's comments on the 'compulsory' membership of the firm under corporate capitalism), we should envisage that under market socialism, given a greater commitment to sustain employment and promote the formation of new firms, 'exit' should be a realistic option for the disgruntled industrial citizen in a way which it is not for the dissatisfied citizen of the nation state. In sum, the prospect of 'too much consensus' may constitute a genuine problem for participative forms of democracy. However, its salience is quite limited under the envisaged circumstances of labour-managed enterprises, especially when we recall that self-management is presented as a mixture of direct and representative democratic forms.

A final and, I think, more intractable problem is the question of who are to be the citizens within an economy of worker-managed enterprises. Put more plainly, is there any way in which a system that relies so heavily upon workplace democracy can avoid giving political priority to the needs and interests of those who are active in the formal economy? There is a long-standing suspicion (retraceable at least to the writings of Beatrice Webb) that enterprise self-management will create workers' fiefdoms that are insensitive to the wider needs of consumers or the national economy. Can the needs of the nation and its citizens be best served, she wondered, by a reform that promises to give the 'sewers to the sewer-workers'? (cited in Beilharz, 1992, p. 64). In an age and, in the case of market socialism, a political theory which has lost faith in the Fabian imperative for planning and public administration, this is not perhaps the strongest argument against workers' self-management. If sewerage (or any other industrial service) is to be provided by independent enterprises (perhaps under contract to a municipal political authority), it will seem better to many socialists that it should be provided by a co-operative rather than by a conventional capitalist firm. Rather more telling is another of the reservations that has traditionally been voiced against syndicalism. This is the suspicion that workers' co-operatives will turn into a sort of workers' 'collective capitalism', in which the interests of workers in the formal economy will be privileged over against the interests of that growing number of citizens who for whatever reason (child-rearing, the provision of informal care, retirement, unemployment, participation in full-time education and so on) are not a part of the employed workforce. Market socialists might prefer a market economy where enterprises are owned and managed by their workers rather than by stockholders and their appointees. But it is not just pedantry which designates such an economy workers' capitalism rather than socialism. For, as far as those *outside* these enterprises are concerned, they might seem to be little different from more traditional capitalist corporations. A social theory which held that *all* of the population (except for a tiny exploiting minority) was being driven into the formal economy might be sanguine about the capacity of a workers' democracy to represent *all* the people. But this does not reflect actual changes in late twentieth-century labour markets. Female labour force participation has risen dramatically since the Second World War, yet, as Anne Phillips observes, 'men and women have a different relationship to work, and a different relationship to time, and *no version of democracy that rests its case on increased participation at work can be neutral between men and women'* (1991, p. 45; emphasis added; OECD, 1985). It is clear that there are other groups in the population who might also be marginalized in a democracy of workers' cooperatives.

In fact, this is a problem which is widely recognized by market socialists. John Roemer, for example, is insistent that in his blueprint of market socialism workers will not in any sense own the enterprises in which they work: 'labour will be hired on labour markets' and the profits of firms 'will be divided, after taxes, more or less equally among all adult citizens' (Roemer, 1992b, p. 453). For others (such as Saul Estrin, 1989), it is a problem that must be confronted by devising a form of social ownership which divides control over economic assets between the immediate producers and the wider community. Yet this carries us back onto the extremely difficult terrain of defining an adequate model of social ownership, a problem which, as we saw in chapter 6, is far from definitively resolved.

Despite the very differing criticisms of the advocates of more direct democracy (who find too little democratization in plans for enterprise self-management) and the neo-liberals (who find too much), I think it is reasonable to suggest that plans for worker self-management do at least in principle promise a significant enhancement of democracy. In Bobbio's usage, they aim to bring some well-established democratic procedures to bear in new places and to challenge the regime of 'descending and hierarchical power' that almost universally characterizes the governance of modern industrial enterprises. Many difficulties remain with this model, but these are eased to the extent that its projected form of participatory democracy does not recommend the workplace as the sole or privileged site of democratic participation and that it envisions a mixture of direct and representative democratic forms. But this last recommendation, and especially the weight it places upon representative democratic institutions, carries its own peculiar difficulties. To what extent has a more democratic governance within the workplace been bought by abandoning national government to unreformed liberal democratic procedures? Does greater participation within the workplace encourage greater involvement in national politics (as Pateman hoped), or dissipate the energies of active citizens in purely parochial affairs (as Dahl fears)? How should the democratic decisions of a sovereign enterprise citizenry be reconciled with the sovereign powers of national (and perhaps supra-national) authorities? It is to these questions of the nature of representative democratic government at the societal level, and its relationship to workplace democracy, that we must now turn.

Market Socialism and Representative Democracy

When we consider the importance of representative democratic institutions to the defence of an order of enterprise self-management and the potential difficulties of reconciling workplace democracy with the more traditional political institutions of liberal democracy, it is perhaps surprising that market socialists have not devoted more attention to the character of these wider representative democratic arrangements. In fact, the most prominent theme in the market socialist treatment of existing liberal democracies has concerned the ways in which reform, and especially the inauguration of social ownership, would change the circumstances in which an institutionally little-altered representative democracy could operate. It has long been argued that powerful organized economic interests in civil society tend to undermine the freedom of action of nominally 'sovereign' national governments, and for many classical commentators (both supporters and opponents), this has meant that a stable democratic society would have to be premised upon a regime of (comparative) social and economic equality. For more recent neo-liberals, this tendency was embodied in the capacity of organized labour to defy the will of democratically elected governments.[9] On the left, by contrast, it has been argued that the economic interests of capital (organized or not) will always predominate over the popular will represented by democratic governments. This is a commonplace of the Marxist critique of parliamentary socialism.[10] More recently, the claim has received support from a less likely quarter in the study of *Politics and Markets* by the American political scientist Charles Lindblom. Here, Lindblom adjusted his earlier endorsement of the pluralist model of representative democratic governance by arguing that, given its strategic importance to industrial performance (and thus to government's income and re-electability), business had a 'privileged position' in the politics of liberal democracy, a sort of 'veto power' over what democratically elected governments could and could not do (Lindblom, 1977, esp. pp. 174–5).

It is this power of private capital to distort or even to subvert the popular will expressed through representative democratic institutions that market socialists claim can be eliminated. To this extent, the greatest reform promised under market socialism is not so much an innovation as, in Habermasian parlance, a 'rectification', restoring the proper patterns of democratic authority and accountability which have been undermined by the power of vested private economic interests (Habermas, 1990b). Of course, this description does not at all detract from the importance of such a reform. Concerted private economic power does indeed constitute a major constraint upon democratic governments (one which, in the neo-liberal view, of course, is perfectly legitimate). Elimination of private capital and stock ownership would address this distortion in the most radical way possible. But the very radical nature of the reform proposed makes it peculiarly hard to envisage. In a global economy, what is there to prevent a devastating disinvestment in a polity which even contemplates the socialization of capital? (This is an issue in the politics of feasible transition to which we turn in chapter 8.) Even if we can imagine such a reform carried through, could we be sure that there would not be either (1) a concentration of economic power in particularly large, successful and/or strategic co-operatives giving them disproportionate leverage over national governments, or (2) an erosion of the independence of workplace democracies and increasing tutelage to an empowered state, precisely to prevent the very tendencies described under (1)?

In fact, and perhaps understandably, most market socialists have been so concerned with defending the *economic* rationality of their programmes that they have failed to carry the agenda of democratic reform much beyond the logic of 'rectification'. A partial exception is John Roemer. In his 'Blueprint for Market Socialism', he envisages a reform in which greater indirect collective control over the economic process is exercised through political parties incorporating more or less specific investment strategies into their electoral platforms. Once elected, a government would shape investment not by imperative planning but by imposing differential interest rates in differing industrial sectors and thus encouraging investment into the desired areas. Indeed, Roemer argues that 'by the adjustment of between five and twenty interest rates, the economy can realize the composition of investment that its planners aim to achieve' (1992b, p. 455). This is an ingenious scheme, but, once gain, it is hard to imagine the circumstances in which it would work, and even more difficult to envisage it functioning as a mechanism of increased popular accountability. Given the extreme volatility of interest rates in recent years, and the extent to which decisions about appropriate levels do not lie with national governments, it is hard to see that there could be any binding relationship between an investment strategy in a party manifesto and the conduct of government.[11]

Beyond 'Rectification': Deliberative and Discursive Democracy

A more substantial exception to the neglect of the *political* dimensions of market socialism is to be found in the work of David Miller, who devotes the final third of his influential study *Market, State, and Community* to the nature of state, democracy and citizenship under market socialism. Democratic market socialism cannot function at the societal level, Miller argues, in the absence of some sense of community. But traditional socialist evocations of the communal ideal are too unitary, too self-denying and too nostalgic to provide a workable model in an advanced industrial society. In fact, 'only a politically organized community can aspire to shape its own future and to distribute resources throughout its membership according to needs' and 'nations are the only form in which overall community can be realized in modern societies' (Miller, 1989, pp. 240, 245). Under these circumstances, the 'only viable form of society-wide community' is common *citizenship* in a nation state (1989, p. 16; see also Miller, 1988). In this invocation, citizenship involves membership of a particular nation state and entails the enjoyment of constitutionally specified ('protective', 'political' and 'welfare') rights (Miller, 1989, pp. 245–6). But 'authentic citizenship' also requires a very different political process and a much more active citizenry than we find under liberal democracy. Miller's account here is built around the contrast between politics as *interest-aggregation*, which he identifies with the largely passive citizenry and plebiscitary politics of existing liberal democracies, and politics as a form of *dialogue*, a political practice in which citizens seek to reach a reasoned consensus over matters of general concern through discussion and deliberation oriented around the common good. 'The deliberative ideal', as Miller describes it, 'starts from the premise that political preferences will conflict and that the purpose of democratic institutions must be to resolve this conflict. But it envisages this occurring through an open and uncoerced discussion of the issue at stake with the aim of arriving at an agreed judgement' (Miller, 1993, p. 75). In line with the advocates of greater democratic involvement that we have already considered, Miller's deliberative democracy places a premium upon active participation, and requires of the ordinary citizen both a greater capacity for reasoned discussion and a greater willingness to orient herself around common rather than personal interests. Politics in the dialogic mode does not exclude representation. Indeed, Miller's aspiration, as he describes it, is not the 'wholesale abolition of the present institutions of liberal democracy but rather a reshaping of those institutions in the light of a different regulative ideal' (1993, pp. 74–5). Even so, it seems that, to satisfy Miller's criteria, these reformed institutions would have to be quite different from those that we find in existing liberal democracies.

Miller is quite unusual in the detailed attention he has devoted to the forms that democracy should take *outside* the workplace under market socialism (see also Cohen, 1988). He has done a considerable service in plotting a reasoned path which avoids the twin dangers of world-historical wishful thinking and unrestrained opportunism. The greatest problem with his account lies in knowing what deliberative democratic institutions would actually look like and how they would work. In fact, Miller's account does contain some guidance on the constitutional arrangements of a deliberative democracy. He is quite explicit that 'in order both for citizenship to be practical and for the market to operate effectively, the socialist state must be formally constituted, internally differentiated, and limited in scope' (1989, p. 17). Above all this requires a 'constitutional state', in which there should be no Hobbesian sovereign, but rather a clear division of governmental powers, inscribed in a written constitution and upheld by a constitutional court. Simple majoritarianism should be qualified by the commitment to due process of law and by the constitutional protection of some forms of individual autonomy. Miller is a little less specific in describing the *institutional* framework for a market socialist deliberative democracy. He is clear that where there are democratic assemblies they should correspond to the general model of discursive or dialogic decision-taking. But, if a commitment to popular participation is to be reconciled with the belief that in the modern world, political community can only be constituted at the level of the nation state, there is a further need to define (1) appropriate forms of representation at the national level and (2) the relations between popular assemblies at differing levels of the political system. In the first case, Miller recommends the 'semi-mandating' of representatives from lower- to higher-level assemblies or the more radical short-cut of some form of sortition. The second problem may be addressed through the formal division of powers under the constitution and/or the commitment to mediation that is presumed to inhere in citizens' willingness to seek out and settle upon the greatest common good. Nonetheless, Miller recognizes that the conflicts between differing levels of governance could be severe and that much weight in practice would rest upon the existence of a widely accepted *culture* of discursive conflict resolution (1989, pp. 271–4, 198–9).

Miller does not set out to offer a fully specified model of a workable market socialist democratic polity and we should hardly expect him to deal with the constitutional niceties of reconciling, for example, the national direction of investment strategy with the self-government of workers' co-operatives. Nonetheless, there must be a suspicion that 'fleshing out' these institutional arrangements would prove extremely difficult. Instructive here is a comparison with John Dryzek's work on *Discursive Democracy* (1990). Despite some important differences, Dryzek shares with Miller a commitment to reconstitute democracy as a discursive process in which participant citizens come together to seek

a reasoned consensus about their collective conduct, motivated principally by the common good and allowing themselves to be persuaded
by 'the forceless force of the better argument'.[12] It is much more a part
of Dryzek's ambitions, however, to describe the ways in which this idea
of discursive democracy could be given an institutional form.

In this context, Dryzek discusses a number of 'pre-figurative' or
'incipient' *discursive designs* in which a discursive rationality is embodied. Dryzek sees discursive institutions anticipated in the conduct
of a range of new social movements and considers a small sample of
cases of 'mediation' and 'regulated negotiation' from within the public
policy experience of the United States (Dryzek, 1990, pp. 40–56). However, he sees the most promising terrain for discursive models in the
international field, where there is (for better or worse) no 'overarching
state or state analogue' to short-circuit the discursive negotiating process. He assesses a number of international environmental problems –
trans-boundary water resource disputes across the US–Canadian border and the global control of whaling – and identifies the *potential* for
resolving these through discursive negotiating procedures. Yet these
examples are not too encouraging. The Garrison water diversion dispute across the US–Canadian border reached 'impasse'. In the case of
international whaling, there is plenty of evidence that it is national
interests rather than 'the forceless force of the better argument' that
drives the policy process (Dryzek, 1990, pp. 90–108; Porter and Welsh
Brown, 1991, pp. 78–82). One does not have to be an unreconstructed
Hobbesian, nor an uncritical devotee of rational choice, to feel (perhaps
regretfully) a little less sanguine than Dryzek about the possibilities of
discursive institutions. In terms of our particular interest here (in the
institutional arrangements of a deliberative market socialist democracy), this highlights the problem of a lack of firm institutional guide-
lines for, and real-world examples of, a feasible discursive or
deliberative democracy. In practice, Dryzek's aspiration to give the
axioms of critical theory an institutional form is rather partially redeemed, and this is before we begin to consider the separate, and still
more intractable, problem of transition to such a discursive order.

Representative Democracy and 'Feasible' Reform?

This does not, however, exhaust the possibilities for reform. Recent
years have seen a remarkable renewal of interest throughout the political left in the possibility of radicalizing (rather than simply replacing)
the institutions of representative and liberal democracy.[13] Not all of this
work is easily reconciled with the aspirations of the market socialists.

Yet the two streams of thought are drawn together by their common roots in the profound crisis of the 'socialist project' discussed in part I. Thus, the re-evaluation of liberal democracy, like the new market socialism, issues, at least in part, from the exhaustion of 'actually existing socialisms' in East and West, from the declining confidence in the traditional discourses of socialism (especially of Marxism in all its myriad forms), and the seemingly ubiquitous failure of the state as an agent of economic planning and social reform. At the same time, in an epoch of historical defeats for socialist parties and organized labour, the language of rights, due process and limited government have seemed increasingly important as a way of *defending* what were once presumed to be impregnable historical gains. Where a monological *socialist idea* has lost not just its appeal but even its coherence, plurality and open-endedness are bound to seem newly attractive.

Amongst the most articulate and thoughtful spokespersons for this process of democratic renewal is David Beetham. 'The core meaning of democracy', he suggests, 'is the popular control of collective decision-making by equal citizens' and 'the key value in terms of which it can be promoted and justified is that of *autonomy*' (1993, p. 61; emphasis added). In promoting this democracy premised on autonomy, there are things of value in the 'paradoxical conjunction of liberal democracy'. Many of these elements are historical gains inherited from liberalism's struggle against the absolutist state, which no socialist version of democracy can afford to abandon. The most important of these are a commitment to individual freedoms (of expression, of movement, of association and so on); the institutional separation of governmental powers, due process and the rule of law; the institution of the representative assembly; a constitutionally limited state, a division between public and private spheres and 'the epistemological premise that there is no final truth about what is good for society'. He insists that 'one thing we have learned by the end of the twentieth century is that attempts to abolish these liberal features in the name of a more perfect democracy have only succeeded in undermining the democracy in whose name they were attacked'. But, at the same time, liberalism has acted historically as a major constraint upon the extension of democracy. In the years before the universalization of the franchise, this was often a struggle over who should enjoy the rights of full citizenship. More generally, it has been an argument about where the legitimate division between public and private spheres should be drawn, with feminists, for example, drawing attention to the ways in which inequalities within the 'private' domain of the family prejudice equality at the formally political level and socialists insisting that structures of private control over the economic process undermine the commitment to formal political equality. Given this ambiguity in liberalism's relationship to democracy, the delicate task facing reformers is to discover how and how far it is 'possible to carry the process of democratization, in the sense of both extending popular control and equalizing the conditions for its exercise, without undermining the conditions for democracy itself' (Beetham, 1993, pp. 56–7, 60).

One stratagem of reformers has been to press the case for a much fuller realization of the democratic elements within existing liberal democracies. The aspiration here is to make liberal democratic government deliver in terms of its own constitutional claims. In Britain, probably the best-known advocacy of such constitutional reform has been that organized around Charter 88 (reprinted in Andrews, 1991, pp. 207–11). This document, replete with appeals to the rule of law and the entrenchment of individual rights, wishes to see, inscribed in a written constitution, a Bill of Rights guaranteeing core civil liberties, a reform of the judiciary and the second chamber, greater control of the executive, a clear division of power between local, regional and national government, enhanced freedom of information and a reformed system of electoral representation. The Charter has not lacked intelligent and thoughtful critics on the left. Some have criticized its exclusive concern with the traditional roster of liberal political rights, to the exclusion of any consideration of economic and social rights. Others fear that, unless the radical inequalities of resources and opportunities in Britain are confronted directly, entrenched rights may simply deliver one more tool into the hands of powerful corporations (Andrews, pp. 205–64). In his turn, Paul Hirst is rather dismissive of movements such as Charter 88 having been successful 'precisely because they have confined themselves to advocating changes that would constitute existing representative democratic best practice' (Hirst, 1993b, p. 14). This last criticism, at least, seems rather harsh. The ambitions of the Charter are limited (presumably in an attempt to command the widest possible support), but in the context of Britain's pitiably inadequate constitutional settlement, the adoption of 'existing representative democratic best practice' would represent a huge step forward. What is most disappointing about the Charter is not, I think, what it proposes (unobjectionable as a minimum programme for large numbers of democratic reformers), but the seemingly marginal impact it has had (despite a great deal of spilt ink) upon the conduct of British government.

Others have sought to pursue the reform agenda with rather more radical intent. Beetham himself, whilst defending representative institutions, insists that these can be improved by instituting more effective control of the executive, ensuring more open government and making elected bodies more *truly* representative, through reforms which would equalize the value of all votes cast and increase the effective opportunity of ordinary citizens to stand for office. At the same time, he recommends changes that would moderate the differential influence upon government that derives from the unequal distribution of resources in civil society, 'limiting the scope that wealth gives to individuals and powerful corporations to purchase political influence through ownership of the media, sponsoring or "retaining" elected representatives, or financing election campaigns'. Less specific is his judgement that 'the electoral process could be extended to other institutions, private as well as public, local and neighbourhood as well as national and supranational'. As to what this might mean for an economy of private ownership, Beetham is a little ambivalent. As a democratic form, market socialism, he concedes, would be much less vulnerable to the criticism of liberals than, say, the traditional Soviet command economy. Nonetheless, given the onus upon the advocates of any socialist programme to provide 'a credible strategy for realizing [it] within the framework of liberal democratic institutions', he favours 'strategies of economic democratization that work with the grain of private property rather than against it'. This may mean opting for something like the Swedish model of wage earners' funds rather than market socialism's system of devolved social ownership (Beetham, 1993, pp. 64–5, 69).

Autonomy is again a key term in David Held's more extensive and ambitious attempt to forge a model of democracy that builds on the insights of both socialist and liberal traditions. Held also recognizes that there are indispensable elements in existing liberal democratic forms – among them, an 'impersonal' structure of public power, a written constitution and a bill of rights, the rule of law, representative electoral institutions and a competitive party system. But he suggests for many of these traditional elements a radically new content. Thus, for example, his 'system of rights' would include not only traditional civil liberties, but also 'a broad bundle of social rights linked to reproduction, childcare, health and education, as well as economic rights to ensure adequate economic and financial resources for democratic autonomy' (Held, 1987, p. 285). Similarly, 'the rule of law' would involve 'a central concern with distributional questions and matters of social justice'. It would entail not just a guarantee of 'formal equality before the law, but also that citizens would have the actual capacity (the health, skills and resources) to take advantage of opportunities before them' (1987, pp. 85–6).

Perhaps the most valuable democratic inheritance from the liberal tradition that Held identifies is the insistence that 'the "separation" of the state from civil society must be a central feature of any democratic political order' (1987, p. 281). The relationship between state and civil society has by now been voluminously described and re-described.[14] The essential insight here is that there should be an arena of public life that lies beyond, and is insulated from, the immediate control of the state and its institutions. Any attempt to collapse this distinction – and to bring all public life within the jurisdiction of the state – is likely to prove to be illiberal at best, and, at its worst, totalitarian. As Held recognizes, it is something of a fiction to speak of state and civil society as institutionally 'separated'. What is important is that the indispensability of both spheres should be recognized, and that along with a recognition of their functional interdependence there should be some constitutional guarantee of their mutual independence. However, Held insists that the aspiration to democratic autonomy can only be redeemed if the institutions of both the existing state and existing civil society are radically reconstituted. The problem, as he conceives it, is twofold:

> the structure of civil society (including private ownership of productive property, vast sexual and racial inequalities) ... does not create conditions for equal votes, effective participation, proper political understanding and equal control of the political agenda, while the structure of the liberal democratic state (including large, frequently unaccountable bureaucratic apparatuses, institutional dependence on the process of capital accumulation, political representatives preoccupied with their own re-election) does not create an organizational force which can adequately regulate 'civil' power centres. (1987, pp. 282–3)

This encourages Held to focus his attention upon a process of *double democratization*, in which both state and civil society are subject to a process of democratic renewal. I have already given some brief indication of the reforms envisaged at the level of the state. Within civil society, two reforms seem of particular importance. First, there is the requirement to equalize the opportunities for both men and women to exercise democratic autonomy. In fact, this provides an excellent example of the circumstances in which 'state and civil society must ... become the condition for each other's democratic development' (Held, 1989, p. 286). For, while such an equalization of opportunities for democratic involvement would clearly require fundamental reforms within civil society, it is clear that these could only be sustained with the benefit of certain guarantees from a reformed but interventionist state.

A second major transformation in civil society would involve curtailment of the powers of private capital. Here Held is quite emphatic: 'In order to create the conditions of political equality, the current distribution of material resources will have to be profoundly altered, [whilst] recognition of the necessity to minimize inequality in the ownership and control of the means of production is fundamental to the possibility of an open, unbiased political agenda' (1987, pp. 293–4). However, he is much more wary about the sorts of institutions that should replace private corporate control of the economy. Whilst neither state nor private ownership has proven very satisfactory, Held has a long list of concerns about co-operative alternatives. Nonetheless, he does endorse 'the strong case for democracy's extension to the sites of work and the corporate enterprise' and concedes, that, whatever its limitations in practice, 'co-operative forms of ownership . . . are likely to be far more compatible with democratic autonomy than either state or private ownership alone' (Held, 1991b, p. 884; Held, 1987, p. 294). Held's case in all these areas is summarized in his own model of 'liberal socialism'.

At present, the *institutional* arrangements of a deliberative or discursive democracy, and the account of possible transition to such a regime, seems too little developed to afford a compelling democratic model for market socialists. By contrast, and whilst far from conclusive, the juxtaposition of market socialism with the 'new liberal democracy' of theorists such as Beetham and Held is highly suggestive. In generating models of a mixed polity of more and less representative institutions and of an interventionist but constitutionally constrained state, these theorists are addressing the sorts of problems of democratization which market socialists have so far largely neglected. At the same time, they are clear that a commitment to democratic autonomy means transforming the patterns of ownership and control of productive property, whilst remaining rather ambivalent about the form this 'socialization of the economy' might take. This might offer an opening to market socialism but, given the reservations entered by both Beetham and Held, perhaps only where a number of other problems in the structure of the co-operative economy and the politics of transition to such a regime can be resolved.

Taming the Socialist State

The final element in the case for market socialism as a form of democratization is its promise to tame the leviathan state. Market socialists are surely right to see the over-extended and domineering state as a major source of the problems and unpopularity of traditional forms of socialism. Certainly, this case has, from time to time, been misrepresented and overstated. The welfare state form, for example, whilst widely attacked as bureaucratic and disciplinary, has under some circumstances been a major source of empowerment to ordinary citizens,

Held's model of liberal socialism or democratic autonomy

GUIDING PRINCIPLE

Individuals should be free and equal in the determination of the conditions of their own lives; that is, they should enjoy equal rights (and, accordingly, have equal obligations) in the specification of the framework which generates and limits the opportunities available to them, so long as they do not deploy this framework to negate the rights of others.

KEY FEATURES

State	*Civil society*
Principle of autonomy enshrined in constitution and bill of rights	Diversity of types of household and of sources of information, cultural institutions, consumer groups etc. (governed by principle of DP)
Parliamentary or congressional structure (organized around two chambers based on PR and SR respectively)	
Judicial system to include specialized forums to test interpretations of rights (SR)	Community services such as childcare, health centres, education, internally organized on principle of DP but with priorities set by users
Competitive party system (recast by public funding and DP)	Self-managed enterprises (nationally owned if vital industries, otherwise socially or collectively owned)
Central and local administrative services, internally organized according to principles of DP with a requirement to coordinate local user demands	A variety of private enterprises to help promote innovation and diversity

GENERAL CONDITIONS

Open availability of information to ensure informed decisions in all public affairs

Overall investment priorities set by government, but extensive market regulation of goods and labour

Minimization of unaccountable power centres in public and private life

Maintenance of institutional framework receptive to experiments with organizational forms

Collective responsibility for mundane tasks and reduction of routine labour to minimum

---

DP Direct participation of particular sets of citizens (involving open meetings, referenda and delegated representatives) in the regulation of an organization.

PR Election of representatives on the basis of a form of proportional representation.

SR Representatives chosen on the basis of statistical representation (that is, a sample of those who are statistically representative of key social categories including gender and race).

Source: Derived from Held (1987, pp. 290–1).

something of which they wanted and needed more, not less. Similarly, it may be a mistake to elide the experiences of 'socialism – East and West' into a single problematic of 'state-administered socialism'. It seems to me that the problems of state dominance in East and West have been qualitatively different, and, at the same time, that the problem of the domineering state in the West is not one that can be exclusively identified with socialist and social democratic forces. Having entered these caveats, it remains clear that the over-reliance amongst several strands of traditional socialism upon a state which has proved to be bureaucratic, intrusive, unresponsive to popular sentiment and, above all, ineffective has been immensely damaging.

These is also some reason to believe that a marketized form of socialism would drastically curtail the powers traditionally identified with the socialist state. Under a 'pure' market socialism, the state would abandon its economic role as the (public) owner of the means of production and as the immediate director of an economy-wide imperative planning. Its role as an employer and a supplier of goods and services would be greatly reduced, and the range of alternatives greatly enhanced. Correspondingly, the responsiveness of social and economic services to the final consumer should, in principle, be much improved. Combined with a formal constitutional order limiting the powers of public agencies and guaranteeing a body of justiciable rights to the citizenry, market socialism seems to promise a state which is more modest in size, ambition and lawful authority.

Amongst contemporary market socialists, no one has carried this logic of diminishing the direct authority of the state further than Julian Le Grand. As we saw in chapter 4, Le Grand envisages withdrawal of the state not only from direct management of the economy, but also from the provision (as opposed to the funding) of most traditional welfare services. Purchasing power, in the form of vouchers or earmarked credits, should be allocated to welfare clients (or their representatives), to buy services from non-public producers. State authorities (national and local) should be confined to funding services or where appropriate bulk-purchasing them on the public's behalf. They should not normally be involved in the *direct* production of any of these services (see Le Grand, 1989; Le Grand and Bartlett, 1993). However, most market socialists envisage a much more substantial continuing role for the state. Indeed, so extensive is the role of the state in Alec Nove's feasible socialism that some commentators deny that he is appropriately described as a market socialist at all (see Martell, 1992). Amongst many of those who would more severely curtail the state's involvement in the productive economy, there is still a reluctance to diminish the state's role in welfare provision. Indeed, some would wish to see services such as health and education *more* effectively insulated from market criteria (see Selucky, 1979). It is important, then, that we should not exaggerate the extent to which market socialism means a withdrawal of the powers of the state. It certainly involves a state which is qualitatively different from the old Soviet model and one whose interventions might be quite different from those of the traditional social democratic welfare state. However, it is not clear that there would be a lot less state under market socialism than under current social democratic regimes. Even Le Grand, who recommends such a reduced role for the state in the production of goods and services, is only able to defend his model, as a form of equitable market *socialism*, by insisting upon the imperative of the state being involved in a substantial and prior redistribution of primary income. In addition, there is the uncertainty, to which we have seen neo-liberal critics return again and again, about the plausibility of a new form of social ownership that is not, in the last instance, a surrogate for ownership by the state.

Is there, then, any way in which a market socialist order might deliver a more wholesale reduction in the powers of the state? One possibility would be to look to another initiative on the left, that is, the advocacy of a form of *associative democracy*.[15] In Paul Hirst's interpretation, associative democracy is seen as an effective response to the impasse of left-of-centre politics which was described in part I. In fact, Hirst understands the contemporary context as one defined by the exhaustion not only of collectivistic state socialism but also liberal democratic capitalism, and he is much less persuaded than are the market socialists that a progressive politics under present circumstances can be reconstructed around an enhanced role for markets. In seeking a new way forward, he prefers to look back to a period before socialist politics had attached itself (so disastrously, as it now seems) to the mechanisms of state authority and more specifically to a revival of the principles of associationalism, 'the most neglected of the great nineteenth-century doctrines of social organization' (Hirst, 1993a, p. 112). In essence, associationalism is a doctrine which holds 'that individual liberty and human welfare are both best served when as many of the affairs of society as possible are managed by voluntary and democratically self-governing associations. It gives priority to freedom in its scale of values [but] contends that freedom can only be pursued effectively by the majority of persons if they are both enabled and supported by society in joining with their fellows in voluntary associations in order to do so' (Hirst, 1993b, p. 24). The main political objective of a revived associationalism is to decentralize and devolve as much of the affairs of society as possible to publicly funded but voluntary and self-governing associations. Under associationalism, a self-governing civil society becomes primary, and the state becomes a secondary (if vitally necessary) public power that ensures peace between associations, protects the rights of individuals and provides the mechanisms of public finance whereby a substantial part of the activities of associations are funded. The activities of the state, central and local, are thus greatly reduced in scope . . . public provision is not reduced, but the form in which it is provided ceases to be directly administered by the state. (Hirst, 1993a, p. 117)

The expectation is that, under associational democracy, 'voluntary self-governing associations gradually and progressively become the primary means of democratic governance of economic and social affairs . . . that power should as far as possible be distributed to distinct domains of authority . . . and that administration within such domains should be devolved to the lowest level consistent with the effective government of the affairs in question' (Hirst, 1993b, p. 20). *L'état providédent* would give way to *l'état régulateur*. As the tasks of the state were drastically reduced, so it might be expected to perform its remaining functions much more effectively.

The associationalist argument deserves serious consideration in its own right. Here, however, I want simply to consider what if anything it might offer for a market socialist account of a tamed state. Since associative democracy is presented by Hirst as an *alternative* to market socialism (amongst other things), it is perhaps not very surprising that the associative model of an attenuated state is not easily transferred into a market socialist regime. Associationalism may offer many useful lessons to market socialists in terms of the co-ordination of voluntarism, self-activity in civil society, the constitutional restraint of the state, the operationalization of subsidiarity and so on. Yet it is hard to see the associative state as a suitable model for a doctrine which promises to institute social ownership and to institutionalize substantial redistribution of income on the basis of a community understood to operate through citizenship at the level of the nation state. Indeed, it is hard to see that the *minimized* state would actually be equal to the reduced agenda it is required to fulfil under associative democracy. The possibility of such a state regime rests, I think, upon a belief that civil society would spontaneously create a combination of voluntary associations that were mutually tolerating (and whose distribution of resources was, in some acceptable sense, equitable), as well as the willingness to provide, in an agreed way, the substantial public funds needed for the underwriting of voluntary self-activity (plus the meeting of statutory welfare minima). This is before we consider the question of how *transition* to such an order might be made possible.

This need not, however, be a matter for too much regret. So much attention has been focused (and understandably) upon the bullying, ogrish, enervating presence of the modern state, that we may have forgotten that civil society is not all sweetness and light. It may be that, recognizing these imperfections in civil society, we are still willing to embrace them rather than allow space to the greater evil of the extended state. But it is difficult to see how a politics which even begins to promise to address systematic inequalities of resources and opportunities in civil society can take this line. No traditional statists, Laclau and Mouffe, in an uncharacteristically plain-speaking moment, insist that in the case of feminist struggle, 'the state is an important means for effecting an advance frequently *against* civil society' (Laclau and Mouffe, 1985, pp. 179–80). We are, I believe, inevitably driven back to David Held's central insight, that for any politics with transformative intent, the reform process must be one of *double democratization*, in which 'state and civil society . . . become the condition for each other's democratic development' (Held, 1987, p. 286). As the discussion thus far should have made clear, this does not at all imply that we should accept the necessity for the state, just as presently constituted. In Britain, above all, the case for reform is overwhelming and here, as Hirst presciently notes, 'constitutional reform and political reform of the main institutions of central government is the pre-condition for *any* form of radical politics' (Hirst, 1993b, p. 40). But if this radical politics is to be the advocacy of a form of market socialism, it seems clear that there will be a very substantial continuing role for the state.

Conclusion

It is perhaps the fact that so many of its advocates have a background in economics rather than political science which explains why the claims of market socialism as a form of democratization have been subject to comparative neglect. This is unfortunate because, as we have seen, by combining market socialist principles with elements drawn from other contemporary accounts of democracy, it is possible to construct a plausible case for market socialism as a sponsor of democratization. We began the chapter by identifying three core claims made about democratic arrangements under market socialism – claims about the extension of participation, the checking of the powers of private capital and the taming of the interventionist state. None of these can be straightforwardly affirmed. Certainly, participation in the workplace is likely to be limited, the neutering of capital hard to envisage and the checking of the powers of the state quite limited. Nonetheless, as a form of mixed democratic regime, combining elements of a reformed liberal democracy with qualified workplace self-government, market socialism does promise, at least in principle, an enhancement of democracy within both state and economy. Indeed, we may feel that market socialism is on rather firmer ground as a political theory of democratization than as an economic theory of socialization. Yet none of this represents much of an advance unless we can deal with the still more vexatious question of the politics of transition. It is to this issue that we turn in the final chapter.

8

Feasible Socialism?

For many of its advocates, the clinching argument in favour of market socialism (said to offset many of its theoretical imperfections and potential inconsistencies) is its promise of enhanced *feasibility*. It is widely accepted that a society operating under market socialism would be far from comprehensively transformed. According to James Yunker, the differences between pragmatic market socialism and capitalism are 'in the larger scheme of economic mechanisms and human affairs . . . so minor as to be almost negligible' (1992, p. 13). Writing of his own model, John Roemer (1991) concedes that the distribution of income under market socialism will continue to be unjust and that market imperatives will tend to encourage the selfish and rivalrous rather than the communal and co-operative features of human nature. Even David Miller, whose view of the compatibility of markets with traditional socialist aims is unusually sanguine, concedes that a marketized form of socialism will mean retrenchment on at least two 'basic socialist goals': the conscious direction of social activities towards common purposes and the promotion of an enlarged sphere of co-operative action (Miller, 1991, p. 406). Yet for virtually all the market socialists what is lost in the *scope* and *purity* of the socialist agenda is more than outweighed by the enhanced *feasibility* that market socialism promises. According to Alec Nove, it is characteristic of 'feasible socialism' that it should describe 'a state of affairs which could exist in some major part of the developed world within the lifetime of a child already conceived, without our having to make or accept implausible or far-fetched assumptions about society, human beings and the economy' (1991, p. 209).

This view of what constitutes a *realizable* socialist agenda clearly owes something to the lived experience of what was 'actually existing socialism' and to the traditional conservative expectation that any attempt wholly to reconstitute society in line with the dictates of Reason prefaces the descent into dystopia. But it owes much more to the belief that practical-minded socialists, starting from where we are now, should not aspire to see the world 'turned upside down', but rather incrementally improved. The reforms that the market socialists envisage may be partial (and for some at least they represent a first step in some much longer process of transition), but they are significant and worthwhile. In addition, it is argued that the more modest are these proposals for reform, the greater are their chances of success.[1] If market socialism is self-consciously less heroic than its traditional forerunners, it is at least, so its advocates insist, 'a workable, feasible sort of socialism' (Nove, 1983, p. ix).

It is this assertion, that market socialism is, above all, a *feasible* sort of socialism, that I want to investigate in this final chapter. We need at the outset to be clear about what this claim to feasibility might mean and, in this context, two senses are of particular importance. First, in response to the perceived weaknesses of traditional forms of a planned economy, there has been an attempt to construct a plausible theoretical model of an economy which would combine markets with social ownership while satisfying certain conventional criteria and standards of evidence derived from a largely neo-classical economics. Here the question is whether or not market socialism provides a model of a socialized market economy that 'works' in theory and according to these standard economic criteria (especially in terms of its perceived efficiency). Much of the discussion in earlier chapters has concerned the development of this model and its plausibility. In the absence of more empirical evidence, and given the very serious disagreements about the conceptual status of the model, it is perhaps best to describe claims to feasibility in this respect as contested but defendable.[2] There is, however, a second, rather broader and still more important aspect of feasibility which is at issue here. For it is clear that market socialism is recommended above all else as the core element in a *political strategy* around which left-of-centre social and political forces could be mobilized. Indeed, as we have seen, one reason for celebrating the 'modesty' of the market socialist agenda is the belief that it is this very moderation which makes it viable as a programme for increasingly beleaguered socialist forces. It is recommended as a socialist programme not for starry-eyed dreamers, but for hard-headed and practical politicians in an era of historic reverses. In this sense, market socialism is feasible socialism because it presents the possibility of prosecuting a socialist political project under existing and seemingly rather unpromising circumstances. It was, after all, this promise (of offering a distinctive socialist project under circumstances where the prevailing twentieth-century forms of socialist practice are held to have failed) that has justified our directing so much attention to the market socialist model.

It is that second sense of feasibility that I want to investigate in this final chapter; and since the 'hard case' for the advocacy of any feasible socialism has always seemed to lie in its account of systemic change, it is upon the process of *transition* to market socialism that I concentrate. In particular, I want to consider the extent to which this account of transition overcomes difficulties which are seen to have blocked the path of more traditional 'roads to socialism' in developed capitalist societies. I begin by considering the market socialists' own account of this transitional process.

The Transition to Market Socialism

Given my specific interest in forms of advocacy of market socialism as a political strategy in the developed West, I confine my consideration of accounts of the transition process to this context. In so doing, it is only fair to point out that many contemporary market socialists see this as the *least* promising ground for such reform in the contemporary world order. We know that earlier forms of market socialism were recommended as a remedy for the defects of pre-existing socialist regimes in the former Soviet bloc (see pp. 82–3 above; Nove, 1983 and 1991). Some commentators have presented contemporary market socialism as an alternative form of market economy for the transformed states of Eastern Europe or, indeed, for China or even Cuba (see Roemer, 1994, p. 122). As in the 'old' Eastern Europe, it is recommended as a way of reforming already-existing social ownership without collapsing into an unmediated form of *laissez-faire* market capitalism. Within the presently capitalist world, John Roemer argues that market socialism may have some chance as a reform trajectory for those developing countries under authoritarian regimes which have so far failed to deliver adequate improvements in the living standards of their working-class and peasant populations.[3] It is less likely to be taken up as an option in the more successful developing capitalist countries (such as Korea and Taiwan). It is *least* likely to appeal under advanced democratic capitalism (in Western Europe, North America and Australasia), where private property relations are most deeply entrenched and where it is more probable that advances will be secured with 'social democratic concessions' rather than the 'nationalization of private assets' (Roemer, 1994, p. 122). (Of course, this perspective will not be especially encouraging for those who have turned to market socialism as a strategy for advanced capitalist societies precisely because of their sense that traditional social democratic political strategies are 'exhausted'.[4]) We should recognize, then, that we are considering the prospects for a transition to market socialism on what many (but not all) of its own advocates consider to be its least promising terrain.

Nonetheless, it is remarkable that market socialists, for whom feasibility is their model's trump card, should have had so very little to say about the trajectory of reform under advanced capitalism. David Miller shows a keen awareness of this problem, noting that 'the major difficulty lies not in the system itself but in finding a path of transition to such an economy' (1991, p. 414). But Miller's own *Market, State, and Community* is predominantly and explicitly a *theoretical* investigation of the foundations of market socialism. Where he does (briefly) comment on the mechanisms of transition, he seems to understand it as a gradual process in which sympathetic governments would support various schemes of profit-sharing and co-determination, enabling workers to buy out their own firms or to form new co-operatives. Any government would, however, face acute difficulties in pursuing this agenda in the wider context of a prevalently capitalist global economy. Miller concludes, rather cautiously:

> Increasing international cooperation may work in favour of such a transition . . . if there continues to be domestic support for greater economic equality and a more participatory style of work organization. But the path will be a long one, and we ought to think of market socialism as a guiding ideal, not as a platform for the next election. (1991, p. 414)

Alec Nove (1983 and 1991), is much more explicitly concerned to lay out the context in which the transition to a 'feasible sort of socialism' would be possible. Yet his commentary on the process of transition in the developed capitalist West is largely confined to a criticism of more traditional socialist strategies for nationalization and for the redistribution of wealth. Of the political process (and bases of support) through which a feasible socialism of the kind he envisages could be realized, he says next to nothing. He insists that 'the danger one foresees is not of a vote to "restore capitalism" ' (Nove, 1991, p. 247). But the prior problem of the political and institutional support which might make it possible to 'vote in socialism' is simply not addressed.[5] Le Grand and Estrin's edited collection of essays on *Market Socialism* (1989) is similarly thin on accounts of the transition process. Perhaps the most substantial discussion comes in Saul Estrin's own essay on 'Workers'

Co-operatives' (1989). Here Estrin considers the differing ways in which social ownership might be introduced. In its most radical variant, he indicates that the socialization of ownership would require the enactment of mandatory workers' control of all productive firms above a certain size and the conversion of all existing equity into interest-earning debenture stock, to be managed by a number of competing state-owned holding companies (Estrin, 1989, pp. 191–2). But this slightly improbable political scenario is itself based upon the prior (and rather grand) assumption that 'a market socialist government [had been] elected to office, with an unambiguous mandate to transform relations in the production sphere' (1989, p. 191).

A notable exception to the reluctance to engage directly with the mechanics of systemic change can be found in James Yunker's *Socialism Revised and Modernized* (1992), which concludes with a prospectus for transition to market socialism in the United States (surely the definitive 'hard case'!). Whilst pragmatism is an organizing theme of Yunker's economic model of market socialism, this can hardly be extended to his account of the process of political change. He insists that 'the campaign toward pragmatic market socialism would basically be a campaign of enlightenment against the force of entrenched ignorance and prejudice.' He envisages this 'enlightenment campaign' being mobilized by 'a special interest group whose central purpose is the achievement of pragmatic market socialism. A tentative name for the group might be the Pragmatic Progress Society'. He continues:

> It would probably be advisable for the Pragmatic Progress Society to prepare draft legislation at a very early stage. A possible title for the draft legislation to establish pragmatic market socialism would be 'An Act for Economic Justice'. The act would outline exceptions to socialization, specify a procedure and timetable for socialization, establish the Bureau of Public Ownership, specify the extent and limitations of the BPO's authority, provide for social dividend distribution of capital property return earned by large-scale, established corporations, and deal with a variety of subsidiary issues such as foreign ownership. (1992, p. 280)

This exemplary legislation 'will enable relatively smooth and rapid implementation of pragmatic market socialism once sufficient political support for the transition has been achieved' (1992, p. 280). Yunker gives some consideration to the (rather ambivalent) support that such a programme might find among professional economists, but not to the (surely extremely improbable) possibility of its being endorsed by, for example, organized labour, newer social movements or even the Democratic Party. If anything, his anticipations of the prognoses for market socialism and its consequences on a global scale are even more ambitious (and speculative).[6] Yunker is a professional economist, who develops his account of a pragmatic market socialist economy with great care and attention to practical detail. It is perhaps unfair to expect him to develop a similar account of the *politics* of transition. Nonetheless, this is an extraordinarily unconvincing exposition of the politics of social change which leaps back over two centuries of organized political action and the almost unanimous judgement of the political science community, to assert the transformative power of sheer moral suasion. Yunker shows considerable courage in his willingness to 'bite the bullet' and offer a prospective account of the transition to market socialism. But his account surely lies towards the 'utopian' rather than the 'pragmatic' pole of political strategy-making.

The Transition to Market Socialism Assessed

For the most part, then, we find contemporary market socialists operating with an extremely sketchy account of the politics of systemic change. Yet this very sketchiness tells us something about the way in which the process of transition under the circumstances of advanced capitalism is understood. We have already seen that the Western market socialists do not claim to be innovators in their account of the *aims* of socialism (see above, p. 85). To this, we should now add that they do not generally wish to offer an innovative account of the *means* through which their distinctive brand of socialism may be inaugurated. Substantially, they endorse the traditional social democratic view of the imperative of following 'the parliamentary-democratic road to socialism'. Certainly, some market socialists advocate significant constitutional reform within particular advanced capitalist polities and some at least see the co-operative enterprise as the site of new forms of democratic self-determination. Yet, however much institutional innovation they may welcome in the future, they are broadly committed to the introduction of market socialist reforms *within* the existing constitutional order. Under the circumstances of advanced liberal-democratic capitalism, revolution (understood as the enforcement of rapid and extra-constitutional change) is seen to be both undesirable and infeasible.

It follows from this, that the market socialist agenda, however radical in intent, will have to be realised gradually and that it will be subject to revision, and even reversal, in response to the duly-constituted will of democratic publics.[7] In this context, market socialism is best understood as expressing the programmatic intention of a socialist party which will seek to gain office and to implement its legislative programme through the institutions of an actually existing liberal democratic state. What distinguishes market socialism from more traditional forms of social democracy cannot then be its account of the transitional process. It is rather the claim that market socialism will have a wider electoral appeal and sustain an efficient and effective economy under circumstances in which the old social democratic agenda of 'Keynesianism plus the welfare state' and the electoral constituency upon which this relied can no longer deliver. What distinguishes market socialism from a more orthodox social democracy (if anything does), is the content of its reform agenda and the potential bases of its political support, *not* the political mechanisms through which this may be realized. But if this is the case, we are bound to enquire whether market socialism really does offer the possibility of a transitional politics which avoids the weaknesses which are widely thought to have halted more traditional social democracy in its tracks.

Market Socialists and the Dilemmas of Electoral Socialism

For just so long as socialism has been identified as the long-term political *aim* of the organized working class (certainly for more than a hundred years), there have been violent disagreements about the legitimate *means* through which this social transformation could be effected. The schism that divided the left in early twentieth-century Europe, for example, is often seen to have expressed above all a disagreement about appropriate *forms of transition* to a prospective socialist destination whose desirability was much less keenly contested.[8] The shorthand in which this dispute is reduced to a confrontation between 'reform or revolution' can be rather misleading. Yet it is important to note that in terms of this division both market socialism and more traditional forms of social democracy belong within that same reformist tendency which has favoured the promotion of socialist goals through the medium of existing constitutional arrangements. Properly understood, contemporary market socialism is more or less uniformly a species of electoral socialism. The issue for us is whether or not it is a form of electoral socialism whose prospects are brighter than those of more traditional social democracy.

Any discussion of the prognoses for electoral forms of socialism, including market socialism, is bound to begin with a consideration of the authoritative work of Adam Przeworski (Przeworski, 1977, 1980 and 1985; Przeworski and Sprague, 1986; Przeworski and Wallerstein, 1988; Przeworski, 1991). In a succession of elegant and economical essays published through the 1980s, Przeworski set out, with considerable analytical rigour, a general argument against the possibility of following an electoral route into socialism. Przeworski's case is developed in terms of a set of strategic dilemmas which have confronted socialists and social democrats operating on the terrain of democratic capitalism. Historically, socialists are said to have faced three strategic questions: whether to work for the advancement of socialism within or outside of the existing institutions of capitalist society; whether to rely exclusively upon the political backing of the working class or to seek multi- or even non-class support; and whether to press for reform of the existing social order or to dedicate all efforts and energies to the complete abolition of capitalism (Przeworski, 1985, p. 3). Przeworski argues that the structure of capitalism and the rules of the democratic game have driven socialists down the social democratic road, resolving these strategic dilemmas in favour of electoral participation, support beyond the working class and the pursuit of immediate reforms within the existing system. But whilst leaders of the worker's movement had little choice but to participate ('electoral abstention has never been a feasible option for political parties of workers'), this participation is subject to a peculiar paradox: 'Participation in electoral politics is necessary if the movement for socialism is to find mass support among workers, yet this very participation appears to obstruct the attainment of final goals' (1985, pp. 10, 13)

Two crucial features underpin this paradox. First, whilst socialist leaders entered into the democratic process believing that they represented the class that either was or was coming to be the overwhelming majority of the population, the working class never does come to constitute a majority of the electorate in any advanced capitalist society. This combination of 'minority status with majority rule' forces social democratic leaders to seek support *beyond* the traditional working class (defined quite narrowly by Przeworski as 'manual wage earners in mining, manufacturing, construction, transport, and agriculture, as well as their inactive adult household members') (Przeworski and Sprague, 1986, p. 35). But this quest for allies means compromising on the maximalist socialist agenda and de-emphasising the politics of class interest. The attempt to broaden the appeal of social democratic parties will prove self-defeating, for the very things that make socialist parties popular beyond the working class are the same things that will *demo*-bilize working-class electors. Thus: 'When socialists seek the support of other people they erode the very sources of their strength among workers. To be effective in elections they cannot remain class-pure and yet they can never cease altogether to be a party of workers. They seem unable to win either way' (Przeworski, 1985, p. 106).

The paradox of participation also has a programmatic dimension. For once socialist leaders are forced to abandon the maximalist ambition of the immediate socialization of capital ownership (which the imperative of finding a supra-class majority requires), they find themselves increasingly committed to the *success* of the existing capitalist economy and thus to securing the well-being of that capitalist class from which the bulk of investment under such an economy must flow. According to Przeworski, 'once private property of the means of production was left intact, it became in the interests of wage-earners that capitalists appropriate profits' (1985, p. 43). Where the investment function is not socialised, the economic well-being of *all* social classes (and with them the electoral prospects of *any* government) is dependent upon meeting the accumulation needs of the investors of private capital. It follows that 'current realization of material interests of capitalists is a necessary condition for the future realization of material interests of any group under capitalism' (1985, p. 139). 'Crises of capitalism' are in no one's interest. Certainly they are not in the interest of workers, since 'economic crises, *when not accompanied by political transformations*, fall on the shoulders of wage-earners' (1985, p. 153; emphasis added).

Przeworski extends this argument to draw the seemingly yet more paradoxical conclusion that the politics of participation may mean that workers, *even if* they believe that socialism is potentially better able to secure their welfare, will still *rationally* choose capitalism in preference to socialism. We have seen that if the politics of class compromise leaves the investment function in private hands, workers' interest in the long-term maximization of their well-being (and income flows) requires them to take an interest in sustaining an environment for long-term capital accumulation. Yet it may also be that even if we suppose that workers' welfare would be better secured under socialism there is never a point at which it is in workers' interests to *initiate* the process of transition to such a transformed social order. This supposition builds upon Przeworski's axiom that the transition from capitalism to socialism would necessarily induce economic crisis and involve passing through a trough (the 'valley of transition': see figure 8.1) in which workers' welfare would be (however temporarily) depressed.

If, as Przeworski supposes, 'the transition to socialism involves a deterioration of workers' welfare and if workers have an option of improving their material conditions by cooperating with capitalists', it follows that 'the socialist orientation cannot be deduced from the material interests of workers' (Przeworski, 1985, p. 177). Even if we suppose that the peak of socialist potential lies above the peak of capitalist potential, whilst workers face the downward slope into the valley of transition their material interests will induce them to favour the status quo, rather than the very uncertain benefits that lie on the sunny but rather distant uplands of a socialist future. Even if the process of tran-

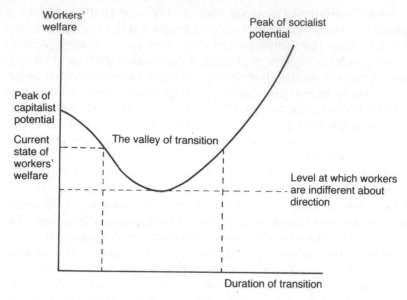

Figure 8.1   The 'valley of transition' (after Przeworski, 1985, p. 178: fig. 13)

sition were somehow to be initiated, Przeworski believes that it would
be impossible under democratic conditions to reach the upward slope
of the transitional trough before the democratic public would insist
upon a reversal of the transitional process (1985, pp. 176ff).[9]

Przeworski Assessed: Class and the Electoral Trade-off

Adam Przeworski's projections seem to evoke a uniquely depressing
future for democratic socialists and *Paper Stones*, his history of electoral
socialism written with John Sprague, closes with the judgement that
'the era of electoral socialism may be over' (Przeworski and Sprague,
1986, p. 185).[10] Yet, while much admired for his clarity and boldness,
Przeworski's conclusions have been firmly resisted and his thesis subjected to a sustained critique.[11] Much of this criticism has focused upon
Przeworski's account of changing class structures, of potential class
alliances and their political consequences. Some have taken exception
to Przeworski's very narrow characterization of the working class
(Przeworski and Sprague, 1986, p. 35; Przeworski, 1985, p. 91). Whilst
this definition underpins his conclusions about the failure of the working class to achieve majority status, it is seen, at the same time, to be
inconsistent with his own theoretical claim that actual class formation
is to some extent an underdetermined process shaped by the more or

less effective strategies of party leaders (Przeworski, 1985, pp. 47–9; Sainsbury, 1990, p. 33). In fact, few of Przeworski's critics balk at the suggestion that the industrial working class has generally come to constitute only a minority (if at times a very substantial one) in developed capitalist societies. But there are much more substantial objections to his further claim that support for social democratic parties beyond this working class can only be secured at the cost of demobilizing the workers *in sensu strictu*. Przeworski is quite explicit about this relationship: 'There exists a trade-off between the recruitment of middle classes and of workers: when socialist parties direct their efforts to mobilizing the support of allies they find it increasingly difficult to recruit and maintain the support of workers' (1985, p. 106).

Przeworski concedes that socialist parties may successfully mobilize both workers and 'non-workers' around programmatic elements that go beyond the immediate interests of the industrial working class (he cites the example of an appeal to 'honest government'). But evoking these supra-class issues (and appealing to 'citizens' or 'the people') means diminishing the electoral appeal to workers *qua* workers, and this must in the longer term damage the capacity of socialist parties to mobilize this core constituency. This trade-off is likely to be especially pronounced where (1) there is a class party to the left of the socialists which may garner the votes of disaffected workers, (2) there are confessional or linguistic parties which may make an appeal on grounds of an alternative identity to workers whose class identity has been blurred by the socialists' supra-class appeal, and (3) there is not a strong and unitary national-level trade union organization which may act as a surrogate for the party in binding workers to their collective identity and interests as proletarians. Przeworski seeks to buttress this theoretical argument by comparing the electoral strategies (and fortunes) of socialist parties where the trade-off is least developed (Denmark, Norway) and most pronounced (Belgium, France, pre-1933 Germany).

A number of commentators resist these claims about an electoral trade-off. Sainsbury (1990), for example, argues that the Scandinavian experience gives limited support to Przeworski's position. The observed patterns of changing electoral support (and the interplay of several variables) are complex, but Sainsbury insists that the trade-off (at least in the period down to 1985), is largely confined to Denmark. Overall she finds 'no consistent relationship between the existence of a trade-off and the left's electoral fortunes' (Sainsbury, 1990, pp. 38–41). Britain, whose Labour Party has suffered such a catastrophic loss of votes in recent years, is not included in Przeworski's formal statistical analyses. Certainly, the party here may have been subject to some sorts of political trade-off but, as King and Wickham-Jones (1990) insist, it is surely a strained reading that understands this haemorrhaging of votes primarily in terms of the Labour Party's loss of traditional proletarians through a supra-class appeal.[12] Mark Lichbach's comparative survey of class voting for five social democratic parties in the period down to 1975 found that some parties would have been best advised to pursue a pure working-class electoral strategy, whilst others would have done better to focus upon appeals to the middle class. Only in the case of the Australian Labor Party, however, was there an unambiguous trade-off between the quest for middle-class and working-class votes (Lichbach, 1984, 439–48).

Possibly the most systematic criticism of Przeworski's class trade-off thesis comes in Herbert Kitschelt's *Transformation of European Social Democracy* (1994). Indeed, Kitschelt seeks to *invert* the logic of Przeworski's position. There do not exist, so he argues, either the political issues or the economic benefits that would make it sensible for a socialist party to appeal exclusively to traditional blue-collar workers (as opposed, for example, to addressing itself to all wage-earners). Indeed, patterns of support for socialist parties amongst 'narrowly defined workers' and their allies show not a *trade-off* but a *bandwagon effect*, with support tending to increase (or decrease) within both groups in tandem. These movements take place not in a context of fixed class positions, electoral opportunities and strategic options but in a context of continuous change in which socialist parties, along with other social and political actors, face a delimited but real range of strategic choices. Ironically, the socialist parties best able to exploit these 'strategic opportunities' are, according to Kitschelt, those which Przeworski had envisaged facing the most acute threat of electoral trade-off. Reviewing the claims made in *Paper Stones*, he argues that 'socialist parties are bound to thrive just under those conditions where Przeworski and Sprague are led to expect . . . the greatest potential for the[ir] demise' (Kitschelt, 1994, p. 56). Under contemporary conditions, those parties which are least 'captured' by a blue-collar constituency, and least strongly identified with the trade unions, are likely to be best able to generate an electorally successful cross-class programmatic appeal. Similarly, historically-strong communist parties have become less a threat (siphoning off disgruntled blue-collar voters) than a resource, whose voters may be wooed by 'renewed' socialist parties. Kitschelt concludes:

> If there is any relation between patterns of class trade-offs . . . and parties' electoral success in the 1980s, it is the *opposite* to that predicted by Przeworski and Sprague. Parties that operate in an environment prone to yield severe trade-offs have improved their electoral performance most. Conversely, parties facing intermediate or mild electoral trade-offs performed worst. (Kitschelt, 1984, pp. 64–5; emphasis added)

Przeworski Assessed: The Problem of Transition

Still more important for us, though less extensively discussed, are the reservations that have been entered against Przeworski's account of the unsustainable costs of transition to some form of democratic socialism. A first response is to argue that the 'valley of transition', which Przeworski among others has identified, can be traversed without abandoning either economic transformation or democracy (or both). Ironically, some indication of this possibility is given in Przeworski's own later treatment (1991) of the possibilities of transition from command to market economies in Eastern Europe. Here, Przeworski restates the problem of the 'valley of transition', but also offers a more elaborate model of the time-frame and several strategies through which reform may take place. The two major paths of transition described by Przeworski correspond to the radical strategy (R) and the gradual strategy (G) in figure 8.2. The radical strategy offers a shorter but deeper economic trough. The gradual strategy sees less depression of economic production, and less overall loss of economic welfare, but is extended over a longer period.

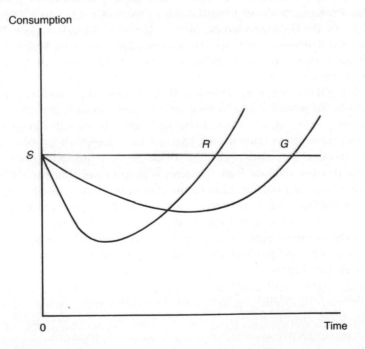

Figure 8.2 Strategies of reform. *S*: starting-point; *R*: radical reform; *G*: gradual reform (after Przeworski, 1991, 163: fig. 4.2)

It would be quite wrong to characterize Przeworski's speculations on the transition from command to market economies as optimistic. Under real-world circumstances, he envisages oscillation between gradualist and radical strategies, repeated policy failures and an active threat to both economic reform and the institutions of democracy. Yet he does at least entertain the possibility of successful transition from one economic system to another passing through a temporary economic downturn, whilst maintaining the institutions of representative democracy. Thus:

> People will vote for the party that proposes to traverse the valley if they believe that their future after reforms will be sufficiently superior to the status quo to compensate for temporary deterioration. And if voters are highly confident about the future, they choose the radical strategy, although it entails a higher social cost than the gradual one. (Przeworski, 1991, p. 164)

Of course, it may well be that the voters' confidence in these circumstances is not rewarded, and this may set in train a process in which the reforms unravel. It may also be that while such electoral support could be mobilized behind the transition from a command to a market economy, it would never be expressed in the expectation of a projected transition from advanced capitalism to market socialism.[13] Nonetheless, Przeworski's amended account of the transitional process does at least raise the possibility of a transformation which embraces both a temporary economic downturn *and* the maintenance of democratic institutions.

A second response is to insist that Przeworski's pessimism here proceeds from over-simplification in his own model and that the logic of *rational choice* has not been applied with sufficient rigour (or in sufficient detail) to disclose the actual (and varying) choices facing social actors under advanced capitalism. Some commentators suggest that in fact he misdescribes the circumstances for collective labour's complicity in its own exploitation and exaggerates the freedom of manoeuvre that is available to particular capital funds. Thus, in terms of generating 'the material bases of consent', whilst the fear of insolvency in circumstances of permanent mass unemployment will certainly influence wage claims, most wage-earners do not negotiate their terms and conditions in a context which makes possible a systematic accommodation with the long-term interests of capital accumulation. Furthermore, the circumstances of 'institutionalized trust' in which longer-term compromises of this kind between capital and labour could be struck are *de*creasingly characteristic of modern employment conditions. Wage-earners may certainly carry the costs of any 'crisis of capitalism', but it may also be that the circumstances for a systematic accommodation of wage-earners to their own long-term interest in the continued circumstances for the optimal accumulation of capital simply do not exist.

At the same time, and despite enhanced international mobility, capital faces its own constraints. According to King and Wickham-Jones, 'disinvestment is costly and will not be undertaken lightly . . . the capitalist has to compare slightly lower future profits [under a social democratic regime] with much lower future profits from disinvestment, lower growth and possibly economic crisis' (King and Wickham-Jones, 1990, p. 407). Private control over investment decisions and enhanced mobility vests enormous powers in capital, but even the representatives of capital are obliged to make decisions about their actions in the light of external constraints, limited options and uncertain knowledge of the future decisions of other important actors (including states, other capitals and even the representatives of organized labour). In the real world, knowledge is far less perfect, the institutional regime less supportive and, correspondingly, choices much less clear-cut than they are in Przeworski's model. Given the levels of uncertainty and strategic ignorance in the 'real world', there may be circumstances in which a social democratic government, even one embarked upon quite fundamental reforms, could manage to sustain levels of investment. Thus, according to Jonas Pontusson, 'it is at least conceivable that a reformist government committed to radical reforms could sustain an adequate rate of investment through a combination of carrots to private investment, sticks to discourage capital flight and hoarding of wealth, and perhaps a partial replacement of private investment by public investment' (1992a, p. 19).

Of course, if this were simply a way of redescribing the political orientation of a radical social democratic strategy carried through under the rubric of the Keynesian Welfare State, it would not so much carry us forward from Przeworski as back to the very problem upon which the whole of this study is based. We have seen that one premise of the market socialists (amongst others) is that it is no longer possible to pursue a politics based upon *shaping* the investment decisions of private capital holders, leaving the state to achieve greater equity through its capacity for redistribution. This is seen as a strategy which will increasingly demobilize social democracy's supporters and fracture the bases of its most promising electoral alliances. However hazy is the market socialists' own account of the politics of transition, they are clear that the issue of the socialization of the investment function has now to be confronted. The decisive challenge in this context is whether a radical transformation of this kind can both attract an initial public mandate and then be carried through whilst retaining sufficient popular support. For such a transformation to be possible, it would seem that economic costs to wage-earners at least must be limited and that the longer the transitional period, the more limited are the costs which this population are likely to be willing to sustain.

This brings us to the third element in the response to Przeworski, that is, the possibility that an appropriate social democratic reform agenda need not pass through a significant period of economic downturn. Just such an account is canvassed in Gosta Esping-Andersen's account of 'the social democratic road to power' in *Politics against Markets* (1985). The challenge, as Esping-Andersen envisages it, is to find a strategy which is consistent with the constitutional demands of liberal parliamentary democracy, and yet is able both to address the question of the *direct* socialization of major economic decision-taking and to avoid the unacceptable costs of transition. His own solution is found in the advocacy of a form of *wage-earners' funds*. There is by now a very extensive literature on wage-earners' funds, both in theory and practice.[14] Here it will be sufficient to note that wage-earner's funds, in the most widely discussed form advocated by Rudolf Meidner (1978), were envisaged as investment funds to be owned collectively by employees (at local, regional or national level). They were to be built up over a prolonged period through the annual transfer of the ownership of a part of the profits reinvested in an enterprise from their previous owners to the employees as a collective. Meidner envisaged that at a transfer rate of 20 per cent per annum this 'creeping socialism' might give wage-earners a controlling share in their enterprises within twenty-five to fifty years (1978, p. 59). In principle, so Esping-Andersen has argued, the Meidner proposal defines a social democratic strategy for implementing *direct* communal or workers' control over economic decision-making but in a *gradualist* form which avoids the threat of capital flight and the trough of economic underproduction and civil unrest which more conventional strategies for transition have always implied. To this extent, it is seen to defy the logic which for Przeworski makes the transition to socialism through electoral means impossible.

Transition to Market Socialism: The Politics of Support

Confronted with the messiness of political reality, the sharply defined lines of Przeworski's theses begin to look a little less clear-cut and repeatedly the rough arithmetic of the electoral process seems to have defied his elegant algebra. But if Przeworski's claims do not prove to be axiomatically true, they nonetheless point up some severe challenges for the advocates of electoral forms of socialism. Here I want to focus more closely upon the capacity of market socialism in particular to respond to these challenges. In such an evaluation, two areas seem to be of especial importance: the politics of support and the politics of transition.

For reasons extensively discussed in part I, I do not regard the challenge posed by 'the declining working class' to be just so severe as Przeworski supposes. It is clear to me why the 'narrowly defined' working class might be thought to have interests that are more un-ambiguously hostile to the interests of capital than any other social grouping (though recent work on the divisions of interest between productive workers in the domestic and export-oriented sectors of the economy makes even this claim far from straightforward).[15] It is less clear why a socialist programme should not be at least as attractive to some groups beyond the working class so defined, for example, among public sector manual workers. Indeed, I am not persuaded that the most salient issue here is one of class structure (at least in the way that Przeworski has understood this). Przeworski's presumptions about the uniquely powerful aspiration to socialism amongst the narrowly de-fined working class seem to proceed from the claim that these are the workers from whom a surplus is extracted for consumption by the rest of society and who *therefore* have the keenest material interest in socialization. Yet support for the maximalist socialist programme has always been limited even within this group, and characteristically they have shared the political ambitions (for full employment, a social wage, an extensive welfare state, and so on) of a much more broadly defined working class. It is probably elsewhere (perhaps amongst sections of the intelligentsia) that we should look for the most sustained support of social ownership. In brief, the narrowly defined working class has never formed a pool of 'maximalist' socialists whose ambitions for the transition to socialism have been frustrated by the dead weight of the socialists' non-working-class electors and historically it is not at all clear that the workers 'narrowly defined' have pursued interests and a political agenda which would clearly mark them off from a working class much more broadly defined (perhaps, for example, around wage-earning status). It follows that changes in the class structure of contem-porary advanced capitalism (and in particular, the decline of the traditional blue-collar manufacturing sector) may be much more a challenge to traditional forms of social democratic accommodation with capitalism (Keynesianism and the welfare state), than they are to a previously viable transition to socialism. It follows further that the (depleting) minority status of the narrowly defined working class is probably not the right place to look for an explanation of the absence of an electoral trajectory into socialism.

This puts a rather different slant on the question of electoral support for social democratic forces. Certainly, the declining number of workers in traditional blue-collar manufacturing and extractive industries depletes a reservoir from which socialist and social democratic parties have traditionally drawn much of their electoral support. But this should not be read as the depletion of a 'core' which previously endorsed a radical strategy for socialization. Nor should we presume that socialist parties (which have rather rarely been 'ghetto' parties of the narrowly defined working class) cannot gather votes from elsewhere. Socialist parties have certainly had difficulty in retaining electoral support, but this is a problem which they have shared with other established parties (including mainstream parties of the right and centre-right), and the very diversity in the record of support for socialist parties since the 1970s suggests that electoral fortunes may not be straightforwardly read off from changes in class structure.[16]

At the end of part I, I suggested that the problem for socialist parties was not that they would be unable to attract electoral support (though recruiting and retaining supporters might become more difficult). The more substantial difficulty was that it seemed socialist parties might now only be able to garner this support by abandoning even a modestly reformist political platform (as in the traditional commitment to 'Keynesianism plus the welfare state'). It is this further challenge which it is said market socialism may be able to overcome. Its advocates claim that market socialism represents an alternative which can deliver not only the possibility of sustained support but also a political programme for socialization under prevailing (and seemingly rather unpromising) economic and political circumstances.

Is it realistic to believe that the market socialist programme could mobilize a coalition of new and old supporters around a distinctive and feasible socialist agenda? If we look first to the strengths of this account, I think it is clear why a politics built upon self-management might appeal to a new (and perhaps expanding) constituency. If, as Kitschelt suggests (1994, p. 27), there has been a libertarian 'tilt' amongst potential supporters of parties of the left (and the 'narrowly defined' working class is in numerical decline), a political economy which promised greater autonomy and self-direction might well reach out to a new (and expanding) group of wage-earners, and offer parties of the left which promoted it an electoral dividend. Similarly, if voters' self-definition now proceeds as much from their experience in the realm of consumption as from their increasingly fragmented occupational identity, it is clear why a socialism which promised to do more than represent the sectional interests of organized producers might have an enhanced appeal. The reliance upon markets under social ownership also promises to deflect much of that hostility to socialism, which is presumed to be generated by its intimate association with an overweening and centralized state. (And we should be mindful that the scepticism of contemporary electorates may be turned quite as much upon the claims of 'benign' transnational corporations as it has been upon the claims of the 'provident' state.) We can also see why, if more traditional socialist strategies are now widely seen not to be viable, there may be electoral advantage in promoting a policy which generates an aura of feasibility. Where the market experience seems to be so ubiquitous, it may well seem to make sense to foster a type of socialism which works with rather than against the logic of markets.

Yet there are some peculiarities in characterizing market socialism as a strategy for a more *popular* socialism. First, whilst we live in a world which seems to be increasingly market-driven and we are all of necessity consumers, a growing part of the population in most advanced capitalist societies is not active in the labour market at all.[17] Market socialism still looks very much like a wage-earners' socialism and to this extent its appeal to those outside the formal economy might actually appear to be rather narrower than that of the traditional Keynesian Welfare State. Secondly, it is not clear that the welfare elements of the state have become just so unpopular. Certainly, there have been rising levels of tax resistance and hostility directed towards particular 'undeserving' welfare recipients, but survey evidence discloses continuing high levels of voters' support for the public provision of key welfare services (including health, education and pensions).[18] Whilst the welfare state faces substantial reform in the coming period, it is not self-evidently clear that the most popular and effective form of this revision will be the dismantling proposed from the New Right. Social democrats may actually have something to gain electorally from standing as the architects of a revised form of state welfare. Thirdly, as Estrin and Le Grand make clear, 'market socialism is race- and gender-blind' (Le Grand and Estrin, 1989, p. 22). They might have added that it lacks any vision of the relationship between socialism and ecology. Yet these are precisely the groups and issues to which, in other contexts, socialists have been advised to address themselves in the quest for new allies and for 'programmatic renewal'. Often, these interests have been seen as potential allies precisely because markets appear *not* to address their concerns. In their differing ways, both feminists and ecologists insist that existing market arrangements fail to address the needs of women and the environment. Of course, there are those who argue that the interests of women and of the environment are best served by reliance upon markets.[19] Socialist-feminists and eco-socialists might be persuaded that such interests could be advanced through the agency of markets, but not, it would seem, unless these markets are themselves constituted and controlled in very particular ways.

This final problem brings us back to the question of market socialism's relationship to the state. I have already argued at some length that the expectation that a marketized form of socialism could be the means for delivering 'socialism with a minimal state' is a myth. In terms of the practical politics of electoral support, it seems clear that no social democratic party would be willing to abandon overnight the potential support of many millions of public sector workers, nor should it abandon its defence of the interests of those whose sole protection against destitution is the support of the state. More than this, I have insisted that a system of market *socialism* will be heavily dependent upon the management of the social and economic framework of the market by the state. Handing over powers to an unreformed civil society will have little appeal to socialists. Markets (along with many other institutions in civil society) will need to be *patrolled*, not necessarily by the state, but almost certainly under the final jurisdiction of the state. It is this that makes reform of state institutions the undiscussed (perhaps even unacknowledged) premise of any move to a market socialist order. Under these circumstances, it would seem to make more sense for social democrats to appeal to a *redefinition* of the relationship of state and civil society (a mutual reform in the sense indicated in the earlier discussion of David Held), rather than to the prospect of a social order wholly under the tutelage of socialized markets.

More generally, it seems that under the right circumstances (which would have to include confidence in the capacity of government to deliver), self-management under social ownership might be *one* plank in a revivified social democratic programme. But in terms of maximizing support, it is hard to see that, under envisageable circumstances, it could be the defining centrepiece of such an electoral strategy.

Market Socialism and the Politics of Transition

This brings us finally and explicitly to pass judgement on the claims of market socialism as an agenda for political *transition*. For a *feasible* socialism, this really is the bottom line. I begin from the rather uncontroversial claim that in the short to medium term the prospects for *any* form of socialism are not very promising and a recognition that the feasibility of any projected political change is necessarily speculative. Given these caveats, it remains the case that amongst the available alternative models, at least in terms of the process of transition, market socialism is peculiarly unpromising. I confine my comments here to two issues: 'the inevitability of gradualism' and the political context of a global economy.

The impetus towards market socialism is often seen to arise from a set of conditions peculiar to the contemporary period, including a declining faith in the historical privileging of socialism, increased electoral volatility, divisions of political interest amongst wage-earning populations, declining respect for the competence of the state. These same circumstances which induce a move towards market socialism seem also to require that now more than ever any social democratic strategy for change must be built upon 'the inevitability of gradualism'. Yet, in the light of our discussion of the nature of the co-operative economy in chapter 6, it would seem that in practice any move to market socialism would require a fairly brief and wholesale transformation. This, interestingly, was Oskar Lange's view (1938, pp. 124–5). It seems also to be supported by Jon Elster's recent (1988) writings on the co-operative economy, which stress the difficulties of 'islands of co-operativism' in a greater capitalist sea. It may thus be that the circumstances for a successful co-operative economy actually require that the great bulk of economic activity should be transferred into the co-operative sector within a comparatively short period. This may do something to redeem the claim that market socialism is a radical doctrine, but under circumstances in which more traditional socialist strategies have had to be abandoned at least in part because of the lack of popular support for large-scale socialization, it is hard to see that this makes it a more *feasible* option. In fact, it is difficult to see how the radical socialization which market socialists proffer is more readily realizable than, say, the very traditional (and largely abandoned) policy of nationalizing the 'commanding heights' within an autarkic economy.

It may be useful here to draw very briefly a contrast with a second 'alternative strategy for social democracy', that is, the advocacy of wage-earners' funds. Wage-earners' funds have also been recommended as a move 'beyond' the traditional politics of Keynesian Welfare States and as a way of confronting directly the question of the socialization of the investment function. Wage-earners' fund socialism has a complex and contested history (see, *inter alia*, Pontusson, 1992a and 1992b; Esping-Andersen, 1985; Higgins and Apple, 1983; Meidner, 1978, 1980 and 1993). Whatever its wider relevance and debilitating weaknesses may be, wage-earners' fund socialism does at least have a coherent account (on paper) of how a radical but *gradualist* strategy for socialization could be effected. The very gradual transfer of ownership through the dividends of growth rather than confiscation was envis-

aged to avoid the problems of capital flight and of an economic downturn in the process of transition to social ownership. Yet, when pursued
as a strategy within the most trenchantly social democratic polity ever
devised (and in the face of vigorous opposition from employers and
others), wage-earners' fund socialism was repeatedly watered down
and then effectively abandoned. My intention here is not to evaluate
the experience of wage-earners' funds in Sweden (about which a great
deal more would have to be said). I confine myself to the judgement
that on favourable terrain a strategy with a much more modest and
gradualist strategy for transition than that espoused by market socialists met with fierce resistance and eventually failed. This does not bode
well for the *feasibility* of the market socialist alternative.

This objection seems the more compelling when we consider it in the
light of the international economic circumstances in which a market
socialist strategy would have to be pursued. There is again an irony
here. Interest in market socialism was largely fuelled by the seeming
impossibility of pursuing a national-based socialist or social democratic strategy (largely because of the disabling effect of international
markets). Thus globalization of economic processes must be seen as
one of the causes of renewed interest in marketized forms of socialism.
Yet the market socialist model is very much one for 'socialism in one
nation state'. It is precisely because incomes policies, full employment
and a national consensus on citizenship (all of which we can find in the
programmes of market socialists) were so difficult to sustain that
socialists found themselves having 'to learn to love the market'. Given
the difficulties of sustaining co-operative enterprises in a wider capitalist environment, it is difficult to see how we could have 'market socialism in one country', but it is still more difficult to see how we might
have market socialism at a global level. What may have helped to make
market socialism look more viable is the expectation that in a self-
managed economy socialism could somehow be produced at the
micro-level within the individual enterprise. The problem is that while
such self-management may well be desirable in itself, and while it may
constitute a more 'social' form of enterprise governance, it is *not* the
same thing as instituting a market socialist regime. There is also no very
compelling account of how the self-managed sector might grow so as to
come incrementally and eventually to a point at which a market socialist regime could be constituted.

Conclusion: A Feasible Socialism?

Market socialism may appear to recommend itself to the 'practical'
wing of social democracy, as a way of reversing the electoral conse-

quences of a decline in the popularity of the traditional socialist agenda. But, in practice, this can probably only be achieved by attaching the label 'market socialism' to what is more properly a 'social market economy' (in which vigorous capitalist economic growth is to be encouraged to permit some increment for the expansion of public services). The proposal at the heart of the market socialist model is the socialization of all but very small-scale capital and this is indeed a very radical intention. It is also quite essential to the defence of market socialism as a strategy for 'socialism with markets'. As we have seen, traditional socialist criticism of the market socialist project is repeatedly deflected by the insistence that its arguments are with capitalist markets not markets-under-socialism. However, if this more radical version of market socialism is to be defended, and this is essential to its defence as an authentically socialist model, it is not clear that it has the quality of enhanced feasibility that its advocates suggest. What makes market socialism seem feasible is its attachment to the *market*, but that which makes it *socialist* is the very thing that renders it infeasible.

Conclusion

At the end of part I, I ventured the judgement that, however sickly the historical left might look, evidence did not point unambiguously towards the world-historical 'death of socialism'. Yet, if the obituaries for socialism were rather premature and over-written, we certainly could discern in the material assessed in these opening chapters a profound challenge to much of what has been the bedrock of traditional socialist and social democratic politics, both in theory and in practice. In the light of this evidence, it seemed reasonable to suppose that any future revival of socialist political fortunes was likely to require a correspondingly profound rethinking of some very basic elements in the socialist idea. Above all, perhaps, it seemed to require a reassessment of socialist attitudes to the state and to the market. In retrospect, socialism's long-standing association with the state has not always been a happy one. In the management of both economic and social life, the state has not delivered the sorts of redistribution of resources and opportunities that socialists had anticipated. Still worse, the particular failings of the state have been frequently redescribed as generic failures of socialism. At the same time, the irrationalities and inefficiencies of the market economy seem to have been dwarfed by the wholesale incompetence of a centrally planned (and socialist) alternative.

It is in this particular context that I have considered the claims made for a revised form of 'socialism-with-markets'. However it is presented, I take it that the market socialist position is defined by the continuing aspiration to give institutional expression to certain core socialist values, in forms which can be built upon existing social institutions and political forces, whilst addressing the most debilitating weaknesses that have undermined earlier invocations of the socialist idea. At its simplest, market socialism promises to salvage socialist aspirations by retaining an economy in which most commodities are allocated through the mechanism of markets whilst bringing capital into social ownership. In this way, we should be able to enjoy all the economic benefits that proceed from having a market economy, without all the disadvantages of living under capitalism. Indeed, the market socialists have sought to turn the tables on their neo-liberal opponents by advertising the market economy (under social ownership) as the best means for redeeming what is seen to be socialism's central commitment to the empowerment of ordinary (working) people.

In parts II and III, I have entered a series of detailed and specific reservations about this account, culminating in what I take to be the most damning indictment – that is, that under any envisageable circumstances this strategy is infeasible. Here, I want to indicate more briefly, and generally, why I think that market socialism cannot form the basis of a revised strategy of the left.

On Markets

It is hard not to be impressed both by the invasive power and the tenacity of markets in the contemporary world and, given certain simple (and rather improbable) assumptions, by the elegance of neo-classical solutions to questions of supply and demand. It seems clear that in any envisageable future (even a socialist one for those blessed with such acutely developed foresight), markets are likely to have an extremely prominent role. The market socialists have tried to make a virtue out of this ubiquity of the market. In an adroit argumentative manoeuvre, they seek to outflank the neo-liberals by accepting much of their argument for markets, while transforming this by introducing a very radical proposal for the social ownership of capital. Yet this skilful move will not, in the end, work, because markets in the market socialist account prove not to be an analogue of markets in the neo-liberal position. For the most committed neo-liberals, the very best social order is one which guarantees the integrity of market-like exchanges between freely-contracting individuals, *irrespective of particular substantive outcomes*. Certainly, many market socialists accept that, in a broad range of circumstances, markets will enhance the individual's freedom of choice. But hardly any would support the further claim that market outcomes, just because they are market outcomes, should be respected, even when these are widely perceived to have pernicious consequences. Most market socialists simply do not accept the premises which commit neo-liberals to market outcomes (whatever these may be). This is not a very remarkable qualification. It is hard to think of any existing regime (including the most neo-liberal) that would adhere to 'the imperatives of the market' in its most demanding form. Yet if markets describe procedures which may legitimately be interfered with, they cannot enjoy the centrality or the authority which attaches to them in 'authentically' neo-liberal explanations. In the end, the market socialist argument for markets is, in ways which for neo-liberals it is not, an argument from utility, and like all such arguments it is provisional and liable to be amended in the light of actual outcomes.

This does not mean that we may not envisage a socialism with a very prominent role for the market. Indeed, markets might be much more ubiquitous than they have been even under existing Western forms of social democracy. If we are dealing not only with optimal procedures in theory but also with 'second-best' options in practice, markets will often seem to offer the 'best second-best' outcome in a range of imperfect real-world situations. But however extensive might be the markets of a marketized socialism, they cannot have the same fundamental status as they have for neo-liberals. Even those market socialists who value the market as authentically a device for delivering an enhancement of freedom qualify this commitment with an attachment to other values. Of course, in practice, even the most 'spontaneous' markets operate within a given constitutional and institutional framework. But, characteristically, those who aspire to 'socialism-with-markets' will want to intervene explicitly (and perhaps repeatedly) to *restructure* the social and institutional framework within which markets can legitimately operate. Socialists and social democrats making much more extensive and imaginative use of markets certainly seems possible. But recasting socialism as a special breed of 'catallaxy with social ownership' does not.

On the State

This brings us to a consideration of the market socialists' position on the state. The difficulties here complement those which I have identified in attitudes to the market. It is clear enough why neo-liberals, given the nature of their commitment to the outcomes of market transactions, should subscribe to a minimal role for the state. We are also aware that it is a part of the market socialists' brief to rid socialism of its pejorative association with an overweening and ineffective state. But there can be little question of socialists simply 'abandoning' the state in the way that the most radical of market socialist prescriptions would seem to indicate. In fact, we have seen that, whatever their 'mission statements' may say, most market socialists' blueprints for institutional reform do, in fact, envisage a very substantial continuing role for the state. Markets will only do the things that market socialists require of them (an ambition which is wholly alien to the neo-liberals), if the social and economic context for market transactions is suitably constructed, and we have seen repeatedly that market socialists allow for markets to operate *only* where the circumstances for their operation have been previously established by some outside force (most characteristically, the state). Le Grand, for example, allows an unusually wide provenance to markets in the welfare area, but wishes this market to be allowed to operate *only* where the state has previously (and repeatedly) reallocated spending power in favour of the least advantaged. Here, as in their discussion of the reordering of markets under socialism, the market socialists have interesting and innovative things to say about the ways in which public interventions may be mediated by and through various 'secondary institutions'. The principal weakness in their position is that, perhaps because of an aspiration to mirror the structure of neo-liberal arguments and to distance themselves from forms of state socialism, they have tended to neglect the nature of state forms under market socialism. It bears repeating that socialists cannot simply abandon the domain of the state. But they are surely not obliged to seek to work with the state 'just as it is'. Indeed, state power is already being reconstituted (not just in the nation state but also at supra-national, regional and local levels), in ways which might be consonant with a revised socialist understanding of the nature and limits of public authority. It is also clear that socialists and social democrats, whatever their commitment to markets, are unlikely to be happy to work with civil society 'just as it is'. It is not just the state or civil society that requires reconsideration, but also the relationship between them. This is perhaps best approached in terms of the process of *double democratization* discussed in chapter 7 (pp. 181–2).

On Social Ownership

It is clear that social ownership lies at the very heart of the market socialist project. Considerable effort and ingenuity have been devoted to specifying the nature of a regime of social property, establishing the possibility of multiple sites of social capital and distinguishing it from ownership by the state or 'the workers'. Yet it remains under-specified and, in Djordjevic's phrase, 'semantically ambivalent' (see above p. 152). This is a serious weakness and it has been seized upon by critics with an unrelenting ferocity. Yet, if the market socialists have still to come up with a compelling answer in this area, it seems to me that they are at least asking the right sorts of questions. The nature of property generally proves to be much more ambiguous than popular sentiment might suggest. Fully specified private ownership proves not to be the norm in market economies, but rather something of a limiting case. Much of the investment upon which existing market economies rely proves not to have come from the pockets of abstaining venture capitalists, but from 'deferred wages' accumulated in large-scale pension funds and from institutions managing the aggregated resources of very large numbers of comparatively small savers (G. Thompson, 1990, pp. 144–6). This is not quite 'the abolition of the capitalist mode of production within the capitalist mode of production' as Marx anticipated it (Marx, 1972, p. 429). But ownership already takes such a plurality of forms, and the instruments of saving and debt management are so varied, that we may certainly hope to be able to generate new forms of ownership which could satisfy at least some of the criteria of social property (see e.g. Roemer, 1992a). Of course, such a regime is unlikely to look much like the classical socialist model of a socialized economy. But in this classical form, the wholesale socialization of ownership has not, as we have seen, met with unqualified success and it is anyway an imperative of contemporary circumstances that we should find forms of change which are gradual and incrementalist. At the same time, seeking changes to the structure of ownership seems unavoidable now, in a way which it did not for Keynesian social democrats in the 1930s and beyond. However gradualist and incrementalist it may be in practice, a revised socialism has little choice but to be radical in so far as it must bring into question the ownership of society's productive assets.

The Future of (Market) Socialism?

As the twentieth century stumbles towards a close, few people will feel at all sanguine about the prospects for socialism; and whilst I have rejected the most apocalyptic stories about its disintegration, this has not been from any conviction that we stand at the threshold of a new era of socialst advance. Have we then reached the point where 'the left' (for want of some better expression) should cast off the dead weight of its socialist baggage and reconstitute itself around some newly minted or, at least, less discredited organizing principle?

In line with what was said in the opening pages of this study, my response would be no, or, at least, not yet. I think it should be clear from the evidence discussed in part I, that great swathes of 'traditional' socialist thinking (on the 'historical mission' of the urban-industrial working class, on the shared identity of 'progressive' causes, on the 'truth' of the socialist case and so on) have, more or less simply, to be abandoned. However, it is also possible to think about socialism not as the summation of these world-historical generalizations, but rather as the 'antidote' to capitalism (albeit one that has been clinically rather ineffective). In the whirlwind of 'creative destruction' that has been unleashed by deconstruction, many of the most familiar landmarks of social and political analysis ('the state', 'society' and, most certainly, 'socialism' and 'capitalism') have been blown away. Yet, amidst the conceptual haze that has followed, I still make out the rather shadowy form, if not of a singular 'capitalism', then certainly of relationships, institutions and practices to which the label 'capitalist' may be usefully applied. So long as it makes sense to study capitalist forms and relations, and to consider alternatives to these, there is value in thinking in socialist terms. In such a context, however, it is better to think of socialist politics not as bringing us to the terminus of humanity's prehistory, but rather as a set of guiding ideas informing what is an open-ended political process.

Despite all the discouraging things written here and elsewhere, the prospects for such a reconstructed socialist politics are not unremittingly bleak. It seems clear that the high tide of the neo-liberal renaissance has passed and this, not least, because so far as it was ever a view that informed political practice, that practice can now be seen substantially to have failed. Commercialization of the life-world continues more or less apace, but this falls some way short of the inception of a societal catallaxy. At the same time, *fin de siècle* global capitalism looks not much prettier than any of its historical predecessors. Indeed, stripped of the favourable contrast with the 'alternative' of World Communism and of the moderating influence of many social democratic institutions, it is in many ways still less attractive. As I suggested earlier in the book, it is probably only the dramatic problems of preexisting forms of socialism that have made contemporary capitalism look such a good bet. And whilst a rather grandly conceived Idea of Socialism may not have much resonance with contemporary publics, it is far less clear that the more mundane embodiments of socialist aspirations are so universally unpopular. Socialist parties, in common with many others, have had difficulty in sustaining electoral support and an active memebership, but we have seen that there is considerable evidence of continuing public endorsement of publicly funded health care, state provision of education, policies to promote full employment, and so on. At the same time, it is curious piece of New Right double-think that supposes that employees who so resent 'the yoke of trade union membership' should forever welcome the existing hierarchical structure of authority within the typical capitalist firm. In fact, there must be a reasonable suspicion that, in some Western countries at least, it is not so much what socialists and social democrats promise, as their inability to deliver, that fuels scepticism amongst the democratic public. Nor can we suppose, as I shall argue below, that *all* of the social, economic and ideological changes of recent times must count decisively and unilaterally against the socialist case.

Beyond Market Socialism?

I argued earlier that one of the characteristic weaknesses of contemporary readings of the socialist experience has been to take the ideological claims of socialists *too* seriously. We know that whilst socialism has been replete with 'big ideas', the ambitions of its practitioners have generally been much more modest. It as as well to recognize, then, that nothing very much may be about to change. In practice and in office, socialist and social democratic politicians in the West may not be well disposed towards bold programmatic change. Finding themselves restored to government, they may well try to pursue, albeit under very different circumstances and in rather different forms, the sorts of policies which have been theirs throughout most of the twentieth century. This is not perhaps such a contemptible ambition. We know that reaching an 'accommodation' with existing social and economic forces has become increasingly difficult, but if 'muddling through' were to bring global capitalist regimes towards Swedish levels of income inequality and unemployment, for example, it would still look like a significant achievement. Yet, in the light of the changes discussed in the opening part of this study, it is extremely difficult to see that such 'muddling through' could offer anything more than very temporary relief and we are bound to look for a more radical and long-sighted way of responding to present circumstances. In my judgement, we cannot be at all confident that market socialism offers a viable basis for such a radical alternative and, curiously enough, given what I have had to say about feasibility, I suspect that this is because market socialists have been *insufficiently* radical in their rethinking of the socialist idea. In a number of areas – on markets, on the state and, above all, on the question of ownership – they have shifted the discussion in some new and promising directions. But to realize the full potential of these initiatives, they need to be carried further forward.

Certainly, much has been gained by confronting deeply-ingrained prejudices within the left (not all of which, however, prove to be unfounded), and imaginatively reconstructing an account of 'markets-under-socialism'. Yet we have seen that, in the end, markets will not quite do all the conceptual work that market socialists anticipate. Though diversity and plurality are celebrated, and seen to be encouraged by their form of a market economy, market socialists are not, in the end, as unconcerned with actual outcomes as are the advocates of a *real* catallaxy. Since the market procedure is not celebrated as of overriding value *in itself*, they cannot properly be redescribed as 'left Hayekians'. But if markets will not then do just so much institutional work as the market socialists have envisaged, this leaves much more space for two further initiatives which I think will bear greater argumentative weight. The first concerns democracy. I have already sought to distance myself from those who insist that the ambitions of socialism can simply be 'rewritten' under the rubric of democracy, but I do hold that a much more radical view of democratization can, at least in principle, contribute to those forms of empowerment to which socialists have aspired. Democratization was discussed at some length in chapter 7, in which I suggested that there were some extremely powerful arguments in favour of extending democracy into the economic sphere (though not exclusively into the workplace), and that, while they have been chronically underdeveloped by the market socialists themselves, socialists would do well to make much fuller use of them. But arguments for democracy may also help in addressing some of the ideological and epistemological objections to socialism that were raised in chapter 3. It is characteristic of the contemporary condition that *all* truth claims or appeals to 'grounded' knowledge are treated sceptically; and socialism (at least in respect of some of its more grandiose epistemological claims) has been one of the principal victims of this scepticism. Yet, under these circumstances of radical uncertainty, we have still to act politically and to make hard choices. One plausible response is to have much greater recourse to pragmatic modes of thought and, indeed, decision-making.[1] Some schools of pragmatism, at least, place preponderant weight upon democracy and consensus-formation ('reasoned' or otherwise) as the most legitimate form of decision-making under radical epistemological uncertainty. Thus the very circumstances which make our knowledge-claims more provisional (and imperil some of the traditional 'truths' of the socialist cause), may dispose towards more pragmatism which, in turn, may favour forms of democratic decision-taking that are consonant with the sorts of economic democratization pursued by market socialists. In fact, the conventional description of democracy as embracing both a 'protective' and a 'developmental' logic captures rather effectively the sorts of qualities we are looking for in a contemporary enhancement of democratic decision-making.

This brings us to the issue of social ownership, the reconsideration of which is, I think, the single greatest strength of the market socialist initiative. There are still plenty of social democrats, perhaps even a growing number, who insist in the classical manner that 'ownership does not matter'. But this (as the avid privatizers of state assets in the 1980s seemed to realize) is surely not correct. Certainly, Keynes held that 'ownership of the instruments of production' was 'not important', whilst Crosland insisted upon 'the growing irrelevance of the ownership of the means of production' (Keynes, 1973, p. 378; Crosland, 1964, p. 34). But both men subscribed to this view precisely because the state *was* able to direct economic activity *without* bringing privately owned economic assets under public control. Circumstances have now changed fundamentally in ways which mean that *indirect* public control of the economy is much less effective. This is not a case for nationalization (beyond those natural monopolies whose public control is not justified on 'socializing' grounds and which would in any saner times be uncontentious). Indeed, nationalization in its traditional forms⁻ is neither very desirable (the Morrisonian public corporations could be considered socialist only if one accepts the view widely attributed to Morrison that socialism is 'what the Labour Party does'), nor at all practicable (we are after all thinking about those circumstances in which global economic forces have drastically undermined the powers of the interventionist nation state). There is, however, a different and much stronger case for some sort of 'social' ownership of society's productive assets. It is absolutely fair that neo-liberal critics should draw attention to the acute difficulties that market socialists have had in defining a workable institutional order in which 'social' ownership is not just a polite word for 'state' ownership. But this is a weakness that might be addressed 'from both ends', recasting the state in more democratic directions and enhancing the effective control of decision-taking at a more local level. We need also to remember that the characteristics of ownership do not unambiguously favour the neo-liberal position. Neo-liberals do particularly well in terms of the *institutional* ordering of existing property regimes, but under scrutiny their *normative* arguments look distinctly wobbly. We should certainly not assume that a closer investigation of the forms of property will necessarily reveal that the right has all the best tunes and the most compelling arguments.

These arguments on democracy and ownership are, I think, greatly strengthened if we turn to one of the (several) issues curiously missing from the market socialist agenda – that is, the 'ecological imperative'. Of course, the precise ecological limits to our activity are unknown and probably unknowable. Yet, whilst we lack knowledge of the *precise* limits upon our appropriation of the external environment, we do know that there *are* such limits, and this should have a profound impact upon our political thinking. For example, it surely further weakens those normative claims to appropriation of private property which rely, in some form, upon leaving 'as much and as good' for appropriation by others. More generally, if we recognize that we face finite collective resources (albeit that these might still be very extensive), and therefore an injunction against unlimited appropriation, we also have a strong *prima facie* argument in favour of greater collective control over humankind's limited resources. This does not necessarily mean a predisposition against markets. Indeed, given what we know about the efficiency features of markets, we may be strongly inclined to use them to deliver particular goods and services. But as those who are sympathetic to both markets and ecological limits have found, markets under these circumstances can only operate in an already politically given context (Pearce, Markandya and Barbier, 1989). Managing a sustainable future may well involve the use of markets, but it cannot be premised upon the institutionalization of a global catallaxy. Under these circumstances, there are ever more pressing reasons for us to seek (democratic) institutional forms through which we can take (equitable) binding and self-limiting decisions.

In these circumstances, the challenge is to deliver policies which accentuate popular elements in the socialist programme in ways which are credible, sustainable and (as I see it consequently) incremental. The market socialists may have much to contribute to this process of revision, but I doubt that market socialism offers in itself a convincing solution.

Notes

Introduction

1 Surely, Michael Novak could no longer claim in the 1990s that 'the most unreported fact of our era is the death of socialism'! (1982, p. 187).

Chapter 1   Socialism's Disappearing Social Base

1 'What the bourgeoisie therefore produces, above all, are its own grave-diggers' (Marx, 1973c, p. 79).
2 Esping-Andersen notes (1992, p. 148 n. 2), that 'in the United States, the average hourly earnings of workers in eating and drinking establishments is only 44 per cent of average hourly manufacturing wages'.
3 It is worth noting that the figures for union densities correlated by Jelle Visser (1992), covering the period down to the end of the 1980s, show a greater decline than is recorded by Blanchflower and Freeman (most notably in the case of France). However, Visser's figures do confirm the considerable divergence between differing countries and the exceptionally low absolute level and severity of decline in the US.
4 At the same time, it is important to note that the failure of the category of wage-earners to provide a satisfactory basis for identifying a 'real' working class does *not* oblige us to see the performance of manual labour as a compelling alternative. See e.g. Eric Olin Wright (1985, pp. 182, 195), who rejects manual labour as a criterion for defining the working class but still identifies 40 per cent of the US labour force (and 43 per cent in Sweden) as 'unambiguously proletarian'.
5 The much broader argument of Adam Przeworski (1985 and 1986), that voting in socialism was always impossible because of the constraints of minority status for the workers in a democratic order that gave

governing power to electoral majorities is considered in ch. 8 below (pp. 195–205).

Chapter 2   The Declining Political Economy of Socialism

1   Whilst Marxists have frequently laid claim to the superiority of scientific socialism over its moralizing forerunners, it has long been argued that even Marxian socialism is replete with moral invocations and other socialist traditions have voiced a quite self-consciously ethical appeal (see Kamenka, 1969; Lukes, 1985; Dennis and Halsey, 1988; Shaw, 1993). Indeed, many of socialism's critics have insisted that it is, above all, a *moral* theory concerned with the realization of 'social justice', and lacking even the most basic rudiments of a coherent *economics* (Hayek, 1982; Lomasky, 1988).

2   The economies of the region were transformed into such close resemblance with one another that to talk of an East European or even a Soviet type of economic system of central planning was for decades justified. All the East European economies have shared certain fundamental *institutional* characteristics: the declared priority of state ownership over other property forms; the organization of the state sector in a hierarchical bureaucracy of branch ministerial management; centralized planning of production by means of mandatory plan targets; the centralized supply of the means of production; and, in various forms, a state monopoly of foreign trade (Sutcla, 1990, pp. 59–60).

3   See also Brus, 1973, 1975, 1980, 1985, 1987, 1989 and 1990; Brus and Laski, 1989a and 1989b.

4   There is an element of shorthand here. Not all social democrats came to 'Keynesian' solutions *via* Keynes, as the influence of the Stockholm School in Swedish experience attests, and not every social democratic movement arrived at these solutions at the same time. Nor do all commentators on the social democratic experience accept the usefulness of the idea of the 'Keynesian Welfare State'. For an important dissenting opinion, see Therborn (1986).

5   An excellent general account of Keynesianism and its relationship to social democracy is provided in Scharpf (1991, esp. pp. 17–37).

6   The definitive statement, in the British tradition at least, is still Crosland (1964).

7   As in ch. 1, the British experience cannot be read as 'typical' still less as the 'vanguard' for other advanced industrialized states. In practice, the experience of the welfare state and of its 'dissolution' has varied substantially throughout the advanced industrial nations (see e.g. Alber, 1988a and 1988b).

8   The most-quoted lines of Callaghan's party address are these: 'We used to think that you could just spend your way out of a recession and increase employment by cutting taxes and boosting government spending. I tell you, in all candour, that the option no longer exists, and that insofar as it did exist, it only worked by injecting a bigger dose of inflation into the economy followed by higher levels of unemployment as the next step.' Cited in Therborn (1986, p. 37).

9 However, it is worth noting that, historically, it was often those (small) countries with 'open' economies that had the most developed welfare states.

Chapter 3   The Ideological and Epistemological Crises of Socialism at the 'End of History'

1 For a clear and sophisticated introduction, see J. Thompson (1990).
2 Indeed, there is a galaxy of competing Marxist explanations of why these societies cannot properly be called socialist (see e.g. Callinicos, 1991).
3 For a fuller account, see Pierson (1986, pp. 133–152).
4 Of course, these same social actors might also become available for other forms of 'the politics of identity' (e.g. racism or religious fundamentalism), which will seem much less benign to those on the left.
5 Consider e.g. the intellectual trajectory of Robert Dahl and Charles Lindblom (Dahl and Lindblom, 1953; Dahl, 1985; Lindblom, 1977 and 1982).
6 The quotation is from Daniel Singer (1988, p. 291).
7 Among the more interesting theoretical commentaries on 1989 and its consequences in the West are Heilbroner (1989), Prins (1990); Furet (1990), Habermas (1990b), Blackburn (1991), Kumar (1992), Therborn (1992), Held (1993).
8 The question of planning is raised again in chs 4 and 5.

Chapter 4   A Model of Market Socialism

1 For a characteristic discussion, see Gillespie and Paterson (1993).
2 For the view that neo-liberals promote the market as an imperfect but 'least worst' mechanism, see Lavoie (1985, pp. 55ff).
3 Elster's own judgement is heavily qualified by his claim that 'market socialism could be compatible with the cooperatives being in a minority' (Elster and Moene, 1989b, p. 26).

Chapter 5   Market Socialism: A 'Contradiction in Terms'?

1 There is a vast literature on 'what equality really means', which I cannot address here. See e.g. Baker (1987); Dworkin (1981); Miller (1993).
2 For a useful introduction to this difficult area, see Reeve (1987), Roemer (1982 and 1985).
3 See von Mises (1951), cited in Nuti (1992, p. 22).
4 For a recent discussion, see Roland and Sekkat (1993).
5 Miller (1989) is an honourable exception, though, as we shall see in ch. 7, there are substantial difficulties with his account of democracy under market socialism.

Chapter 6   The Political Economy of Labour Management

1   See e.g. Miller (1989), Selucky (1979), Elster and Moene (1989a). At the same time, it is important to note that other market socialists remain deeply sceptical of the desirability of reorganizing enterprises along self-managing lines (Roemer, 1992a; Yunker, 1990a).

2   On the scale of British co-operatives, see Estrin and Perotin (1987).

3   Among the most important contributions are Vanek (1970, 1972 and 1975); Ward (1958 and 1967); Meade (1988a and 1988b); Domar (1966 and 1989); Horvat et al. (1975); Horvat (1976 and 1982); Dreze (1976). Good secondary accounts can be found in Stephen (1982); Steinherr (1983); Estrin (1983); Bonin and Putterman (1987). A less technical discussion of many of the issues can be found in Fanning and O'Mahony (1983); and Fanning and McCarthy (1986).

4   For a general discussion of co-operatives in socialist countries, see Bonin and Putterman (1987, pp. 156–161). For an account of the co-operative movement in Eastern Europe *before* the introduction of state socialism, see Balawyder (1980).

5   Of course, Hungary might be taken as an alternative model of a 'real-world' market socialist economy. But, it fact, Hungary was, at least in principle, much further from being a worker-managed economy (see Swain, 1992).

6   It is worth repeating here that not *all* market socialists accept that workers' self-management would be a central feature of a market socialist order.

7   See e.g. Horvat (1982); Fanning and McCarthy (1986); Elster (1988). I shall, however, seek to give due weight to those criticisms which would apply equally to co-operative enterprises within either capitalist *or* labour-managed economies.

8   For a review of the wealth of modified Illyrian models see Mygind (1986) and Steinherr (1983).

9   Beatrice Webb reserved her most withering scorn for this gravest disorder of workers' self-management: 'Consider a railway managed on the system of the porters choosing the station master, the station master choosing the traffic superintendent, the whole body of employees choosing the board of directors! Those who have watched the inner workings of associations of this mould have realized the impossibility of this form of government in a highly organized industry' (B. Potter, 1891, p. 153).

10 Adam Przeworski and John Sprague (1985 and 1986), offer a similar though more general argument about the impossibility of securing democratic support for socialism in the face of its transitional costs. See pp. 197–8 below.

11 Of course, this is *not* to say that the judgement of these critics is necessarily true. A cursory comparison of the state of the world's underground transport systems, for example, would suggest that attitudes to common property may be subject to considerable cross-cultural variation.

12 Djordjevic concludes: Under 'nationalization . . . the working class continues to exist, often in a sense losing its autonomy and especially its historic right . . . to institute self-management. This "right" is, on behalf of the workers, taken over by the state [giving] rise to old and new

forms of social and political alienation and mythology' (Djordjevic, 1966, pp. 81–2).

13 The mildest suggestion of property reform has often been enough to invoke the image of the respectable middle classes systematically excluded from the quiet enjoyment of their homes by an army of parasitic squatters. For a discussion of the psychology of ownership and possessiveness, see Trasler (1982).

14 Waldron's discussion runs to nearly 500 pages. For those whose time is short, Waldron obligingly summarizes his major arguments and conclusions on pp. 3–5.

15 The classical source on differing types of rights is Hohfeld, *Fundamental Legal Conceptions* (1919). On the issue of socialism and self-ownership, see Kernohan (1987 and 1988); Cohen (1990).

16 Where the market socialist position is explicitly discussed by Waldron, his response is somewhat ambivalent (1988, pp. 9–11, 320–2).

17 Of course, this qualification does not prevent Gray from going on to dismiss market socialism as 'an unworkable absurdity' (1992, p. 54).

18 A rather simpler objection to this arrangement is that on an economy-wide scale it simply would not work. It is difficult to know how one might prove/disprove this claim without trying it! Here I am solely concerned with the theoretical question of whether such an arrangement should be understood as a 'restoration of capitalism'.

Chapter 7   Democracy and State under Market Socialism

1 See, *inter alia*, Barber (1984); Dahl (1985); Burnheim (1985); Held (1987); Gould (1988); Dahl (1989); Dryzek (1990); Phillips (1991); Held (1993). For influential forerunners, see Pateman (1970); Macpherson (1977a). Also of interest are Arneson (1992 and 1993).

2 Some make it quite clear that their aspiration for extended participation is exclusively *political*, and has very little to do with the legislation of socialism. Barber (1984, especially pp. xv–xvi, 252–7), is a good example; though even his position is somewhat qualified by hostility to corporate capitalism and an enthusiasm for *markets* rather than for market capitalism.

3 See, *inter alia*, Dahl (1956, 1961, 1971, 1985 and 1989). For a brief appreciation of Dahl's remarkable intellectual biography, see Held (1991b).

4 This general case for democracy is still more fully and more explicitly established in the magisterial *Democracy and its Critics* (Dahl, 1989).

5 Many neo-liberals do not, of course, wish to see democracy extended at all. Hayek is perhaps the most articulate spokesperson for the view that 'only limited government can be decent government' and that, if it is not to undermine both itself and the prior values of liberty, democracy must be restrained by insulating the economic sphere form control by the *demos* (Hayek, 1982, vol. 2, p. 102). On the ways in which workplace democracy would institutionalize exploitation, see Arnold (1992). On the general neo-liberal case for limited democracy, see ch. 5 above and Pierson (1993a).

6 For the classical statement of this view, see Rousseau (1968); for two distinctive contemporary treatments of the case against representation, see Barber (1984); Burnheim (1985).

7   The famous original is, of course, John Locke's. Rejecting the Hobbesian argument that men could only be secure against each others' predations by surrendering all their protective powers to an unrestrained sovereign, he insisted: 'This is to think that Men are so foolish that they take care to avoid what Mischiefs may be done them by *Pole-cats*, or *Foxes*, but are content, nay think it Safety, to be devoured by *Lions*' (Locke, 1963, p. 372).

8   For an especially clear and sensible discussion of this potential problem as manifest in feminist politics, see Phillips (1991, pp. 146ff).

9   The discourse of 'ungovernability' reached fever pitch in the mid-1970s. If anything, it was more a reflection of the contingent and defensive strength of the organized labour movement in the post-war period, under circumstances of full employment which have long since passed. For a discussion, see King (1987); Pierson (1991a).

10 Marx (1973b); Lenin (1960); Luxemburg (1970); Miliband (1961); for a commentary, see Pierson (1986).

11 A simple if graphic example is given by the experience of John Major's UK Conservative government, which, in the wake of intense speculative pressure, was forced on 16 Sept., 1992 to abandon its membership of the Exchange Rate Mechanism of the European Monetary System, an institution which had six months previously been described in its election manifesto as 'central to our counter-inflation discipline' (*Conservative Manifesto*, 1992, p. 6). At what stage and by what imaginable mechanism might the government have been held to account for this policy reversal?

12 Not the least of the differences between Dryzek and Miller is the insistence of the former that discursive institutions should be located in opposition to, and not within, the state. It is also probably fair to say that Dryzek is more directly indebted to the tradition of critical theory than is Miller.

13 Any survey of these initiatives is likely to include Beetham (1993); Bobbio (1987a and 1987b); Bowles and Gintis (1986); Campbell (1983); J. Cohen (1983); Cunningham (1987); Esping-Andersen (1985); Gould (1988); Held (1987 and 1993); Held and Hall (1989); Held and Pollitt (1986); Hindess (1983); Hirst (1986); Keane (1984, 1988a and 1988b); Laclau and Mouffe (1985); Mouffe (1992); Offe (1985); Phillips (1991); Poulantzas (1978).

14 For a compendious overview, see Arato and Cohen (1992).

15 For a representative sample, see Matthews (1989); Cohen and Rogers (1992); Martell (1992); Cohen and Rogers (1993); Hirst (1993b).

Chapter 8   Feasible Socialism?

1   According to James Yunker (1992, p. 278), 'what the moderately stated case for pragmatic market socialism loses in terms of drama and rhetorical force, it (one hopes) more than gains in terms of basic credibility and plausibility'.

2   For the view that what Alec Nove, at least, proposes is 'really an "efficient" socialism, no more "feasible" than traditional central planning, undistinguishable from the capitalist mixed economy', see Nuti (1992, p. 20).

3   Roemer (1994, pp. 123–4) cites, as rather differing examples, South Africa, El Salvador, Mexico and Brazil.

4   For a definitive account of the 'exhaustion' of traditional social democratic strategy, see Esping-Andersen (1985). Not all market socialists share Roemer's perspective. David Miller, for example, argues that 'market socialist ideas might seem to stand a greater chance of success in well-established market economies, where working under market constraints is a familiar experience, but where many employees find themselves frustrated by the hierarchical structure of the traditional capitalist firm' (Miller, 1991, p. 414).

5   It is interesting to note that the publication of the second edition of *Feasible Socialism* (in 1991) finds Nove rather less certain that a vote to restore capitalism is so very improbable.

6   On market socialism as an aspect of world government, see Yunker (1985).

7   On the benefits of reversibility, see Yunker (1992), pp. 281–4.

8   See Pierson (1986); Hindess (1983). Certainly the idea of transition became increasingly irrelevant for many post-war social democrats, (such as Anthoy Crosland in Britain), for whom, if socialism was not yet established, traditional capitalism had certainly already been transcended (see Crosland, 1964).

9   For a more trenchantly Leninist account of the problem of transition, see Emmanuel (1979).

10 In response to those critics who insist that Przeworski's ruminations upon social democracy must make him a Leninist, Przeworski responds that he is 'a follower not of Vladimir Illych but of that other great Russian socialist thinker, Georgij Konstantinowich Pessim' (Przeworski, 1985, p. 239).

11 Notable critiques include Higgins and Apple (1983), Lichbach (1984), King and Wickham-Jones (1990), Sainsbury (1990), Kitschelt (1993 and 1994).

12 It is not clear why socialist parties may not seek to mobilize support around the shared interests of wage-earners, a group which is far more extensive than Przeworski's 'workers in the narrow sense'.

13 Certainly Przeworski recognizes that the special circumstances for such a transition may never apply in practice to any of the regimes in transition from command to market economies in Eastern Europe.

14 See e.g. Esping-Andersen (1985); Meidner (1980); Pontusson (1992a and b); Pierson (1991a and b); Meidner (1993).

15 Swenson (1991). See also Dunleavy and Husbands (1985).

16 For a concise discussion, see Kitschelt (1994, pp. 41–7).

17 Przeworski (1977) was one of the first to draw attention to this.

18 For a brief discussion see Pierson (1991a), Taylor-Gooby (1989).

19 Even some of those who are keenest to argue for a market-directed response to environmental problems insist that this is only possible within the context of a previously established (state) framework. See e.g. Pearce, Markandya and Barbier (1989).

Conclusion

1   Here I use 'pragmatic' not in its degenerate and pejorative sense of 'unprincipled' or 'opportunistic', but in something closer to its earlier philosophical sense of thought oriented around practice and experience.

Bibliography

Aglietta, M. 1979: *A Theory of Capitalist Regulation*. London: New Left Books.

Alber, J. 1988a: Is there a crisis of the welfare state? Cross-national evidence from Europe, North America, and Japan. *European Sociological Review*, 4 (3), 181–207.

Alber, J. 1988b: Continuities and changes in the welfare state. *Politics and Society*, 16 (4), 451–68.

Albertsen, N. 1988: Postmodernism, post-Fordism, and critical social theory. *Environment and Planning D: Society and Space*, 6, 339–65.

Andrews, G. (ed.) 1991: *Citizenship*. London: Lawrence and Wishart.

Arato, A. and Cohen, J. 1992: *Civil Society and Political Theory*. London: MIT Press.

Aristotle 1946: *The Politics*. Oxford: Clarendon.

Arneson, R. J. 1992: Is socialism dead? A comment on market socialism and basic income capitalism. *Ethics*, 102, 485–511.

Arneson, R. J. 1993: Socialism as the extension of democracy. *Social Philosophy and Policy*, 10 (2), 145–71.

Arnold, N. S. 1987a: Marx and disequilibrium in market socialist relations of production. *Economics and Philosophy*, 3, 23–47.

Arnold, N. S. 1987b: Why profits are deserved. *Ethics*, 97 (2), 387–402.

Arnold, N. S. 1989: Marx, central planning and utopian socialism. *Social Philosophy and Policy*, 6 (2), 160–99.

Arnold, N. S. 1992: Equality and exploitation in the market socialist community. *Social Philosophy and Policy*, 9 (1), 1–28.

Baker, J. 1987: *Arguing for Equality*. London: Verso.

Balawyder, A. (ed.) 1980: *Cooperative Movements in Eastern Europe*. London: Macmillan.

Barber, B. 1984: *Strong Democracy: Participatory Politics for a New Age*. Berkeley: University of California Press.

Bardhan, P. and Roemer, J. E. (eds) 1993a: *Market Socialism*. Oxford: Oxford University Press.

Bardhan, P. and Roemer, J. E. 1993b: Introduction. In Bardhan and Roemer (1993a), pp. 3–17.

Barone, E. 1935: The ministry of production in the collectivist state. In Hayek (1935), pp. 245–91.

Barr, N. 1987: *The Economics of the Welfare State*. London: Weidenfeld and Nicolson.

Barr, N. 1992: Economic theory and the welfare state: an interpretation. *Journal of Economic Literature*, 30 (June), 741–803.

Bartlett, W. and Pridham, G. 1991: Co-operative enterprises in Italy, Portugal and Spain: history, development and prospects. *Journal of Interdisciplinary Economics*, 4, 33–59.

Bartlett, W., Cable, J., Estrin, S., Jones, D. C. and Smith, S. C. 1992: Labor-managed cooperatives and private firms in North Central Italy: an empirical comparison. *Industrial and Labor Relations Review*, 46 (1), 103–18.

Beck, P. A. 1984: The dealignment era in America. In R. J. Dalton, S. C. Flanagan and P. A. Beck, *Electoral Change in Advanced Industrial Democracies: Realignment or Dealignment?* Princeton, NJ: Princeton University Press, pp. 240–66.

Becker, L. C. 1977: *Property Rights: Philosophic Foundations*. London: Routledge and Kegan Paul.

Beetham, D. 1993: Four theorems about the market and democracy. *European Journal of Political Research*, 23, 187–201.

Beilharz, P. 1992: *Labour's Utopias: Bolshevism, Fabianism, Social Democracy*. London: Routledge.

Bell, D. S. and Criddle, B. 1988: *The French Socialist Party: The Emergence of a Party of Government*, 2nd edn. Oxford: Clarendon.

Ben-Ner, A. and Neuberger, E. 1990: The feasibility of planned market systems: the Yugoslav visible hand and negotiated planning. *Journal of Comparative Economics*, 14, 768–90.

Berend, I. T. 1989: *The Hungarian Economic Reforms: 1953–1988*. Cambridge: Cambridge University Press.

Bergson, A. 1966: Socialist economics. In A. Bergson, *Essays in Normative Economics*. Cambridge, Mass.: Harvard University Press; first published in 1948, pp. 193–236.

Bergson, A. 1967: Market socialism revisited. *Journal of Political Economy*, 75, 655–73.

Bergson, A. 1987: Comparative productivity: the USSR, Eastern Europe and the West. *American Economic Review*, 77 (3), 342–57.

Bergson, A. 1989: *Planning and Performance in Socialist Economies: The USSR and Eastern Europe*. London: Unwin Hyman.

Berki, R. N. 1975: *Socialism*. London: Dent.

Berlin, I. 1969: *Four Essays on Liberty*. Oxford: Oxford University Press.

Berman, K. V. and Berman, M. D. 1989: An empirical test of the theory of the labor-managed firm. *Journal of Comparative Economics*, 13, 281–300.

Bernstein, E. 1909: *Evolutionary Socialism*. London: Independent Labour Party.

Beveridge, W. H. 1944: *Full Employment in a Free Society*. London: George Allen and Unwin.

Blackburn, R. 1991: *After the Fall: The Failure of Communism and the Future of Socialism*. London: Verso.

Blanchflower, D. and Freeman, R. 1992: Unionism in the United States and other advanced OECD countries. *Industrial Relations*, 31 (1 Winter), 56–79.

Bobbio, N. 1987a: *The Future of Democracy: A Defence of the Rules of the Game*.

Cambridge: Polity.

Bobbio, N. 1987b: *Which Socialism? Marxism, Socialism and Democracy.* Cambridge: Polity.

Bonin, J. P. and Fukuda, W. 1986: The multifactor Illyrian firm revisited. *Journal of Comparative Economics*, 10, 171–80.

Bonin, J. P. and Putterman, L 1987: *Economics of Cooperation and the Labor-Managed Economy.* London: Harwood.

Bowles, S. and Gintis, H. 1986: *Democracy and Capitalism: Property, Community and the Contradictions of Modern Social Thought.* London: Routledge and Kegan Paul.

Boyne, R. and Rattansi, A. 1990: Introduction. In R. Boyne and A. Rattansi, *Postmodernism and Society.* London: Macmillan, pp. 1–43.

Brada, J. C. and Estrin, S. 1990: Advances in the theory and practice of indicative planning. *Journal of Comparative Economics*, 14, 523–30.

Bradley, K. and Gelb, A. 1986: Cooperative labour relations: Mondragon's response to recession. *Industrial Relations Journal*, 17, 177–97.

Braverman, H. 1974: *Labour and Monopoly Capital.* New York: Monthly Review Press.

Brewer, A. 1988: Technical Change in Illyria. *Journal of Comparative Economics*, 12 (3), 401–15.

Brittan, S. 1975: The economic contradictions of democracy. *British Journal of Political Science*, 5 (2), 129–59.

Broekmeyer, M. J. (ed.) 1970: *Yugoslav Workers' Self-management.* Dordrecht: D. Reidel.

Bruno, M. and Sachs, J. D. 1985: *Economics of Worldwide Stagflation.* Oxford: Blackwell.

Brus, W. 1972: *The Market in a Socialist Economy.* London: Routledge and Kegan Paul.

Brus, W. 1973: *The Economics and Politics of Socialism.* London: Routledge and Kegan Paul.

Brus, W. 1975: *Socialist Ownership and Political Systems.* London: Routledge and Kegan Paul.

Brus, W. 1980: Political systems and economic efficiency. *Journal of Comparative Economics*, 4, 40–55.

Brus, W. 1985: Socialism – feasible and viable? *New Left Review*, 153, 43–62.

Brus, W. 1987: Market socialism. In J. Eatwell, M. Milgate and P. Newman (eds), *The New Palgrave Dictionary of Economics*, vol. 3. London: Macmillan.

Brus, W. 1989: Evolution of the communist economic system: scope and limits. In V. Nee and D. Stark, *Remaking the Economic Institutions of Socialism* (Stanford, Calif.: Stanford University Press), pp. 255–77.

Brus, W. 1990: The 'March into Socialism'. In H. Flakierski and T. T. Sekine, *Socialist Dilemmas: East and West.* Armonk, NY: Sharpe, pp. 28–38.

Brus, W. and Laski, K. 1989a: *From Marx to the Market: Socialism in Search of an Economic System.* Oxford: Clarendon.

Brus, W. and Laski, K. 1989b: Capital Market and the problem of full employment. *European Economic Review*, 33 (2, 3), 439–47.

Bukharin, N. and Preobrazhenksy, F. 1969: *The ABC of Communism.* Penguin: Harmondsworth.

Burke, E. 1910: *Reflections on the Revolution in France.* London: Dent.

Burnham, W. D. 1989: The Reagan heritage. In G. M. Pomper et al. (eds), *The Election of 1988.* Chatham, NJ: Chatham House, pp. 1–32.

Burnheim, J. 1985: *Is Democracy Possible? The Alternative to Electoral Politics.* Cambridge: Polity.

Butler, D. and Stokes, D. 1974: *Political Change in Britain* rev. edn. London: Macmillan.

Callinicos, A. 1990: Reactionary postmodernism. In Boyne and Rattansi (1990), pp. 97–118.

Callinicos, A. 1991: *The Revenge of History: Marxism and the East European Revolutions.* Cambridge: Polity.

Campbell, T. C. 1983: *The Left and Rights: A Conceptual Analysis of the Idea of Socialist Rights.* London: Routledge and Kegan Paul.

Caresvic, M. 1974: Social property in the drafts of the constitutions. *Socialist Thought and Practice*, 14 (2), 3–17.

Central Statistical Office (CSO) 1991: *Social Trends 21.* London: HMSO.

Chiplin, B. and Coyne, J. 1977: *Can Workers Manage?* London: IEA.

Christman, J. 1988: Entrepreneurs, profits and deserving market shares. *Social Philosophy and Policy*, 6 (1), 1–16.

Cohen, G. A. 1990: Marxism and contemporary political philosophy, or: Why Nozick exercises some Marxists more than he does any egalitarian liberals. *Canadian Journal of Philosophy*, suppl. vol., 16, 363–87.

Cohen, G. A. 1992: The future of a disillusion. In J. Hopkins and A. Savile (eds), *Psychoanalysis, Mind and Art: Perspectives on Richard Wollheim.* Oxford: Blackwell, pp. 142–60.

Cohen, Jean 1983: *Class and Civil Society: The Limits of Marxian Theory.* Oxford: Martin Robertson.

Cohen, J. 1988: The economic bases of deliberative democracy. *Social Philosophy and Policy*, 6 (2), 25–50.

Cohen, J. and Rogers, J. 1992: Associations and democracy. *Social Philosophy and Policy*, 10 (2), 282–312.

Cohen, J. and Rogers, J. 1993: Associative democracy. In Bardhan and Roemer (1993), pp. 236–52.

Cole, G. D. H. 1945: *A Century of Co-operation.* London: Allen and Unwin.

Cole, G. D. H. 1953: *Socialist Thought – the Forerunners 1779–1850.* London: Macmillan.

Comisso, E. T. 1979: *Workers' Control under Plan and Market: Implications of Yugoslav Self-management.* London: Yale University Press.

Commission of the European Communities 1991: *Employment in Europe.* Luxembourg: Office for Official Publications of The European Communities.

Crewe, I. 1984: The electorate: partisan dealignment ten years on. In H. Berrington (ed.), *Change in British Politics.* London: Frank Cass, pp. 183–215.

Crewe, I. 1985: Great Britain. In I. Crewe and D. Denver, *Electoral Change in Western Democracies.* London: Croom Helm, pp. 100–50.

Crewe, I. 1987: A New Class of Politics. *Guardian*, 15 June 1987.

Crewe, I. 1991: Labor force changes, working class decline, and the labour vote: social and electoral trends in postwar Britain. In Piven (1991), pp. 20–46.

Crewe, I. 1993: Voting and the electorate. In P. Dunleavy, A. Gamble, I. Holliday and G. Peele (eds), *Developments in British Politics 4.* London: Macmillan, pp. 92–122.

Crosland, A. 1964: *The Future of Socialism.* London: Cape.

Cunningham, F. 1987: *Democratic Theory and Socialism.* Cambridge: Cambridge University Press.

Dahl, R. 1956: *A Preface to Democratic Theory.* Chicago: University of Chicago Press.

Dahl, R. A. 1961: *Who Governs? Democracy and Power in an American City*. New Haven, Conn.: Yale University Press.

Dahl, R. A. 1971: *Polyarchy: Participation and Opposition*. New Haven, Conn.: Yale University Press.

Dahl, R. A. 1985: *A Preface to Economic Democracy*. Cambridge: Polity.

Dahl, R. A. 1989: *Democracy and its Critics*. New Haven, Conn.: Yale University Press.

Dahl, R. and Lindblom, C. 1953: *Politics, Economics and Welfare*. New York: Harper and Row.

Dahrendorf, R. 1990: *Reflections on the Revolution in Europe*. London: Chatto and Windus.

Deakin, N. 1987: *In Search of the Postwar Consensus*. London: Suntory – Toyota International Centre for Economics and Related Disciplines, LSE.

De Jasay, A. 1990: *Market Socialism*. London: IEA.

Demsetz, H. 1967: Toward a theory of property rights. *American Economic Review: Proceedings and Papers*, 57, 347–59.

Denemark, D. 1990: The political consequences of Labour's New Right agendas: findings from the Fendalton Survey, 1987. *Political Science*, 42 (1), 62–82.

Dennis, N. and Halsey, A. H. 1988: *English Ethical Socialism: Thomas More to R. H. Tawney*. Oxford: Clarendon.

Department of Employment (UK) 1991–4: *Employment Gazette*, June.

Department of Health and Social Security (DHSS), UK 1985: *The Reform of Social Security*, Cmnd. 9517, vol 1. London: HMSO.

Devine, P. 1988: *Democracy and Economic Planning: The Political Economy of a Self-Governing Society*. Cambridge: Polity.

Dickinson, H. D. 1933: Price formation in a socialist community. *Economic Journal*, 43 (June), 237–50.

Djordjevic, J. 1966: A contribution to the theory of social property. *Socialist Thought and Practice*, 24 (Oct. – Dec.), 73–110.

Djordjevic, J., Jogan, S., Ribicic, M. and Vratusa, A. (eds) 1982: *Self-management: The Yugoslav Road to Socialism*. Belgrade: Jugoslovenski Pregled.

Dobb, M. 1955: *On Economic Theory and Socialism: Collected Papers*. London: Routledge and Kegan Paul.

Dobson, A. 1990: *Green Political Thought*. London: Unwin Hyman.

Domar, E. D. 1966: The Soviet collective farm as a producer cooperative. *American Economic Review*, 56, 734–57.

Domar, E. D. 1989: *Capitalism, Socialism, and Serfdom*. Cambridge: Cambridge University Press.

Dreze, J. H. 1976: Some theory of labour management and participation. *Econometrica*, 44, 1125–39.

Dryzek, J. S. 1990: *Discursive Democracy: Politics, Policy and Political Science*. Cambridge: Cambridge University Press.

Dunleavy, P. and Husbands, C. T. 1985: *British Democracy at the Crossroads: Voting and Party Competition in the 1980s*. London: Allen and Unwin.

Dworkin, G. 1981: What is Equality? (Parts 1 and 2), *Philosophy and Public Affairs*, 187–246, 283–345.

Dyker, D. A. 1990: *Yugoslavia: Socialism, Development and Debt*. London: Routledge.

Electoral Studies: 1982–

Ellerman, D. 1990: *The Democratic Worker-Owned Firm: A New Model for the East and West*. London: Unwin Hyman.

Ellman, M. 1989: *Socialist Planning*, 2nd edn. Cambridge: Cambridge University Press.

Elson, D. 1988: Market socialism or socialization of the market? *New Left Review*, 172, 3–44.

Elster, J. 1988: From here to there, or: If co-operative ownership is so desirable, why are there so few co-operatives? *Social Philosophy and Policy*, 6 (2), 93–111.

Elster, J. 1989: Self-realisation in work and politics: the Marxist conception of the good life. In Elster and Moene (1989a), pp. 127–58.

Elster, J. and Moene, K. O. 1989a: *Alternatives to Capitalism*. Cambridge: Cambridge University Press.

Elster, J. and Moene, K. O. 1989b: Introduction. In Elster and Moene (1989a), pp. 1–35.

Emmanuel, A. 1979: The state in the transitional period. *New Left Review*, 113/14, 111–31.

Engels, F. 1987: Anti-Dühring. In K. Marx and F. Engels, *Collected Works*, vol. 25. (London: Lawrence and Wishart).

Esping-Andersen, G. 1985: *Politics against Markets*. Princeton, NJ: Princeton University Press.

Esping-Andersen, G. 1990: *The Three Worlds of Welfare Capitalism*. Cambridge: Polity.

Esping-Andersen, G. 1992: The emerging realignment between labour movements and welfare states. In M. Regini (ed.), *The Future of Labour Movements*. London: Sage, pp. 133–49.

Estrin, S. 1983: *Self-Management: Economic Theory and Yugoslav Practice*. Cambridge: Cambridge University Press.

Estrin, S. 1989: Workers' co-operatives: their merits and their limitations. In Le Grand and Estrin (1989), pp. 165–92.

Estrin, S. and Holmes, P. 1990: Indicative planning in developed economies. *Journal of Comparative Economics*, 14, 531–54.

Estrin, S. and Perotin, V. 1987: Cooperatives and participatory firms in Great Britain. *International Review of Applied Economics*, 1, 152–75.

Estrin, S. and Winter, D. 1989: Planning in a market socialist economy. In Le Grand and Estrin (1989), pp. 100–38.

Estrin, S., Jones, D. C. and Svejnar, J. 1987: The productivity effects of worker participation: producer cooperatives in Western economies. *Journal of Comparative Economics*, 11 (1), 40–61.

Eurostat 1988: *Basic Statistics of the Community*, 26th edn. Luxembourg: Statistical Office of the European Communities.

Eurostat 1989a: *Rapid Reports: Population and Social Conditions*. Luxembourg: Statistical Office of the European Communities.

Eurostat 1989b: *Labour Force Survey, 1987*. Luxembourg: Statistical Office of the European Communities.

Eurostat 1990: *Some Statistics on Services*. Luxembourg: Statistical Office of the European Communities.

Eurostat 1993: *Basic Statistics of the Community*, 30th edn. Luxembourg: Statistical Office of the European Communities.

Fanning, C. M. and McCarthy, T. 1986: A survey of economic hypotheses concerning the non-viability of labour-directed firms in capitalist economies. In S. Jansson and A. B. Hellmark, *Labor-owned Firms and Workers' Cooperatives*. Aldershot: Gower, pp. 7–50.

Fanning, C. and O'Mahony, D. 1983: The worker co-operative. In Kennedy

(1983), pp. 11–29.

Fay, C. R. 1908: *Cooperation at Home and Abroad*. London: P. S. King.

Field, F. 1989: *Losing Out: The Emergence of Britain's Underclass*. Oxford: Blackwell.

Flakierski, H. 1989: *The Economic System and Income Distribution in Yugoslavia*. Armonk, NY: Sharpe.

Fleurbaey, M. 1993: Economic democracy and equality: a proposal. In Bardhan and Roemer (1993), pp. 266–78.

Flora, P. (ed.) 1987: *State, Economy and Society*, 2 vols. London: Macmillan.

Frankel, P. E. 1989: *Socialism*. Oxford; Blackwell.

Friedman, M. 1962: *Capitalism and Freedom*. Chicago: University of Chicago Press.

Fukuyama, F. 1989: The end of history? *The National Interest*, Summer, 3–18.

Fukuyama, F. 1992: *The End of History and the Last Man*. London: Hamish Hamilton.

Furet, F. 1990: From 1789 to 1917 and 1989: looking back at revolutionary traditions. *Encounter*, Sept., 3–7.

Furubotn, E. and Pejovich, S. 1970: Property rights and the behaviour of the firm in a socialist state: the example of Yugoslavia. *Zeitschrift für Nationalökonomie*, 30, 431–54.

Galbraith, J. K. 1990: Revolt in our time: the triumph of simplistic ideology. In Prins (1990), pp. 1–11.

Gamble, A. 1988: *The Free Economy and the Strong State: The Politics of Thatcherism*. London: Macmillan.

Garton Ash, T. 1990: *We the People*. Cambridge: Granta.

Geras, N. 1990: Seven types of obloquy: travesties of Marxism. *Socialist Register*, 1–34.

Gilbert, B. B. 1966: *The Evolution of National Insurance in Great Britain*. London: Michael Joseph.

Gillespie, R. and Paterson, W. E. 1993: *Rethinking Social Democracy in Western Europe*. London: Frank Cass. (Originally appeared as *West European Politics*, Special Issue, 16 (1), Jan. 1993.)

Glennerster, H., Power, A. and Travers, T. 1991: A new era for social policy: a new enlightenment or a new Leviathan? *Journal of Social Policy*, 20 (3), 389–414.

Goldthorpe, J. H. (ed.) 1984: *Order and Conflict in Contemporary Capitalism*. Oxford: Oxford University Press.

Goodin, R. E. and Le Grand, J. 1987: *Not Only the Poor: The Middle Classes and the Welfare State*. London: Allen and Unwin.

Gorz, A. 1982: *Farewell to the Working Class: An Essay on Post-Industrial Socialism*. London: Pluto.

Gough, I. 1979: *The Political Economy of the Welfare State*. London: Macmillan.

Gould, C. 1988: *Rethinking Democracy: Freedom and Social Cooperation in Politics, Economy, and Society*. Cambridge: Cambridge University Press.

Gouldner, A. 1980: *The Two Marxisms*. London: Macmillan.

Gray, J. 1984: *Hayek on Liberty*. Oxford: Blackwell.

Gray, J. 1988: Against Cohen on proletarian unfreedom. *Social Philosophy and Policy*, 6 (1), 77–112.

Gray, J. 1992: *The Moral Foundations of Market Institutions*. London: IEA.

Greenberg, E. S. 1984: Producer cooperatives and democratic theory: the case of the plywood firms. In R. Jackall and H. M. Levin, *Worker Cooperatives in America*. London: University of California Press.

Grunebaum, J. O. 1987: *Private Ownership*. London: Routledge and Kegan Paul.

Habermas, J. 1972: *Knowledge and Human Interests*. London: Heinemann.

Habermas, J. 1981: Modernity versus postmodernity. *New German Critique*, 22, 3–14.

Habermas, J. 1987: *The Philosophical Discourse of Modernity*. Cambridge: Polity.

Habermas, J. 1990a: The new obscurity: the crisis of the welfare state and the exhaustion of utopian energies. In J. Habermas, *The New Conservatism*. Cambridge: Polity, pp. 48–70.

Habermas, J. 1990b: 'What does socialism mean today? The rectifying revolution and the need for new thinking on the Left'. In R. Blackburn, *After the Fall*. London: Verso, pp. 25–46.

Hall, S. and Jacques, M. (eds) 1989: *New Times: The Changing Face of Politics in the 1990s*. London: Lawrence and Wishart.

Hankiss, E. 1990: *East European Alternatives*. Oxford: Clarendon.

Hardin, R. 1982: *Collective Action*. Baltimore: Johns Hopkins University Press.

Harrington, M. 1987: *The Next Left: The History of the Future*. London: Tauris.

Harrington, M. 1989: Markets and plans: is the market necessarily capitalist? *Dissent*, 36 (1), 56–70.

Harrop, M. and Shaw, A. 1989: *Can Labour Win?* London: Unwin/Fabian.

Harvey, D. 1989: *The Condition of Postmodernity*. Oxford: Blackwell.

Hassan, I. 1985: The culture of postmodernism. *Theory, Culture and Society*, 2 (3), 119–31.

Hayek, F. 1935: *Collectivist Economic Planning*. London: Routledge and Kegan Paul.

Hayek, F. 1940: Socialist calculation: the 'competitive solution'. *Economica*, 7, 125–49.

Hayek, F. 1944: *The Road to Serfdom*. London: Routledge and Kegan Paul.

Hayek, F. 1982: *Law, Legislation and Liberty*, 3 vols. London: Routledge and Kegan Paul.

Hayek, F. 1990: *The Fatal Conceit*. London: Routledge and Kegan Paul.

Heath, A. et al. 1985: *How Britain Votes*. Oxford: Pergamon.

Heath, A. et al. 1991: *Understanding Political Change: The British Voter 1964–1987*. Oxford: Pergamon.

Heilbroner, R. 1989: The triumph of capitalism. *New Yorker*, 23 Jan.

Held, D. 1980: *Introduction to Critical Theory*. London: Hutchinson.

Held, D. 1987: *Models of Democracy*. Cambridge: Polity.

Held, D. 1991a: Democracy, the nation-state and the global system. In D. Held, *Political Theory Today*. Cambridge: Polity, pp. 197–235.

Held, D. 1991b: Review essay: The possibilities of democracy. *Theory and Society*, 20, 875–89.

Held, D. 1992: Liberalism, Marxism and democracy. In S. Hall, D. Held and A. McGrew, *Modernity and its Futures*. Cambridge: Polity, pp. 13–47.

Held, D. 1993: *Prospects for Democracy*. Cambridge: Polity.

Held, D. and Hall, S. 1989: Left and rights. *Marxism Today*, June, 16–23.

Held, D. and Pollitt, C. (eds) 1986: *New Forms of Democracy*. London: Sage.

Higgins, W and Apple, N. 1983: How limited is reformism? A critique of Przeworski and Panitch. *Theory and Society*, 12 (5), 603–30.

Hindess, B. 1983: *Parliamentary Democracy and Socialist Politics*. London: Routledge and Kegan Paul.

Hirst, P. 1986: *Law, Socialism and Democracy*. London: Allen and Unwin.

Hirst, P. 1993a: Associational democracy. In Held (1993), pp. 112–35.

Hirst, P. 1993b: *Associative Democracy: New Forms of Economic and Social Governance*. Cambridge: Polity.

Hobbs, P. and Jefferis, K. 1990: So how many cooperatives are there? In G. Jenkins and M. Poole (eds), *New Forms of Ownership*. London: Routledge, pp 289–302.

Hobsbawm, E. 1981: *The Forward March of Labour Halted?* London: Verso.

Hodge, C. C. 1993: The politics of programmatic renewal: postwar experiences in Britain and Germany. In Gillespie and Paterson (1993), pp. 5–19.

Hohfeld, W. N. 1919: *Fundamental Legal Conceptions*. New Haven, Conn.: Yale University Press.

Honoré, A. M. 1961: Ownership. In A. G. Guest (ed.), *Oxford Essays in Jurisprudence*. Oxford: Oxford University Press, pp. 107–47.

Hoover, K. and Plant, R. 1989: *Conservative Capitalism in Britain and the United States: A Critical Appraisal*. London: Routledge.

Horvat, B. 1976: *The Yugoslav Economic System*. White Plains, NY: IASP.

Horvat, B. 1982: *The Political Economy of Socialism*. Armonk, NY: Sharpe.

Horvat, B., Markovic, M., Supek, R. and Kramer, H. (eds) 1975: *Self-governing Socialism: A Reader*, 2 vols. White Plains NY: IASP.

Hyman, R. 1992: Trade unions and the disaggregation of the working class. In M. Regini (ed.), *The Future of Labour Movements*. London: Sage, pp. 150–68.

Jenkins, P. 1987: *Mrs Thatcher's Revolution: The Ending of the Socialist Era*. London: Cape.

Jessop, Bob 1991: The welfare state in the transition from Fordism to post-Fordism. In B. Jessop, H. Kastendiek, K. Nielsen and O. K. Pedersen, *The Politics of Flexibility*. London: Edward Elgar, pp. 82 105.

Jones, B. 1968: *Co-operative Production*. London; repr. New York: Augustus Kelley.

Jones, D. C. 1982a: British producer cooperatives, 1948–1968: productivity and organizational structure. In Jones and Svejnar (1982), pp. 175–98.

Jones, D. C. 1982b: The United States of America: a survey of producer co-operative performance. In Stephen (1982), pp. 53–73.

Jones, D. C. 1983: Producer co-operatives in industrialised Western Economies. In Kennedy (1983), pp. 31–60.

Jones, D. C. 1985: The economic performance of producer cooperatives within command economies: evidence for the case of Poland. *Cambridge Journal of Economics*, 9, 111–26.

Jones, D. C. and Svejnar, J. (eds) 1982: *Participatory and Self-managed Firms: Evaluating Economic Performances*. Lexington, Mass.: Lexington Books.

Jones, D. C. and Svejnar, J. 1985: Participation, profit sharing, worker ownership and efficiency in Italian producer cooperatives. *Economica*, 52, 449–65.

Kaldor, M. 1991: After the Cold War. In M. Kaldor, *Europe from Below: An East–West Dialogue*. London: Verso, pp. 27–42.

Kalecki, M. 1971: *Selected Essays on the Dynamics of the Capitalist Economy 1933–1970*. Cambridge: Cambridge University Press.

Kamenka, E. 1969: *Marxism and Ethics*. London: Macmillan.

Kardelj, E. 1979: Social ownership and socialist self-management. *Socialist Thought and Practice*, 19 (2), 46–57.

Katz, M. 1986: *In the Shadow of the Poorhouse*. New York: Basic Books.

Kautsky, K. 1920: *Terrorism and Communism*. London: George Allen and Unwin.

Kautsky, K. 1964: *The Dictatorship of the Proletariat*. Ann Arbor, Mich.: University of Michigan Press.

Kavanagh, D. 1990: *Thatcherism and British Politics: The End of Consensus?*, 2nd edn. Oxford: Oxford University Press.

Kavanagh, D. and Morris, P. 1989: *Consensus Politics from Attlee to Thatcher*. Oxford: Blackwell.

Keane, J. 1984: *Public Life and Late Capitalism: Toward a Socialist Theory of Democracy*. Cambridge: Cambridge University Press.

Keane, J. 1988a: *Democracy and Civil Society*. London: Verso.

Keane, J. (ed.) 1988b: *Civil Society and the State*. London: Verso.

Keane, J. and Owens, J. 1986: *After Full Employment*. London: Hutchinson.

Keizer, W. 1989: Recent reinterpretations of the socialist calculation debate. *Journal of Economic Studies*, 16 (2), 63–83.

Keman, H. 1993: Theoretical approaches to social democracy. *Journal of Theoretical Politics*, 5 (3), 291–316.

Kennedy, L. (ed.) 1983: *Economic Theory of Co-operative Enterprises: Selected Readings*. Oxford: Plunkett Foundation for Co-operative Studies.

Keohane, R. O. 1984: *After Hegemony: Cooperation and Discord in the World Political Economy*. Princeton, NY: Princeton University Press.

Kernohan, A. 1987: Democratic socialism and private property. *Studies in Political Economy*, 22, 145–66.

Kernohan, A. 1988: Capitalism and self-ownership. *Social Philosophy and Policy*, 6 (1), 60–76.

Kesselman, M. 1982: Prospects for democratic socialism in advanced capitalism: class struggle and compromise in Sweden and France. *Politics and Society*, 11 (4), 397–438.

Keynes, J. M. 1973: *The General Theory of Employment, Interest and Money*. London: Macmillan.

King, D. S. 1987: *The New Right: Politics, Markets and Citizenship*. London: Macmillan.

King, D. and Wickham-Jones, M. 1990: Social democracy and rational workers. *British Journal of Political Science*, 20 (3), 387–413.

Kitschelt, H. 1993: Class structure and social democratic party strategy. *British Journal of Political Science*, 23, 299–337.

Kitschelt, H. 1994: *The Transformation of European Social Democracy*. Cambridge: Cambridge University Press.

Kolakowski, L. 1978: *Main Currents of Marxism*, 3 vols. Oxford: Oxford University Press.

Kornai, J. 1980: The dilemmas of a socialist economy. *Cambridge Journal of Economics*, 4 (2), 147–57.

Kornai, J. 1986: The Hungarian reform process. *Journal of Economic Literature*, 24 (4), 1687–737.

Kornai, J. 1988: Individual freedom and the reform of the socialist economy. *European Economic Review*, 32 (2–3), 233–67.

Kornai, J. 1990a: *Vision and Reality, Market and State: Contradictions and Dilemma Revisited*. New York: Harvester Wheatsheaf.

Kornai, J. 1990b: *The Road to a Free Economy*. London: Norton.

Kornai, J. 1993: Market socialism revisited. In Bardhan and Roemer (1993), pp. 42–68.

Korpi, W. 1983: *The Democratic Class Struggle*. London: Routledge and Kegan Paul.

Korpi, W. 1989: Power, politics, and state autonomy in the development of social citizenship: social rights during sickness in eighteen OECD countries since 1930. *American Sociological Review*, 54 (3), 309–28.

Kumar, K. 1992: The revolutions of 1989: socialism, capitalism and democracy. *Theory and Society*, 21, 309–56.

Laclau, E. 1990: *New Reflections on the Revolution of our Time*. London: Verso.

Laclau, E. and Mouffe, C. 1985: *Hegemony and Socialist Strategy: Towards a Radical Democratic Politics*. London: Verso.

Ladd, E. C. 1981: The brittle mandate: electoral dealignment and the 1980 Presidential election. *Political Science Quarterly*, 96 (1), 1–25.

Lafferty, W. M. 1990: The political transformation of a social democratic state: as the world moves in, Norway moves right. *West European Politics*, 13 (1), 79–100.

Lambert, P. 1963: *Studies in the Social Philosophy of Co-operation*, Manchester: Cooperative Union.

Lane, J.-E. and Ersson, S. O. 1987: *Politics and Society in Western Europe*. London: Sage.

Lange, O. 1938: On the economic theory of socialism. In O. Lange and F. M. Taylor, *On the Economic Theory of Socialism*. Minneapolis: University of Minnesota Press, pp. 55–143.

Lash, S. and Urry, J. 1987: *The End of Organized Capitalism*. Cambridge: Polity.

Lavoie, D. 1981: A critique of the standard account of the socialist calculation debate. *Journal of Libertarian Studies*, 5, 41–87.

Lavoie, D. 1985: *Rivalry and Central Planning*. Cambridge: Cambridge University Press.

Lavoie, D. 1986: The market as a procedure for discovery and conveyance of inarticulate knowledge. *Comparative Economic Studies*, 28 (1), 1–19.

Lavoie, D. 1990: Computation, incentives and discovery: the cognitive function of markets in market socialism. *Annals of the American Academy of Political and Social Science*, 507, 72–9.

Le Grand, J. 1989: Markets, welfare, and equality. In Le Grand and Estrin (1989), pp. 193–211.

Le Grand, J. and Bartlett, W. (eds) 1993: *Quasi-Markets and Social Policy*. London: Macmillan.

Le Grand, J. and Estrin, S. (eds) 1989: *Market Socialism*. Oxford: Clarendon.

Leeman, W. A. 1977: *Centralized and Decentralized Economic Systems: The Soviet-Type Economy, Market Socialism, and Capitalism*. Chicago: Rand McNally College.

Lemke, C. and Marks, G. 1992: *The Crisis of Socialism in Europe*. London: Duke University Press.

Lenin, V. I. 1960: *The Proletarian Revolution and the Renegade Kautsky*. In *Collected Works*, vol. 28, pp. 227–326. London: Lawrence and Wishart.

Lerner, A. P. 1937: Statics and dynamics in socialist economics. *Economic Journal*, 47 (June), 253–70.

Lerner, A. P. 1944: *The Economics of Control*. New York: Macmillan.

Lichbach, M. 1984: Optimal strategies for socialist parties: does social class matter to party fortunes? *Comparative Political Studies*, 16 (4), 419–52.

Lindblom, C. 1977: *Politics and Markets*. New York: Basic Books.

Lindblom, C. 1982: The market as prison. *Journal of Politics*, 44, 324–36.

Locke, J. 1963: *Two Treatises of Government*. Cambridge: Cambridge University Press.

Lomasky, L. E. 1988: Socialism as classical political philosophy. *Social Philosophy and Policy*, 6 (2), 112–38.

Lowi, T. J. 1985: An aligning election, a Presidential plebiscite. In M. Nelson (ed.), *The Elections of 1984*. Washington, DC: CQ Press, pp. 277–301.

Luard, E. 1991: *Socialism without the State*, 2nd edn. London: Macmillan.

Lukes, S. 1985: *Marxism and Morality*. Oxford: Oxford University Press.

Lukes, S. 1990: Socialism and capitalism, Left and Right. *Social Research*, 571–8.

Luxemburg, R. 1961: *The Russian Revolution and Leninism or Marxism*. Westport, Conn.: Greenwood.

Luxemburg, R. 1970: *Reform or Revolution*. New York: Pathfinder.

Lydall, H. 1984: *Yugoslav Socialism: Theory and Practice*. Oxford: Clarendon.

Lyotard, J.-F. 1984: *The Postmodern Condition*. Manchester: Manchester University Press.

McCarney, J. 1993: Shaping ends: reflections on Fukuyama. *New Left Review*, 202, 37–53.

McKay, D. 1993: *American Politics and Society*, 3rd edn. Oxford: Blackwell.

Mackie, T. T. and Rose, R. 1991: *The International Almanac of Electoral History*, 3rd edn. London: Macmillan.

McLennan, G. 1989: *Marxism, Pluralism and Beyond: Classic Debates and New Departures*. Cambridge: Polity.

Macpherson, C. B. 1977a: *The Life and Times of Liberal Democracy*. Oxford: Oxford University Press.

Macpherson, C. B. 1977b: *Property: Mainstream and Critical Positions*. Toronto: University of Toronto Press.

Mandel, E. 1978: *From Stalinism to Eurocommunism*. London: New Left Books.

Mandel, E. 1986: In defence of socialist planning. *New Left Review*, 159, 5–37.

Mandel, E. 1988: The myth of market socialism. *New Left Review*, 169, 108–20.

Mann, M. 1993: *The Sources of Social Power*, vol. 2. Cambridge: Cambridge University Press.

Marquand, D. 1988: *The Unprincipled Society: New Demands and Old Politics*. London: Fontana.

Marquand, D. 1991: The life after death of socialism. *Guardian*, 5 June.

Marquand, D. 1993: After socialism. *Political Studies*, 61, 43–56.

Marshall, G., Rose, D., Newby, H. and Vogler, C. 1989: *Social Class in Modern Britain*. London: Unwin Hyman.

Martell, L. 1992: New ideas of socialism. *Economy and Society*, 21 (2), 152–71.

Marx, K. 1972: *Capital*, vol. 3. London: Lawrence and Wishart.

Marx, K. 1973a: *Capital*. Harmondsworth: Penguin.

Marx, K. 1973b: The Eighteenth Brumaire of Louis Bonaparte. In K. Marx, *Surveys from Exile*. Harmondsworth: Penguin, pp. 143–249.

Marx, K. 1973c: The Communist Manifesto. In *The Revolutions of 1848*. Harmondsworth: Penguin, pp. 62–98.

Marx, K. 1974: The civil war in France. In *The First International and After*. Harmondsworth: Penguin, pp. 187–268.

Marx, K. 1975: On the Jewish Question. In *Early Writings*. Harmondsworth: Penguin, pp. 211–41.

Matthews, J. 1989: *The Age of Democracy*. Melbourne: Oxford University Press.

Matthews, R. C. O. 1968: Why has Britain had full employment since the war? *Economic Journal*, 78 (3 Sept.), 555–69.

Meade, J. 1964: *Efficiency, Equality and the Ownership of Property*. London: Allen and Unwin.

Meade, J. 1988a: The theory of labour-managed firms and profit sharing. In J. Meade, *The Collected Papers of James Meade*, vol. 2. London: Unwin Hyman, pp. 158–82.

Meade, J. 1988b: Labour managed firms in conditions of imperfect competition.

In J. Meade, *The Collected Papers of James Meade*, vol. 2. London: Unwin Hyman, pp. 192–200.

Meidner, R. 1978: *Employee Investment Funds*. London: Allen and Unwin.

Meidner, R. 1980: Our concept of the third way: some remarks on the socio-political tenets of the Swedish labour movement. *Economic and Industrial Democracy*, 1 (3), 343–69.

Meidner, R. 1993: Why did the swedish model fail? *Socialist Register*, 211–28.

Merkel, P. 1992: After the golden age: is social democracy doomed to decline? In Lemke and Marks (1992), pp. 136–70.

Michels, R. 1962: *Political Parties*. New York: Free Press.

Milenkovitch, D. D. 1971: *Plan and Market in Yugoslav Economic Thought*. London: Yale University Press.

Milenkovitch, D. D. 1984: Is market socialism efficient? In A. Zimbalist (ed.), *Comparative Economic Systems*. Boston: Kluwer-Nijhoff, pp. 65–107.

Miliband, R. 1961: *Parliamentary Socialism*. London: Merlin.

Miller, D. 1981: Market neutrality and the failure of co-operatives. *British Journal of Political Science*, 11, 309–29.

Miller, D. 1988: In what sense must socialism be communitarian? *Social Philosophy and Policy*, 6 (2), 51–73.

Miller, D. 1989: *Market, State, and Community: Theoretical Foundations of Market Socialism*. Oxford: Clarendon.

Miller, D. 1991: A vision of market socialism. *Dissent*. Summer, 406–14.

Miller, D. 1993: Deliberative democracy and social choice. In Held (1993), pp. 74–92.

Miller, D. and Estrin, S. 1985: Market socialism: a policy for socialists. In I. Forbes, *Market Socialism*. London: Fabian Society, pp. 3–12.

Mitchell, B. R. 1975: *European Historical Statistics 1750–1970*. London: Macmillan.

Miyazaki, H. and Neary, H. M. 1983: The Illyrian firm revisited. *Bell Journal of Economics*, 14 (1), 259–70.

Mouffe, C. (ed.) 1992: *Dimensions of Radial Democracy*. London: Verso.

Mouzelis, N. P. 1990: *Post-Marxist Alternatives: The Construction of Social Orders*. London: Macmillan.

Murrell, P. 1983: Did the theory of market socialism answer the challenge of Ludwig von Mises? A reinterpretation of the socialist controversy. *History of Political Economy*, 15 (1), 92–105.

Mygind, N. 1986: From the Illyrian firm to the reality of self-management. In S. Jansson and A.-B. Hellmark, *Labor-owned Firms and Workers' Cooperatives*, Aldershot: Gower, pp. 73–104.

Novak, M. 1982: *The Spirit of Democratic Capitalism*. New York: Simon and Schuster.

Nove, A. 1983: *The Economics of Feasible Socialism*. London: Allen and Unwin.

Nove, A. 1987: Markets and socialism. *New Left Review*, 161, 98–104.

Nove, A. 1988: Socialism, capitalism, and the Soviet experience. *Social Philosophy and Policy*, 6 (2), 235–51.

Nove, A. 1989: The role of central planning under capitalism and market socialism. In J. Elster and K. O. Moene, *Alternatives to Capitalism*. Cambridge: Cambridge University Press, pp. 98–109.

Nove, A. 1991: *The Economics of Feasible Socialism Revisited*, 2nd edn. London: Allen and Unwin.

Nozick, R. 1974: *Anarchy, State and Utopia*. New York: Basic Books.

Nuti, D. M. 1992: Market socialism: the model that might have been but never was. In A. Aslund, *Market Socialism*. Cambridge: Cambridge University Press, pp. 17–31.

Oakeshott, R. 1978: *The Case for Workers' Co-ops*. London: Routledge and Kegan Paul.

OECD 1977: *Towards Full Employment and Price Stability*. Paris: OECD.

OECD 1985: *The Integration of Women into the Economy*. Paris: OECD.

OECD 1988: *The Future of Social Protection*. Paris: OECD.

OECD 1991: *Quarterly Labour Force Statistics*, 2.

Offe, C. 1984: *Contradictions of the Welfare State*. London: Hutchinson.

Offe, C. 1985: *Disorganized Capitalism*. Cambridge: Polity.

Offe, C. 1987: Democracy against the welfare state? *Political Theory*, 15 (4), 501–37.

O'Neill, J. 1988: Markets, socialism, and information: a reformulation of a Marxian objection to the market. *Social Philosophy and Policy*, 6 (2), 200–10.

Padgett, S. 1993: The German Social Democrats: a redefinition of social democracy or Bad Godesburg mark II. In Gillespie and Paterson (1993), pp. 20–38.

Panitch, L. 1986: The impasse of social democratic politics. In L. Panitch, *Working Class Politics in Crisis*. London: Verso, pp. 1–55.

Panitch, L. 1990: The 'Depoliticization of the Economy' or the 'Democratization of Politics'. In H. Flakierski and T. T. Sekine, *Socialist Dilemmas: East and West*. Armonk, NY: Sharpe, pp. 107–27.

Pateman, C. 1970: *Participation and Democratic Theory*. Cambridge: Cambridge University Press.

Parry, R. 1986: United Kingdom. In P. Flora (ed.), *Growth to Limits*, vol. 2. Berlin: De Gruyter, pp. 155–240.

Pearce, D., Markandya, A. and Barbier, E. B. 1989: *Blueprint for a Green Economy: A Report*. London: Earthscan.

Pejovich, S. 1990: A property-rights analysis of the Yugoslav miracle. *Annals of the American Academy of Political and Social Science*, 507, 123–32.

Pfouts, W. and Rosefielde, S. 1986: The firm in Illyria: market syndicalism revisited. *Journal of Comparative Economics*, 10, 160–70.

Phillips, A. 1991: *Engendering Democracy*. Cambridge: Polity.

Pierson, C. 1986: *Marxist Theory and Democratic Politics*. Cambridge: Polity.

Pierson, C. 1990: The 'Exceptional' United States: first new nation or last welfare state? *Social Policy and Administration*, 24 (3), 186–98.

Pierson, C. 1991a: *Beyond the Welfare State?* Cambridge: Polity.

Pierson, C. 1991b: Welfare states and social democracies: redefining Sweden's social democratic road to power. *Research in Political Sociology*, 5, 277–97.

Pierson, C. 1993a: Democracy, markets and capital: are there necessary economic limits to democracy? In Held (1993), pp. 179–99.

Pierson, C. 1993b: Social policy. In P. Dunleavy, A. Gamble, I. Holliday and G. Peele (eds), *Developments in British Politics 4*. London: Macmillan, pp. 246–66.

Pierson, C. 1994: Continuity and discontinuity in the emergence of the 'post-Fordist' welfare state. In R. Burrows and B. Loader (eds), *Towards a Post-Fordist Welfare State?* London: Routledge.

Pimlott, B. 1988: The future of the Left. In R. Skidelsky (ed.), *Thatcherism*. Oxford: Blackwell, pp. 79–92.

Piven, F. F. (ed.) 1991: *Labor Parties in Postindustrial Societies*. Cambridge: Polity.

Plant, R. 1984: *Equality, Markets and the New Right*. London: Fabian Tract 494.

Plant, R. 1989: Socialism, markets and end states. In Le Grand and Estrin (1989), pp. 50–77.

Pollard, S. 1967: Nineteenth-century co-operation: from community building to shopkeeping. In A. Briggs and J. Saville, *Essays in Labour History*. London: Macmillan, pp. 74–112.

Pontusson, J. 1992a: *The Limits of Social Democracy: Investment Politics in Sweden*. London: Cornell University Press.

Pontusson, J. 1992b: At the end of the Third Road: Swedish social democracy in crisis. *Politics and Society*, 20 (3), 305–32.

Popper, K. 1961: *The Poverty of Historicism*. London: Routledge and Kegan Paul.

Popper, K. 1962: *The Open Society and its Enemies*. Routledge and Kegan Paul.

Porter, G. and Welsh Brown, J. 1991: *Global Environmental Politics*. Boulder, Colo.: Westview.

Potter, B. 1891: *The Co-operative Movement in Great Britain*. London: Swan Sonnenschein.

Poulantzas, N. 1975: *Classes in Contemporary Capitalism*. London: New Left Books.

Poulantzas, N. 1978: *State, Power, Socialism*. London: Verso.

Price, R. and Bain, G. S. 1988: The labour force. In A. H. Halsey (ed.), *British Social Trends since 1900*. London: Macmillan, pp. 162–201.

Prins, G. 1990: *Spring in Winter: The 1989 Revolutions*. Manchester: Manchester University Press.

Prout, C. 1985: *Market Socialism in Yugoslavia*. Oxford: Oxford University Press.

Przeworski, A. 1977: Proletariat into a class: the process of class formation. *Politics and Society*, 7 (4), 343–401.

Przeworski, A. 1980: Social democracy as an historical phenomenon. *New Left Review*, 122, 27–58.

Przeworski, A. 1985: *Capitalism and Social Democracy*. Cambridge: Cambridge University Press.

Przeworski, A. 1991: *Democracy and the Market: Political and Economic Reforms in Eastern Europe and Latin America*. Cambridge: Cambridge University Press.

Przeworski, A. and Sprague, J. 1986: *Paper Stones: A History of Electoral Socialism*. London: University of Chicago Press.

Przeworski, A. and Wallerstein, M. 1988: Worker's welfare and the socialization of capital. In M. Taylor (ed.), *Rationality and Revolution*. Cambridge: Cambridge University Press, pp. 179–205.

Rawls, J. 1972: *A Theory of Justice*. Oxford: Oxford University Press.

Reeve, A. 1986: *Property*. London: Macmillan.

Reeve, A. (ed.) 1987: *Modern Theories of Exploitation*. London: Sage.

Reeve, A. 1991: The theory of property: beyond private *versus* common property. In D. Held (ed.), *Political Theory Today*. Cambridge: Polity, pp. 91–114.

Rein, M. 1985: Women, employment and social welfare. In R. Klein and M. O'Higgins, *The Future of Welfare*. Oxford: Blackwell, pp. 37–58.

Roemer, J. E. 1982: *A General Theory of Exploitation and Class*. Cambridge, Mass.: Harvard University Press.

Roemer, J. E. 1985: *Analytical Marxism*. Cambridge: Cambridge University Press.

Roemer, J. E. 1991: Market socialism: a blueprint. *Dissent*, Fall, 562–9.

Roemer, J. E. 1992a: Can there be Socialism after Communism? *Politics and Society*, 20 (3), 261–76. (Reprinted in Bardhan and Roemer (1993a), pp. 89–107.)

Roemer, J. E. 1992b: The morality and efficiency of market socialism. *Ethics*, 102 (Apr.), 448–64.

Roemer, J. E. 1994: *A Future for Socialism*. Cambridge, Mass.: Harvard University Press.

Roland, G. and Sekkat, K. 1993: Market socialism and the managerial labor market. In Bardhan and Roemer (1993a), pp. 204–15.

Rousseau, J. J. 1968: *The Social Contract*. Harmondsworth: Penguin.

Rutland, P. 1985: *The Myth of the Plan*. London: Hutchinson.

Rutland, P. 1988: Capitalism and socialism: how can they be compared? *Social Philosophy and Policy*, 6 (1), 197–227.

Ryan, A. 1982: The romantic theory of ownership. In Hollowell, P. (ed.), *Property and Social Relations*. London: Heinemann Educational, pp. 52–68.

Ryan, A. 1984: *Property and Political Theory*. Oxford: Blackwell.

Sainsbury, D. 1990: Party strategies and the electoral trade off of class-based parties. *European Journal of Political Research*, 18, 29–50.

Sainsbury, D. 1993: The Swedish Social Democrats and the legacy of continuous reform: asset or dilemma? *West European Politics*, 16 (1), 39–61.

Sartori, G. 1987: *The Theory of Democracy Revisited: Part One: The Contemporary Debate*. Chatham, NJ: Chatham House.

Scharpf, F. W. 1991: *Crisis and Choice in European Social Democracy*. Ithaca, NY: Cornell University Press.

Schmidt, M. G. 1983: The welfare state and the economy in periods of economic crisis: a comparative study of 23 OECD nations. *European Journal of Political Research*, 17 (6), 641–59.

Schneider, W. 1981: The November 4th vote for president: what did it mean? In A. Ranney, *The American Election of 1980*. Washington, DC: American Enterprise Institute for Public Policy Research, pp. 212–62.

Schuller, A. 1988: *Does Market Socialism Work?* London: Centre for Research into Communist Economies.

Schumpeter, J. 1976: *Capitalism, Socialism and Democracy*. London: Allen and Unwin.

Selbourne, D. 1990: *Death of the Dark Hero: Eastern Europe, 1987–90*. London: Cape.

Selucky, R. 1979: *Marxism, Socialism and Freedom: Towards a General Democratic Theory of Labour-Managed Systems*. London: Macmillan.

Sen, A. 1985: The moral standing of the market. *Social Philosophy and Policy*, 2 (2), 1–19.

Shapiro, D. 1989: Reviving the socialist calculation debate: a defence of Hayek against Lange. *Social Philosophy and Policy*, 6 (2), 139–59.

Share, D. 1989: *Dilemmas of Social Democracy in the 1980s*. London: Greenwood.

Shaw, E. 1993: Towards renewal? The British Labour Party's policy review. In Gillespie and Paterson (1993), pp. 112–32.

Shonfield, A. 1965: *Modern Capitalism: The Changing Balance of Public and Private Power*. Oxford: Oxford University Press.

Sik, O. 1967: *Plan and Market under Socialism*. White Plains, NY: Rienner.

Sik, O. 1976: *The Third Way*. London: Wildwood House.

Sik, O. 1985: *For a Humane Economic Democracy*. New York: Praeger.

Singer, D. 1988: *Is Socialism Doomed? The Meaning of Mitterand*. Oxford: Oxford University Press.

Skidelsky, R. 1979: The decline of Keynesian politics. In C. Crouch (ed.), *State and Economy in Contemporary Capitalism*. London: Croom Helm, pp. 55–87.

Smart, B. 1993: *Postmodernity*. London: Routledge.

Smith, T. W. 1989: Inequality and welfare. In R. Jowell, B. Witherspoon and L. Brook, *British Social Attitudes: 6th Report*. Aldershot: Gower, pp. 59–86.

Sombart, W. 1976: *Why Is There No Socialism in the US?* Armonk, NY: Sharpe.

Stalin, J. 1955: *The Task of Business Executives. In Works*, vol. 13. Moscow: Foreign Language Publishing Press, pp. 31–44.

Stauber, L. G. 1987: *A New Program for Democratic Socialism: Lessons from the Market-Planning Experience in Austria*. Carbondale, Ill.: Four Willows.

Steinherr, A. 1983: The labour-managed economy: a survey of the economics literature. In Kennedy (1983), pp. 123–50.

Stephen, F. H. 1982: *The Performance of Labour-Managed Firms*. London: Macmillan.

Sutela, P. 1990: The marketization of Eastern Europe. In R. J. Hill and J. Zielonka (eds), *Restructuring Eastern Europe: Towards a New European Order*. London: Edward Elgar, pp. 59–75.

Swain, N. 1992: *Hungary: The Rise and Fall of Feasible Socialism*. London: Verso.

Swenson, P. 1991: Labor and the limits of the welfare state: the politics of intraclass conflict and cross-class alliances in Sweden and West Germany. *Comparative Politics*, 23 (4), 379–99.

Taylor, F. 1929: The guidance of production in a socialist state. *American Economic Review*, 19 (Mar.), 1–8.

Taylor-Gooby, P. 1985: *Public Opinion, Ideology and State Welfare*. London: Routledge and Kegan Paul.

Taylor-Gooby, P. 1989: The role of the state. In R. Jowell, B. Witherspoon and L. Brook, *British Social Attitudes: 6th Report*. Aldershot: Gower, pp. 35–58.

Therborn, G. 1986: *Why Some Peoples Are More Unemployed than Others*. London: Verso.

Therborn, G. 1989a: Two thirds, one third society. In Hall and Jacques (1989), pp. 103–15.

Therborn, G. 1989b: States, populations and productivity: towards a political theory of welfare states. In P. Lassman (ed.), *Politics and Social Theory*. London: Routledge, pp. 62–84.

Therborn, G. 1992: The life and times of socialism. *New Left Review*, 194, 17–32.

Thomas, A. 1990: 'UK worker cooperatives 1989: towards the 10,000 jobs mark? In *Yearbook of Co-operative Enterprise*. Oxford: Plunkett Foundation.

Thomas, H. 1982: The performance of the Mondragon cooperatives in Spain. In Jones and Svejnar (1982), pp. 129–51.

Thomas, H. and Logan, C. 1982: *Mondragon*. London: Allen and Unwin.

Thompson, G. 1990: *The Political Economy of the New Right*. London: Pinter.

Thompson, J. 1990: *Ideology and Modern Culture*. Cambridge: Polity.

Thompson, N. 1988: *The Market and its Critics: Socialist Political Economy in Nineteenth Century Britain*. London: Routledge.

Tilton, T. 1990: *The Political Theory of Swedish Social Democracy*. Oxford: Clarendon.

Tomlinson, J. 1990: *Hayek and the Market*. London: Pluto.

Trasler, G. 1982: The psychology of ownership and possessiveness. In P. Hollowell (ed.), *Property and Social Relations*. London: Heinemann, pp. 32–51.

Turner, B. S. 1990: The end of organized socialism? *Theory, Culture and Society*, 7, 133–44.

Vanek, J. 1970: *The General Theory of a Labor Managed Economy*. Ithaca, NY: Cornell University Press.

Vanek, J. 1972: *The Economics of Workers' Management*. London: Allen and Unwin.

Vanek, J. (ed.) 1975: *Economic Self-Management: Economic Liberation of Man*. Harmondsworth: Penguin.

Visser, J. 1992: The strength of union movements in advanced capitalist democracies: social and organizational variation. In M. Regini (ed.), *The Future of Labour Movements*. London: Sage, pp. 17–52.

von Mises, L. 1935: Economic calculation in the socialist commonwealth. In Hayek (1935), pp. 87–130.

von Mises, L. 1951: *Socialism: An Economic and Sociological Analysis*. New Haven, Conn.: Yale University Press.

Waldron, J. 1988: *The Right to Private Property*. Oxford: Clarendon.

Walzer, M. 1970: A day in the life of a socialist citizen. In M. Walzer, *Obligations: Essays in Disobedience, War and Citizenship* (Cambridge, Mass.: Harvard University Press), pp. 229–38.

Ward, B. 1958: The firm in Illyria: market syndicalism. *American Economic Review*, 48, 566–89.

Ward, B. 1967: *The Socialist Economy: A Study of Organizational Alternatives*. New York: Random House.

Wattenberg, M. P. 1991: *The Rise of Candidate Centred Politics*. Cambridge, Mass.: Harvard University Press.

Webber, D. 1986: Social Democracy and the re-emergence of mass unemployment in Western Europe. In W. E. Paterson and A. H. Thomas, *The Future of Social Democracy*. Oxford: Clarendon, pp. 19–58.

Wilson, W. J. 1987: *The Truly Disadvantaged: The Inner City, the Underclass, and Public Policy*. London: University of Chicago Press.

Wood, E. M. 1986: *The Retreat from Class: A New 'True' Socialism*. London: Verso.

Wood, E. M. 1989: Rational choice Marxism. *New Left Review*, 177, 41–88.

Wright, E. O. 1985: *Classes*. London: Verso.

Wright, E. O. 1993: Class analysis, history and emancipation. *New Left Review*, 202, 15–35.

Xavier, R. 1989: *The Hungarian Model: Planning and the Market in a Socialist Economy*. Cambridge: Cambridge University Press.

Yunker, J. A. 1985: Practical considerations in designing a supernational federation. *World Futures*, 21, 159–218.

Yunker, J. A. 1988: Risk-taking as a justification for property income. *Journal of Comparative Economics*, 12 (1), 74–88.

Yunker, J. A. 1990a: A new perspective on market socialism. *Comparative Economic Studies*, 30 (2), 69–116.

Yunker, J. A. 1990b: Ludwig von Mises on the 'Artificial Market'. *Comparative Economic Studies*, 32 (1), 108–40.

Yunker, J. A. 1992: *Socialism Revised and Modernized: The Case for Pragmatic Market Socialism*. London: Praeger.

Zevi, A. 1982: The performance of Italian producer cooperatives. In Jones and Svejnar (1982), pp. 239–51.

Index